Peabody Journal of Education

Camilla Benbow, Dean, Peabody College
James Guthrie, Editor
Michele Thompson, Coordinating Editor
Matthew Springer, Associate Editor

Peabody Journal of Education

Volume 79, Number 2, 2004

Commemorating the 50th Anniversary of *Brown v. Board of Education*: Reconsidering the Effects of the Landmark Decision

(*continued*)

PEABODY JOURNAL OF EDUCATION, 79(2), 1–4

Guest Editor's Preface

Kenneth K. Wong
Department of Leadership, Policy, and Organizations
Peabody College of Vanderbilt University

Fifty years ago in the landmark *Brown v. Board of Education* decision in May 1954, the U.S. Supreme Court challenged the legitimacy of maintaining a public school system that was based on the doctrine of "separate but equal." The unanimous decision ruled that state-sponsored dual systems of schools that were segregated by race were unconstitutional. The Court recognized "public education in the light of its full development" (p. 492) as a social institution that could not continue to operate under the doctrine of separate but equal. This landmark decision argued that public education is "a principal instrument" (p. 493) in preparing any child for social and economic life. Racial "segregation with the sanction of law" (p. 494), ruled the Court, was unconstitutional. Ruling on a case in Delaware in 1955 (often referred to as *Brown II*), the Court urged public schools to admit students on a "racially nondiscriminatory basis with all deliberate speed."

Implementation of the 1954 and subsequent Court decisions, however, has proven to be difficult. Southern resistance was followed by northern opposition to busing. There was also a shift in the legal paradigm toward a more restrictive federal role. The 1968 Court decision in *Green v. County School Board of New Kent County* outlined the procedure for lifting desegregation orders once districts could prove that de jure segregation had been remedied. By the 1990s, desegregation orders had been lifted and districts declared "unitary" across the country. Further, in 1974 the Supreme Court

Requests for reprints should be sent to Kenneth K. Wong, Peabody College of Vanderbilt University, Department of Leadership, Policy, and Organizations, Peabody Box 514, 230 Appleton Place, Nashville, TN 37203-5721. E-mail: ken.wong@vanderbilt.edu

limited the reach of *Brown* to state-sponsored de jure segregation and effectively excluded the suburbs from metropolitan-wide desegregation orders in *Milliken v. Bradley.* Since the mid- and late 1990s, federal courts have ruled against voluntary efforts to address de facto segregation based on racial classifications. In *Eisenberg v. Montgomery County School District,* the Supreme Court let stand a Fourth Circuit decision that struck down a voluntary transfer policy that used race as a classification. Despite these changes in the legal paradigm, the *Brown* decision remains the foundation that affirmed the nation's commitment to meet the challenge of dismantling racial segregation in our public schools.

This landmark decision has clearly shaped contemporary American public education. From a policy perspective, *Brown* signaled an activist federal direction not only on racial desegregation but on equal educational opportunity more generally. The passage of the 1965 Elementary and Secondary Education Act established a new policy paradigm where the federal government began to set standards on local schooling services. Intergovernmental relations have been reshaped by federal–state and federal–district conflicts over the implementation of *Brown* and its subsequent remedies.

In light of the 50th anniversary of the *Brown* decision, the *Peabody Journal of Education* commissioned a multidisciplinary group of researchers to commemorate and to reassess the educational effects of the Court decision. The articles are grounded in theories and methods of several disciplines, including law, philosophy, economics, political science, sociology, and public policy. Taken as a whole, the researchers examine the way the Court frames racial inequity and whether the proposed remedy (which followed first by permissive and then active implementation) is consistent with the institutional and legal context at the time of the ruling. In addressing these questions, the authors pay particular attention to the nature of the constitutional argument, the use of social science evidence in shaping judicial decisions, the political economy of policy development and implementation in addressing racial desegregation, and the ongoing challenge of ensuring equality of schooling opportunity for our increasingly diverse student population.

The first 3 articles reconsider the meaning and effects of *Brown* in the proper institutional context. James W. Guthrie and Matthew G. Springer place *Brown* in the context of stability and changes in major court decisions over the last 50 years. In light of *Brown*'s promise and limitations, the authors see the need to rethink current public policies to narrow the racial gap. The article proposes strategies that not only emphasize schooling resources but also focus on student outcomes. Rebecca L. Brown, a legal scholar who clerked for Supreme Court Associate Justice Thurgood Marshall in 1985, reaffirms the historic significance of the 1954 decision. In response to skeptics of *Brown*, the article provides several reasons why our society is better off because of the decision. Particularly important was the National Association for the Advancement of Colored People's strategy in 1954 to tie the "interests of the powerless with those of the powerful to achieve better laws for all." Lucius T. Outlaw Jr., a philosopher, reexamines the core assumption of *Brown*, which considered that racial segregation was detrimental primarily to Black children but not to White children. The article challenges the readers to broaden the legacy of *Brown* by rectifying this widely accepted, yet one-sided concern of racial desegregation.

The next four articles examine the ongoing challenge of addressing the interplay of race, class, status, and equal educational opportunities. Jaekyung Lee, drawing on 3 decades of achievement trends in the National Assessment of Educational Progress, conducts a comprehensive assessment of the racial gap in mathematics. Although Black and Hispanic students have made academic gains over the last 30 years, racial gaps have tended to widen in the last decade. This disturbing trend, from Lee's perspective, calls for new efforts to enhance equity and justice in our educational system. Economist Charles T. Clotfelter focuses on the role of private schools in racial segregation, particularly in the South. To avoid interracial exposure, White enrollment in private schools was highly correlated to minority population in southern counties. However, the article shows that private schools, when compared with schools within the public sector, do not constitute a major factor for racial segregation at the national level. From a policy perspective, Ryane McAuliffe Straus conducts a detailed analysis of newspaper reporting on school desegregation in Los Angeles, particularly with regard to the development of magnet school programs between 1976 and 1999. Applying the policy framework of "social construction," Straus found that news reference to desegregation has declined steadily. Instead, magnet schools are increasingly seen as programs of academic excellence in the broader climate of standards-based accountability. In light of the role of social science in shaping *Brown* and other Court decisions, Kenneth K. Wong and Anna C. Nicotera revisit *Brown* and the 1966 report on Equality of Educational Opportunity (known as the Coleman report; Coleman et al., 1966). The article aims to connect social science research to the changing socioeconomic and institutional patterns that have frustrated governmental efforts to enhance equal educational opportunity. The authors observe that social science research will continue to serve its social function in shaping the debate in equal educational opportunity.

The final set of articles explores the challenge of diversity. Kent D. Syverud, a legal expert who testified before the Supreme Court on affirmative action in higher education institutions, articulates the educational benefits of diversity. He observes that "when a critical mass of underrepresented minority students is present, racial stereotypes lose their force." Special education researchers Festus E. Obiakor and Cheryl A. Utley study the challenge of educating students who are culturally diverse learners with exceptionalities. Despite *Brown*, the authors found that public schools continue to "devalue behavioral, learning, cultural, and linguistic styles different from [the] mainstream." Sociologists Daniel B. Cornfield and Angela Arzubiaga map the global immigration pattern to cities in the United States. In their detailed study of immigrant groups in the Nashville, Tennessee, metropolitan area, the researchers differentiate integrating and segmenting tendencies. Their findings suggest broad policy implications in terms of supporting immigrant children and their families toward integrating into the school system. In short, this volume not only commemorates the significance of *Brown* but also enriches our understanding of the equity challenge in our changing society.

References

Brown v. Board of Educ., 347 U.S. 483 (1954).
Brown v. Board of Educ., 349 U.S. 294 (1955).
Coleman, J. S., Campbell, E. Q., Hobson, C. J., McPartland, J., Mood, A. M., Weinfeld, F. D., & York, R. L. (1966). *Equality of educational opportunity.* Washington, DC: U.S. Government Printing Office.
Elementary and Secondary Education Act of 1965, P.L. No. 89-10 (1965).
Green v. County School Board, 391 U.S. 430 (1968).
Milliken v. Bradley, 418 U.S. 717 (1974).
Montgomery County Public Schools v. Eisenberg, 197 F.3d 123 (4th Cir. 1999).

PEABODY JOURNAL OF EDUCATION, *79*(2), 5–32

Returning to Square One: From *Plessy* to *Brown* and Back to *Plessy*

James W. Guthrie and Matthew G. Springer
Department of Leadership, Policy, and Organizations
Peabody College of Vanderbilt University

This essay describes significant legal and policy system changes in America's 50-year crusade to curtail or eliminate racially segregated public school. In hindsight, a more forceful initial policy system stance regarding judicial enforcement might well have resulted in greater desegregation success. However, after 5 decades of judicial and operational compliance trial and error, United States public schools presently appear almost as racially segregated as before the landmark case, *Brown v. Board of Education of Topeka, Kansas* (1954, 1955). In effect, over the 50 years since 1954, the nation has ricocheted from *Plessy v. Ferguson* (1896) to *Brown* and, practically if not constitutionally, back to *Plessy*. The contemporary cause of school segregation rests more with income and housing patterns than with explicit apartheid policies. Regardless of cause, however, even if there now exists something much closer to equal educational opportunity than was true 50 years ago, there clearly is not anything close, nationally, to racial parity of educational achievement. Mindful of the remaining achievement gap, this article posits that it is time to reconsider past policies built almost exclusively around busing and achieving physical mixes of Black and White students. Instead, it is now time to rely on new strategies involving elevated expectations, explicit learning standards, notions of financial "adequacy," and effective accountability. In effect, it is time to mea-

Requests for reprints should be sent to James. W. Guthrie, Peabody College of Vanderbilt University, Department of Leadership, Policy, and Organizations, Peabody Box 514, 230 Appleton Place, Nashville, TN 37203-5721. E-mail: jwgxiii@bellsouth.net

sure racial policy progress by student successes, not by transportation and school resource processes.

May 17, 2004, marks the 50th anniversary of *Brown v. Board of Education of Topeka, Kansas* (1954, 1955). Envisioned as the death knell of systematic school segregation, the cases are assuredly among the most influential judicial actions in the history of the United States. A twin set of decisions is involved. The initial set, referred to as *Brown I*, unanimously ruled that separate educational facilities for Black and White students were inherently inequitable, however similar physically. Such separate facilities violated the United States Constitution's 14th Amendment's equal protection clause and denied Blacks equal educational opportunity. The second set, referred to as *Brown II*, promulgated a plan to dismantle legally permitted racial segregation in schools. As testament to their collective influence, these cases had been cited within 40 years after issuance in more than 2,250 separate federal court cases (Vergon, 1994).

The purpose of this article, and that of its companions in this special issue of the *Peabody Journal of Education*, is to commemorate the 50th anniversary of the Supreme Court's ruling by revisiting and examining *Brown*'s historical significance and its education policy legacy. As with most retrospective efforts, the authors can make no claim that they would have been equally prescient 50 years ago at the time the U.S. Supreme Court issued these decisions. These 21st century insights and assertions are a product of experience during the intervening period. Social science, law, education policy, and historical analyses have also contributed to America's collective understanding over this time.

This article classifies *Brown*'s significance, legacy, and possible future into five distinct stages, four of which represent noteworthy trends in the school desegregation movement: first, resistance; second, reinforcement; third, reaction; and fourth, resegregation. Stage 5, reconception, poses a different model, an education reform strategy now rendered possible by ways of conceiving schooling that were unavailable 50 years ago.

Stage 1 is characterized by high levels of White desegregation resistance, little to no racial integration change, and a lack of leadership among key constituents. Stage 2 proved the most successful in eliminating systematic school racial segregation through uniform and aligned judicial, congressional, and executive branch interventions. By the end of this period, a new national political consensus had emerged, however, and with it a shift throughout Stage 3 toward more conservative congressional and judicial policy making as well as a corresponding de-emphasis of judicial control over desegregation. Here, racial desegregation began to stagnate.

Stage 4 was dominated by a paradigmatic shift away from court-ordered oversight of local education agencies' progress in sustaining desegregation and toward the "going unitary" phenomenon.[1] The burgeoning "unitary" movement is representative of conditions that continue through the present and imparts social science disagreement and policy solution discord between racial desegregation stalwarts and community empowerment and neighborhood school advocates. Stage 5 is posited by this article as a possible new definition of *desegregation*, a definition that emphasizes school academic performance.

Despite episodic setbacks, *Brown*'s 50-year progeny has produced much that is right in American education. Now, in retrospect, it may be time to forego past policies built almost exclusively around busing, resource equality, and achieving physical mixes of Black and White students. It is time instead to rely on new strategies involving elevated expectations, explicit learning standards, notions of financial "adequacy," and effective accountability. In effect, it is time to measure racial policy progress by student success, not by transportation process.

Historical Context and Foundation for *Brown*

Judicially permissible school segregation emerged in America as early as 1850 when the Massachusetts Supreme Court, under the leadership of Chief Justice Lemuel Shaw, ruled that Massachusetts's code permitted policymakers and local education agencies to segregate facilities by race. The ruling, *Roberts v. City of Boston* (1850), was eventually overturned, however, in 1855 by the Massachusetts legislature.

It was not until after the post–Civil War "Reconstruction Era" that the iniquitous *Plessy v. Ferguson* (1896) decision formally introduced "Jim Crow" laws to the Nation.[2] The U.S. Supreme Court ultimately maintained that, as long as equal facilities were provided to citizens, classification of

[1]The meaning of unitary status has changed over time (DeLacy, 1997; McCarthy, 1991). Typically, unitary status means a school district has "complied in good faith" with existing desegregation process standards and has operated to remove patterns of segregation (Harvard Civil Rights Project, 2002). When districts attain unitary status they are no longer subject to state or federal judicial supervision and local control is reinstated to the district level (Bennet, 1996; Gordon & Bartz, 1993).

[2]Jim Crow laws derived the name from an 1828 song written by Thomas Dartmouth Rice in the 1820s entitled "Jim Crow." Dartmouth was a minstrel of sorts and used the song during short solo skits in which he grossly exaggerated Black stereotypes. Over time, the phrase became commonly used as a racial epithet and, later, to describe the systematic segregation of Blacks from Whites (see the Jim Crow Museum of Racist Memorabilia, Ferris State University, Big Rapids, Michigan).

individuals by race was neither a violation of the 14th Amendment's equal protection clause nor inhibitory of the Black community's advancement. The historical precedent set in *Plessy* subjugated Black citizens and engendered racial segregation aboard trains, in restaurants, in restrooms, in theaters, in housing developments, and in schools. Government officials, businesses, and citizens across all levels gerrymandered zoning regulations, school district attendance boundaries, and housing regulations, causing minority families to bear the brunt of social dislocation (Halpern, 1995).

In response to *Plessy*-authorized inequities, social activists and grassroots organizations emerged. Leaders such as W. E. B. DuBois, Thurgood Marshall, Charles Houston, and Ida B. Wells-Barnett struggled throughout the *Plessy* era for equal pay, school and recreational facilities, libraries, and health services. The National Association for the Advancement of Colored People (NAACP), the most prominent of these grassroots organizations, was established in 1909 and became instrumental in advocating the rights of its minority constituency. The ongoing organization of the Black community provided solace and protection for its residents and emboldened activists to challenge social injustices, encouraging all to struggle against suppression and backlash.

The 1948 reelection of President Harry S. Truman and a series of vanguard court cases involving racial inequality in higher education further set the stage for *Brown*. Truman (1947, as cited in Patterson, 2001) stated

> The extension of civil rights today means not protection of the people against the government, but protection of the people by the government. ... We must make the federal government a friendly, vigilant defender of the rights and equalities of all Americans. And again I mean all Americans. (p. 1)

And on the judicial front, cases challenging the inferiority of Black educational facilities and opportunities to those available to Whites were won—for example, *Sipuel v. Board of Regents of the University of Oklahoma* (1948), *Sweatt v. Painter* (1950), and *McLaurin v. Oklahoma State Regents for Higher Education* (1950).

By 1954, bolstered by the leadership and legal vision of Thurgood Marshall and America's changing political climate, the NAACP's Legal Defense and Educational Fund brought a collection of five cases involving K–12 education before the U.S. Supreme Court. This time, the plaintiffs challenged the constitutional basis for systematic school segregation that

Plessy set forth in 1896 and not the comparative equality of separate educational facility attributes.

The leading case, *Brown v. Board of Education of Topeka, Kansas* (1954), involved Linda Brown, who was denied admission to her neighborhood elementary school. Linda had to "leave home at 7:40 in the morning, walk through dangerous railroad switching yards, and cross Topeka's busiest commercial street to board a bus that took her to [a] school that opened at 9:00" (Patterson, 2001, p. 32). The local, White-only school in Kansas, to which 7-year-old Linda sought admission, was named, ironically, after Massachusetts senator and Black rights activist Charles Sumner, the lead attorney in *Roberts v. City of Boston* (1850) more than a century earlier (Kluger, 1976).

The other four cases brought before the U.S. Supreme Court in the *Brown* package have received far less attention but are by no means irrelevant. *Davis v. County School Board of Prince Edward County* (1954) was born of a group of students and community activists who led a sit-in in the small town of Farmville, Virginia. The sit-in lasted 10 days until NAACP attorney Oliver Hill met with community organizers and filed suit on their behalf, claiming that the separate Black educational facilities in Farmville were substandard in comparison to the White facilities (Kluger, 1976). The second case, *Bolling v. Sharpe* (1954), involved 11 Black junior high students who were turned away from a local White-only school, thereby forcing them to attend an inadequate all-Black facility. The third, *Briggs v. Elliott* (1951, 1952), was filed on behalf of 20 Black families in Clarendon County, South Carolina. Even though the South Carolina court ruled in favor of the plaintiffs, the court called only for Black facilities to be made commensurate with the modern, White-only institutions. The plaintiffs countered by appealing for desegregation. Finally, *Belton v. Gebhart* (*Bulah v. Gebhardt*) (1952) sought integration because of the disparity with respect to teacher credentials, student–teacher ratios, academic and extracurricular offerings, and so forth between White and Black schools.

Just after noon on May 17, 1954, Chief Justice Earl Warren delivered the Supreme Court's opinion in *Brown v. Board of Education* (1954). In his account of Warren's ruling, Patterson (2001) wrote

> two-thirds of the way through his opinion, Warren had built up suspense among listeners. He had not indicated what the Court had decided. Finally, he did. He asked, "Does the segregation of children in public schools solely on the basis of race ... deprive the children of the minority group of equal educational opportunity?" He answered, "We believe that it does." A few passages later he added perhaps the most

> widely quoted lines of his opinion. "To separate them [Black children in grade and high schools] from others of similar age and qualifications solely because of their race generates a feeling of inferiority as to their status in the community that may affect their hearts and minds in a way unlikely ever to be undone." (p. 66)

Cheers filled the courtroom that reverberated throughout the nation. The judicial system had forever changed the American sociopolitical landscape.

Stage 1: Resistance

Rapid, or even successful, implementation of new edicts has traditionally proven an elusive achievement. Understanding the complexity of change, and in consideration of the volatile and divisive nature inherent in *Brown I*'s virtual abolishment of the separate but equal doctrine, the Supreme Court scheduled a second case, *Brown II*, as a means to address the challenge of how to rid a fractious culture of America's educational apartheid. The Court entertained briefs from the Attorney General of the United States, state attorneys general, and other key constituents in hopes of gaining clarity.

Arkansas, Florida, Maryland, North Carolina, Oklahoma, and Texas were among historically segregationist states submitting arguments in *Brown II* (Kluger, 1976). Florida provides a poignant example of the issues with which the Supreme Court has to wrestle. The "Sunshine State" spent $10,000 on an opinion poll that revealed 75% of the state's White leaders dissented from *Brown I*; 30% disagreed violently with *Brown I*; and only 13% of police officers said they would enforce desegregation law (Kluger, 1976).

On May 31, 1955, the Supreme Court delivered its decision in *Brown II*. It was evident the Court had reached an impasse in its deliberations. The Court's decision placed responsibility for the oversight of the education system's "prompt and reasonable start toward full compliance" in the hands of the lower courts (*Brown v. Board of Education of Topeka, Kansas*, 1955). The Court requested, furthermore, that the education system move with "all deliberate speed" (*Brown v. Board of Education of Topeka, Kansas*, 1955). These two elements enabled districts to postpone desegregation and equal educational opportunity, as the high court's resolution was devoid of systemic accountability. This lack of forceful federal leadership coupled with extensive White resistance, political skullduggery, and the adroitness of negatively disposed state and local policymakers at circumventing accountability effectively thwarted the first stage of systematic school desegregation before it had even begun. Indeed, "between 1955 and 1957, at least 120 state statutes were passed in an effort to nullify the Supreme Court's desegregation ruling" (Martin, 1957, as cited in Fleming, 1975, p. 9).

Of Southern segregationist campaigns in contradistinction to the *Brown* ruling, Arkansas Governor Orval Faubus incited the most volatile. In 1954, the local Little Rock, Arkansas, school board approved a desegregation plan to be implemented at the start of the 1957–1958 academic year. The plan intended to desegregate fully the city by 1963, but it lacked community engagement, effective support from local leadership, and overarching strategy. One day prior to the plan's implementation, Governor Faubus dispatched the state's National Guard to prohibit Blacks from entering the all-White Central High School. By the close of school in 1958, Little Rock segregationists had "provoked 43 bomb scares and threatened to kill the school superintendent" (Patterson, 2001, p. 112) among a host of other violent tactics aimed at preserving racial polarity. Arguments as to how to desegregate Little Rock raged in the court system well into the 1960s but with little avail. In 1963, less than 1% of Little Rock's Black student population attended junior or senior high schools that were formerly all-White (Patterson, 2001), and on more than one occasion, federal troops were dispatched to Little Rock to protect the rights of Black schoolchildren and subdue demonstrations (Russo, Harris, & Sandidge, 1994).

James Kilpatrick, the staunch segregationist and highly influential newspaper editor from Richmond, Virginia, championed interposition as a means for states to resist court-ordered desegregation. Interposition was a "long-lost constitutional interpretation that compels states to 'interpose' their own authority in order to protect citizens from unjust actions of the federal government" (Forrest, 1994, p. 16). On March 12, 1956, 19 senators and 89 representatives from Southern states enacted the Southern Manifesto (1956), a decree largely based on interposition reasoning. The manifesto stated that its endorsers would "use all lawful means to bring about a reversal of [the *Brown*] decision which is contrary to the Constitution and to prevent the use of force in its implementation" (Southern Manifesto, 1956, p. 4516).

In concert with the Southern Manifesto (1956), Virginia Senator Harry F. Byrd launched the Massive Resistance, a segregationist campaign subsequently approved by the state's General Assembly in 1956. The legislation permitted the state not only to discontinue funding schools that permitted racial integration but also to subsidize private school education through vouchers. Providing public funds for private institutions was in violation of Virginia's Constitution until a timely referendum—a 2,835 to 350 popular vote—abolished Section 141 of Virginia's Constitution in January of

1957 (Peeples, 1963). Two years after the Massive Resistance's inception, Virginia Governor Lindsay Almond shut down schools in Front Royal, Charlottesville, and Norfolk, refusing to integrate their respective White populations with Blacks while approving vouchers for White residents to help them subsidize private education. In 1959, though, the Virginia court ruled that Almond's action violated the 14th Amendment and ordered the reopening of the public school system.

Other less politically charged districts simply instituted freedom-of-choice plans to "satisfy" the Supreme Court's order, as opposed to enacting massive legislative campaigns. Under freedom-of-choice plans, students and their families could select the school they would like to attend. Imbedded in these plans, however, were pupil placement laws, daunting levels of bureaucracy, and other inhibitory elements that ensured sustained racial separation (Gordon, 1994). Gordon further noted that pupil placement laws used psychological and academic measures to evaluate whether a student met specific criteria to attend a designated school. In conjunction with high levels of White resistance, this practice of employing caveat-laden legislation thwarted Blacks from seeking placement in previously all-White institutions under most freedom-of-choice plans.

Though considered by many to be more liberal than the Deep South in its desegregation stance, Nashville, Tennessee, was also plagued by White resistance to the desegregation movement. Nashville's school board implemented a formal desegregation plan in 1957, targeting integration of one grade per year beginning with the first grade. By design, all grades would be integrated upon the initial integrated class's reaching its senior year in 1969. In 1957, less than 1% of African American first graders were enrolled in previously all-White schools (Halberstam, 1998, as cited in Goldring, Cohen-Vogel, & Smrekar, 2003). Six years after the implementation of Nashville's plan, less than 800 Black students were enrolled in previously all-White schools (Halberstam, 1998, as cited in Goldring et al., 2003). Many political officials, and almost all Black families, acquiesced in the face of the strength and ferocity of the White community's resistance to change. It was not only Nashville's agents of change, though, that had witnessed and suffered a decline in vigilance and zeal. Indeed, the NAACP's national membership had plummeted from 450,000 members in 1948 to fewer than 80,000 in 1957 (Patterson, 2001). Although many more citizens most likely supported the keystone organization's work, it is evident that the NAACP had been increasingly isolated and weakened by widespread White resistance.

Growing concerns of imminent court intervention into the racially biased school desegregation policy compelled segregationists to spawn in a second arena. District officials began manipulating real estate and financial marketplaces. Realtors, for instance, falsified racial composition figures for neighborhoods, and bankers discriminated against Blacks when making mortgage loans, thus limiting housing options for Blacks and forcing them to reside in overcrowded inner-city housing (Halpern, 1995; Massey & Denton, 1993). Urban renewal plans in the 1950s and 1960s, whether corrupt or overtly supportive of Black subjugation, "signaled devaluation and abandonment rather than renewal" (Halpern, 1995).

Black families also met considerable resistance if they moved into White communities. For example, a Black family's move into a White housing development in Chicago incited rioting that forced the family to move (Halpern, 1995). Moreover, these families found it difficult to find work, as the economy was controlled and protected by White, dominant-class citizens (Kerner Commission, 1968). Systematic racial steering on the part of segregationists preserved racial imbalance and perpetuated the economic inequality between White and Black citizens. For decades to come, racially isolated neighborhoods would be at the center of the desegregation maelstrom.

Leadership and federal intervention proved integral components in district and state efforts that scored higher ratios of success when implementing *Brown*'s decree. As noted by Patterson (2001), the Baltimore City school system had anticipated the *Brown* decision and, prior to the Supreme Court's ruling, held diversity training workshops. In the fall of 1955, Baltimore implemented its own desegregation plan. Baltimore's plan garnered support from school-affiliated constituents as well as from members of the city's other professional communities (Patterson, 2001). In fact, the local housing authority simultaneously discontinued segregated public housing when the Baltimore school system began to integrate. This is not to say, though, that the Baltimore plan was a panacea with respect to school desegregation. The plan did meet resistance. However, the positive role of the Baltimore community's leadership resulted in a process significantly different than the experience of those areas in the nation that remained under segregationist rule.

The capacity and willingness of public officials to resist desegregation and circumvent *Brown II*'s Court directives resulted in little to no positive desegregation progress during Stage 1 of the post-*Brown* era. State and local officials enacted freedom-of-choice plans and pupil placement laws, authorized closing of schools facing integration, provided vouchers to White families to attend private institutions, and manipulated housing and business markets to keep Black and White families separated. Although there were a modest number of judicial interventions during this period characterized by segregationist resistance, school board discriminatory practices largely went uninterrupted while *Brown II*'s ambiguous time frame rendered many judicial interventions benign.

Stage 2: Reinforcement

The 2nd decade following the Brown decision marked a watershed period. It was the first time since 1954 that the United States' judicial, executive, and congressional branch activities "moved with unparalleled and sometimes passionately cooperative determination to promote desegregation in schools" (Patterson, 2001, p. 137). For the next decade, it was a combination of judicial, executive, and congressional intervention and leadership that made it appear as though "all deliberate speed's" moment in time had ended and *Brown*'s progeny would finally bear the fruit of systematic school desegregation.

Judicial Intervention

Throughout the second post-*Brown* decade, the judicial system's involvement in, and influence on, school desegregation took new form: "The issuance of negative injunctions and approval of voluntary desegregation measures through the early sixties gave way," according to Vergon (1988), "to increasingly affirmative injunctions ... that were ... judged by their objective effectiveness rather than the subjective good faith of their proponents" (p. 29). A survey conducted by the U.S. Commission on Civil Rights exemplified the efficacy of this judicial intervention. The commission (1977) found that between 1966 and 1975, 37% of previously segregated districts desegregated because of judicial mandates and intervention. The changing nature and increased number of court system injunctions, mandates, and judgments—involving equal educational opportunity, freedom-of-choice plans, cross-district busing, and de facto segregation cases—set the stage for a reinforcement period characterized by systematic school desegregation.

In 1964, the U.S. Supreme Court wielded its considerable influence over the evolving desegregation melee for the first time. *Griffin v. County School Board of Prince Edward County* (1964) involved Virginia's politically charged Prince Edward County. In 1959, Prince Edward County had closed its public school system in defiance of both *Brown*'s decree for systematic school desegregation and the Virginia court system's 1959 declaration that Governor Almond's publicly funded private school voucher plan in Front Royal, Charlottesville, and Norfolk was unconstitutional.

Unlike Front Royal, Charlottesville, and Norfolk, Prince Edward County had maneuvered the court system, keeping its school doors shuttered and resisting distribution of public funds earmarked to finance students' private education. Monies donated by private interest groups to special private school scholarship funds were allocated instead to White families based on need. When the U.S. Supreme Court finally intervened, it declared that

> the time for mere "deliberate speed" has run out, and that phrase can no longer justify denying these Prince Edward County school children their constitutional rights to an education equal to that afforded by the public schools in the other parts of Virginia. (*Griffin v. County School Board of Prince Edward County*, 1964, p. 11)

The *Griffin* decision signaled the Court's newfound interest and involvement in defining and protecting the equal educational opportunity of Black students.

Over the next several years, the judiciary system heard numerous cases involving school desegregation. The Court ruled on faculty assignment procedures (e.g., *Bradley v. School Board, City of Richmond*, 1964), student transfer policies (e.g., *Rogers v. Paul*, 1965), and the extent to which school desegregation plans met constitutional standards (e.g., *United States v. Jefferson County Board of Education*, 1966). It was not until 1968, however, that the Supreme Court, in one of the most influential judicial interventions involving school desegregation, finally adjudicated a contextual meaning for systematic school desegregation.

The case, *Green v. County School Board of New Kent County* (1968), involved the freedom-of-choice plan of New Kent County, Virginia. In order to remain eligible for federal financial assistance under President Johnson's Civil Rights Act of 1964, the small town of New Kent County operated two schools, New Kent and Watkins. The plan ostensibly enabled students to choose which school to attend. As was the case with most freedom-of-choice initiatives, though, the plan did little to promote desegregation. In fact, 3 years after implementation, only 15% of New Kent County's Black students attended the predominantly White New Kent School and not a single White student attended the all-Black Watkins School (*Green v. County School Board of New Kent County*, 1968). New Kent's freedom-of-choice plan had proven to be little more than a means by which the district obtained federal funds and avoided judicial intervention.

In 1968, the U.S. Supreme Court ruled that New Kent County's freedom-of-choice plan was not a "sufficient step to 'effectuate a transition' to a unitary system" and that "rather than further the dismantling of the dual system, the plan ... operated simply to burden children and their parents" (*Green v. County School Board of New Kent County*, 1968). New Kent County was required to "formulate a new plan and ... fashion steps which promise realistically to convert promptly to a system without a 'White' school and a

'Negro' school, but just schools" (*Green v. County School Board of New Kent County*, 1968, p. 4). The Court not only mandated desegregation of the student population but also emphasized that New Kent County's desegregation remedies address extracurricular activities; staff, student, and faculty assignment procedures; equity of facilities; and modes of transportation. The formulation within *Green* of these six factors provided plaintiffs with benchmarks by which to measure district compliance with desegregation and, moreover, with the leverage of court rulings to mandate defined outcomes (Gordon, 1994). Indeed, the six criteria defined by the court, commonly referred to as *Green factors*, served as a basis for measurement and evaluation of district desegregation mandates compliance over several following decades.

On September 5, 1969, the U.S. Supreme Court announced an immediate end to *Brown II's* "all deliberate speed" dictum. *Alexander v. Holmes County School Board of Education* (1969) centered on 33 school districts in Mississippi and their operation of a dual school system under the guise of a freedom-of-choice plan. The Court unanimously declared operation of dual education systems constitutionally impermissible, stating "the obligation of every school district is to terminate dual school systems at once and to operate now and hereafter only unitary schools" (*Alexander v. Holmes County School Board of Education*, 1969a, p. 1). Justice Hugo L. Black wrote

> There are many places still in this country where the schools are either "White" or "Negro" and not just schools for all children as the Constitution requires. In my opinion there is no reason why such a wholesale deprivation of constitutional rights should be tolerated another minute. (*Alexander v. Holmes County School Board of Education*, 1969b, p. 4)

The ruling's demand for celerity forced many schools in the middle of the academic year to close existing dual school systems and reassign pupils in order to meet desegregation standards. Most districts instated pupil reassignment plans or the pairing and clustering of attendance zones to achieve racial balance. For some districts, however, the lack of proximity between home and school made it difficult to meet desegregation standards. To a flurry of protest, busing became the norm in resolving the challenge of racially isolated housing developments as well as increased distances between schools and their students' residences.

In what would evolve into one of the most notorious desegregation cases, North Carolina's Federal District Judge James B. McMillan ruled that the Charlotte–Mecklenburg County school systems' "freedom-of-choice plan had not fulfilled its 'affirmative duty' to desegregate the system" (Orfield & Eaton, 1996, p. 180). Charlotte–Mecklenburg was, and remains, a racial doughnut. Its urban area, the doughnut's center, was predominantly populated by minorities; surrounding suburban regions were populated largely by Whites. In addressing the racially isolated configuration of Charlotte–Mecklenburg, Judge McMillan ruled that intradistrict busing must be used to overcome racial isolation and promote balance.

In April 1971, in reviewing Judge McMillan's 1969 *Charlotte–Mecklenburg* decision, the U.S. Supreme Court attempted to attenuate the controversy surrounding desegregation mandates and remedies. The Court not only unanimously affirmed intradistrict busing as an appropriate remedy for achieving racial balance but also declared that existing racial imbalances would not be protected if rooted in any past or present acts deemed discriminatory (Orfield, 1978). *Swann v. Charlotte–Mecklenburg County Board of Education* (1971) was intended to mitigate the busing controversy; in reality, *Swann* became the focal point of contentious debate for more than a decade.

Keyes v. School District No. 1, Denver, Colorado (1973) was the first desegregation case tried outside of the South. Empowered by the *Swann* decision 2 years earlier, *Keyes* plaintiffs challenged the Denver school district's authority over, and intent in, the placement of schools and district boundaries. As noted by Gordon (1994), they argued that both the location of schools and Denver's existing district boundaries resulted in the placement of a great majority of minority students in racially isolated schools of inferior quality. In a divided decision, the Court ruled in favor of plaintiffs. According to Russo et al. (1994), the *Keyes* decision

> established what is, in effect, a spatial presumption in defining desegregation. Even though public education in Denver was not segregated by state law or constitution, the Court found that effects of the Denver school board's actions resulted in a segregated core of inner-city schools that was inferior to the predominantly White schools elsewhere in the district. (p. 304)

Keyes set a new standard for holding districts legally responsible for consequences of their policies; however, the ruling also earmarked the end of favorable judicial interventions post-*Brown*.

Executive and Congressional Interventions

The United States' 36th President, Lyndon Baines Johnson, and his Great Society Program constructed a cornerstone for executive and congressional branch policies and interventions involving school desegregation. The Civil Rights Act of 1964 and the expanded Department of Health,

Education, and Welfare (HEW) role in overseeing school district desegregation compliance, coupled with the Elementary and Secondary Education Act (ESEA) of 1965, effectuated far greater equal educational opportunity for minority students. The unification and alignment of these policies with judicial interventions provided the organizational solidarity facilitating change. It was truly the first time since 1954 that the nation's most influential institutions and individual leaders operated collectively to reinforce *Brown*.

On July 2, 1964, the Civil Rights Act (1964) was enacted after surviving the longest Senate filibuster in American history. The Civil Rights Act contained 11 titles designed to

> enforce the constitutional right to vote, to confer jurisdiction upon U.S. district courts to provide injunctive relief against discrimination in public accommodations, to authorize the Attorney General to institute suits to protect constitutional rights in public facilities and public education, to extend the Commission on Civil Rights, to prevent discrimination in federally assisted programs, to establish a Commission on Equal Employment Opportunity, and for other purposes. (p. 3)

This watershed legislation both legally codified articles protecting the rights of minority citizens and groups and politically united a diverse spectrum of constituents in a common cause.

HEW was created in 1953 and became the largest of the nation's 12 executive departments before being separated into two divisions in 1979 by Congress.[3] In 1965, when John W. Gardner, a celebrated public intellect of the period, was appointed by President Johnson as HEW's secretary, the president expanded the department's supervisory role. HEW, under Office of Civil Rights compliance official David Seeley, began actively to monitor and enforce district compliance with desegregation mandates to ensure all students enrolled in a public education system were afforded an equal education opportunity and that district's eliminated vestiges of unconstitutional discrimination (U.S. Commission on Civil Rights, 1977, 1979, 1981).

During that same year, the ESEA Act (1965), designed by then-Commissioner of Education Francis Keppel, also was endorsed. ESEA was launched "to stimulate innovation, to strengthen the states, to link research with the schools, and to make the problems of the poor the nation's num-

[3]The separation of HEW into a Department of Education and a Department of Health and Human Services was the fulfillment of an election campaign promise made to the National Education Association by President Jimmy Carter in exchange for that organization's political endorsement of his candidacy.

ber one education priority" (Murphy, 1971, p. 36). Title I of ESEA allocated historically unmatched amounts of federal resources to underprivileged and disadvantaged children through compensatory education programs in hopes of providing better educational opportunities.

Working in tandem with Title VI of the Civil Rights Act and HEW, Title I's substantial federal allocations helped promote district compliance with desegregation standards. That is, Title VI gave the federal government the legal right to withhold Title I's federal monies from public school districts if they did not comply with school desegregation mandates or operated unconstitutionally segregated schools, and HEW became the primary marshal in monitoring district compliance.

School districts often misused Title I allocations, and HEW struggled to find staff qualified to monitor widely dispersed funds (Washington Research Project, 1969). However, the effectiveness of monetary coercion on district compliance with desegregation mandates cannot be disregarded. Between 1966 and 1971, a survey of district superintendents identified HEW as the No. 1 reason (more so than the court system) for desegregation compliance (U.S. Commission on Civil Rights, 1981). Over approximately the same period, federal financial assistance filtered through Title I rose 444% from approximately \$2.7 to \$14.7 billion (National Center for Education Statistics, 2001). Although a correlation between increased federal funding and district compliance does not necessarily imply causation, the impact that monetary coercion played in reinforcing desegregation is difficult to overlook.

The political alignment of congressional, judicial, and executive branches' policies, activities, and systematic approach to reinforce *Brown*'s decree not only helped to dismantle segregation but started to eliminate vestiges of White society's resistance to the desegregation movement. Indeed, by the end of the 1962–1963 academic year, less than 1% of Black students in the primary 11 southern states (Alabama, Arkansas, Florida, Georgia, Louisiana, Mississippi, North Carolina, South Carolina, Tennessee, Texas, and Virginia) attended desegregated schools (Leeson, 1974). By 1973, more than 91% of these Black students attended desegregated schools (Leeson, 1974).

Stage 3: A Reactionary Political Paradigm

Stage 3, a nearly antithetical portrait of Stage 2, was characterized by a gradual shift toward more conservative executive, congressional, and judicial policy making as well as a corresponding de-emphasis of governmental control over educational activities and heightened desegregation controversy among, and across, America's diverse citizenry. Uprooted were congressional enactments and judicial mandates that previously countered segregationist philosophies and exemplified the liberalism of President Johnson's Great Society program. With Richard M. Nixon's successful campaign for President in 1968, an entirely new variety of seed was sown in the executive branch's garden. However, the effects of this ideological shift did not come to fruition until the mid-1970s.

Judicial, Executive, and Congressional Interventions

The judicial, executive, and congressional branches' involvement in, and influence over, school desegregation was once again a driving force in *Brown*'s progeny. Judicial impact was evident not only in notable court decisions but also in U.S. Supreme Court justice appointments. These elements greatly impacted the judicial system's organizational dynamics and behavior, while congressional enactments deliberately undermined *Brown*'s progress.

Since 1953, the U.S. Supreme Court under Chief Justice Earl Warren's leadership had set radical new precedents that transformed judicial decision-making and gained the court a reputation for "liberal judicial activism." President Nixon, however, vowed systematically to dampen the U.S. Supreme Court's liberal constitutional interpretations. Nixon's campaign speeches condemned the U.S. Supreme Court, his diatribes targeting, in particular, Chief Justice Warren's leadership. The result was the division of viewpoints amid judicial, congressional, and executive branch activities and the dissolution of a shared sense of purpose among these branches. When given the chance, Nixon planned to appoint justices to the U.S. Supreme Court who would help restore a conservative climate.

In an odd twist of fate, Nixon was able to execute his promise almost immediately. For the first time since Warren G. Harding, U.S. Supreme Court turnover enabled Nixon to appoint four justices in his first term as president (Patterson, 2001). With several controversial constitutional issues such as school desegregation, the death penalty, affirmative action, abortion, and welfare rights lurking on the Court's docket, Nixon's reinstitution of conservative judicial decision making caused significant political unrest (Patterson, 2001).

President Nixon's appointees (Warren E. Burger, Harry Blackmun, Lewis Powell Jr., and William Rehnquist) did not immediately commit to restoring conservative constitutional interpretation and judicial decision making. Warren E. Burger was not blind to the whirlwind of criticism and fear surrounding his appointment as Chief Justice and the radically new composition of the court. Rather than hastily advancing Nixon's platform, Burger struck a balance among executive branch objectives, established judicial precedent, and the nation's political climate. In fact, the Court unanimously supported affirmative action in the workplace (*Griggs v. Duke Power Co.,* 1971) and legalized abortion (*Roe v. Wade,* 1973). By 1974, however, the Burger Court was established, and when issues of de jure and de facto segregation and busing reached the docket, its conservative leanings began to blossom.

By 1974, *Milliken v. Bradley* had worked its way through district and federal courts to the U.S. Supreme Court docket. The class action suit, brought forth by the NAACP, alleged that racial isolation of minority students in the Detroit, Michigan, public school system was a result of discriminatory district zoning and pupil assignment procedures (U.S. Commission on Civil Rights, 1974). Plaintiffs sought implementation of a plan utilizing cross-district busing to desegregate the system. However, in a 5–4 decision, the U.S. Supreme Court ruled that "the relief ordered by the District Court and affirmed by the Court of Appeals was based upon erroneous standards and was unsupported by record evidence that acts of the outlying districts had any impact on the discrimination found to exist in the Detroit schools" (p. 11). Therefore, they rejected cross-district busing as a means of achieving racial balance and overcoming residential segregation. Of interest, four of the five votes in favor of the defendant were Nixon appointees. Although *Milliken* reached the U.S. Supreme Court for a second time on remand in 1977, the catalytic power of the case's initial dismissal mitigated most, if not all, of desegregation's past momentum and advancement.

Congressional statutes and judicial intervention further dismantled the framework of desegregation's progress. The Equal Education Opportunity Act of 1974 required districts to "exhaust all other means before approving busing to effect school desegregation" (p. 1). In 1976, not only did the court system prohibit the Office of Civil Rights and HEW from blocking federal funds to schools that refused to bus students but the Nixon administration began using HEW to defend actions counter to desegregation progress (Orfield, 1978; Vergon, 1990). Moreover, the collective effect of informal and formal actors, whose opinions cut across racial, class, and political lines, polarized desegregation.

Throughout the mid- to late 1970s, the dissonance between advocates and proponents of desegregation propelled educational policy, and busing in particular, to the forefront of domestic politics. Few causes have evoked a more passionate response. Not unlike the 1957 insurrection in Little Rock, Boston erupted in ethnic outrage and racial riots in the fall of 1974. U.S. District Judge W. Arthur Garrity had ordered Boston to desegregate through mass busing. No account of Boston's controversy is more revealing than J. Anthony Lukas's (1985) Pulitzer Prize winning novel, *Common Ground*. Lukas traced the lives of three Boston families as the city mobilized boycotts, initiated desegregation information centers, and voiced discontent with Judge Garrity's commission. Indeed, Judge Garrity's decision was so controversial that the population and racial composition of Boston's school system went from approximately 90,000 students with a 65% White component in 1974 to 57,000 students with a 32% White component by the early 1980s (Overbea, 1982). Boston embodied the effect of executive, judicial, and congressional branch agendas and practices when converged with opposing social ideologies.

In 1981, Ronald Reagan's presidential election brought a second storm surge of conservative political, economic, and social policy. President Reagan espoused New Federalism and a publicly funded voucher program to encourage competition and efficiency. Moreover, reduction in federal oversight of K–12 schools and elimination of the Department of Education were proposed to increase local control. In essence, federal government involvement in desegregation and local school board policy became almost nonexistent. Stage 3's reactionary paradigm had taken hold, preventing further discernible advancement and, conversely, creating a stalemate.

Stage 4: Resegregation

Stage 4 was born out of the resultant stalemate. Relying on "good faith compliance," the federal government conceded control to local governments and policymakers. Despite resistance from desegregation advocates, in the absence of federal enforcement many areas across the nation shifted away from aggressive policies that maintained racially mixed schools. In 1991, the U.S. Supreme Court—in what would be the first of a trilogy of court cases brought before the nation's high court—forever changed the legacy of *Brown*.

In 1984, Oklahoma City, Oklahoma's school board adopted a pupil reassignment policy, the Student Reassignment Plan (SRP), and pursued its implementation during the 1985–1986 academic year through a two-pronged approach. First, SRP proposed to eliminate mandatory busing of elementary grades (K–4) to alleviate the disproportionate burden of busing on Black urban youth. Second, SRP strove to promote greater parental involvement in schools by bringing schools back to the neighborhood. The plan, however, resegregated many of the district's elementary schools. Indeed, 33 of Oklahoma City's 64 elementary schools became racially isolated upon effectuation (i.e., a single race constituted more than 90% of the student body) whereas 31 schools remained racially mixed (*Board of Education of Oklahoma City Public Schools v. Dowell*, 1991).

After 7 years of intense arbitration, litigation, and remanding the case reached the U.S. Supreme Court. It had been nearly a decade since the U.S. Supreme Court had heard a case involving desegregation. In 1991, the U.S. Supreme Court ruled, in a 5–3 decision, that local education agencies could be released from both court-ordered busing and court oversight if they complied in "good faith" (p. 3) with desegregation regulations and "extinguished all vestiges" (p. 3) associated with segregation. The meaning and implication of Oklahoma City's unitary classification proved paramount in triggering the Court's shift away from future involvement in, and oversight of, the school desegregation movement.

Within 10 months of the Oklahoma decision, a second case testing the definition of achieving unitary status, *Freeman v. Pitts* (1992), was presented before the U.S. Supreme Court. Located just outside of Atlanta, Georgia, the DeKalb County School System (DCSS) housed approximately 450,000 residents and operated more than 90 schools serving approximately 75,000 students (Schmidt, 1991). Almost 50% of DCSS's students were Black, and more than half of these students attended schools that were greater than 90% Black (Walsh, 1992). The isolation of Blacks in distinct geographic pockets was largely due to Blacks' migrating south out of Atlanta in search of greater economic opportunity as well as the White community's flight to the north of the city (Walsh, 1992).

Prior to the case's reaching the U.S. Supreme Court, a Georgia court of appeals found that DCSS had successfully met four (i.e., student assignment, transportation, physical facilities, and extracurricular activities) of the six *Green* factors. The 11th Circuit Court of Appeals, however, refused to grant DCSS unitary status and release it from court-ordered desegregation because the system had not met and maintained unitary requirements regarding faculty assignment and resource allocation. The court of appeals concluded that even though the *Green* factors might be "administratively awkward, inconvenient, and even bizarre in some situations" (p. 5), the suburban Atlanta school system must sustain desegregation in all six categories for an adequate period of time before obtaining unitary status (*Freeman v. Pitts*, 1992).

On March 31, 1992, the U.S. Supreme Court overruled the 11th Circuit Court's decision. The U.S. Supreme Court unanimously agreed that a district cannot be held liable for segregation that results from private choice. In his opinion, Justice Kennedy wrote, "It is beyond the authority and beyond the practical ability of the federal courts to try to counteract these kinds of continuous and massive demographic shifts" (*Freeman v. Pitts*, 1992, pp. 7–8). The Court also permitted DCSS incrementally to terminate individual *Green* factors on its path to obtaining unitary status. The U.S. Supreme Court's ruling not only reinstated DeKalb County's school plan, declared unconstitutional almost a year earlier, but also redefined how a district could make a transition to unitary status.

Missouri v. Jenkins (1995) was the third in the trilogy of 1990 going-unitary court cases. Kansas City, Missouri, operated a magnet school plan, costing nearly $200 million a year, to attract White students living outside of Kansas City into city schools in order to meet desegregation guidelines (*Missouri v. Jenkins*, 1995; Weiler, 1998). The magnet school movement started in the 1970s and flourished during the 1980s. It represented a political compromise of sorts by merging school choice and desegregation policy to satisfy multiple constituencies' perspectives (Goldring and Smrekar, 2000). However, the changing legal and political climate made magnet schools race conscious admission policies controversial and various constituents contended that Kansas City's magnet program attracted few White students, put an undue tax burden on state residents, and improperly suborned district control to federal officials (Goldring & Smrekar, 2000; Weiler, 1998). The U.S. Supreme Court ruled as follows:

> The State of Missouri could not be required to provide funding for programs and various kinds of school improvement activities, or to pay for a plan aimed at attracting White students from suburban districts for an undetermined amount of time, simply because minority student achievement scores remained below the national average. The State could only be required to do what is practicable for remedying the vestiges of past discrimination; it was not responsible for remedying inequities that may exist between students within schools. (Weiller, 1998, pp. 6–7)

Although the ruling in *Jenkins* did not dismantle Kansas City's magnet program, it rejected the efforts of lower courts to maintain the program (Orfield & Yun, 1999).

The evolution of the Court's rulings, from *Board of Education of Oklahoma City Public Schools v. Dowell* (1991) to *Freeman v. Pitts* (1992) and *Missouri v. Jenkins* (1995), represents an epic tipping point in the desegregation movement. No longer fettered by stringent oversight and court-ordered desegregation plans, local education agencies increasingly sought relief from desegregation guidelines and dismantled their desegregation plans. Indeed, many large urban school districts, once invigorated by landmark judgments, sought to be and have been declared "unitary," including those in Denver, Colorado; Wilmington, Delaware; Savannah and Atlanta, Georgia; Kansas City, Kansas; Oklahoma City, Oklahoma; Nashville, Tennessee;

and Austin, Texas (Weiller, 1998). At the same time, other districts have called an end to or phased out their desegregation plans, including Buffalo, New York; Las Vegas, Nevada; Mobile, Alabama; Minneapolis, Minnesota; Cleveland, Ohio; and Seattle, Washington (Orfield & Yun, 1999). The impact of judicial intervention in declaring school districts to be unitary and releasing them from court prescribed desegregation standards, coupled with the de-emphasis of federal enforcement of desegregation, has engendered much social science discord.

Desegregation advocates contend that the judicial system is promoting "resegregation, added inequality, reduced opportunity, and a flight from diversity" by declaring local education agencies unitary (Goldring, Crowson, Laird, & Berk, 2002; Orfield & Eaton, 1996). In the last decade, the racial demographics in the United States' school-age population have changed significantly while integration has reverted to figures representative of the early 1960s. Indeed, from 1968 to 1996 the relative proportion of Hispanic and Black students enrolled in public schools has increased 5.76%, whereas the percentage of Anglos has decreased 5.71% (Orfield, Bachmeier, James, & Eitle, 1997). In 1996–1997, it was projected that 68.8% and 74.8% of U.S. Black and Latino students attended predominantly minority schools, respectively (Orfield & Yun, 1999).

Goldring et al. (2003) completed a comprehensive empirical study on the impact of going unitary for racially isolated urban schools. Through the support of the W. T. Grant Foundation, they drew from census data, health and police department records, and geographic information systems mapping software to analyze the Metropolitan Nashville Public Schools district. The Goldring research team concluded that racially isolated Black schools are predominantly situated in high-risk neighborhoods with the poorest economic conditions. Their data further indicate that racially isolated minority neighborhoods are significantly more likely to consist of residents with low levels of education, contain limited human and financial capital, experience high numbers of liabilities (e.g., teen birth, drug arrests, weapons arrests, domestic violence arrests, etc.), and lack institutional assets (e.g., licensed child care programs, community centers, youth service organizations, churches, hospitals, libraries, and colleges and universities). These findings not only highlight disparities found in many urban centers but reflect a sobering reality of the lack of social, political, economic, and human capital in many urban school districts.

Community empowerment and neighborhood school movement advocates believe now is the time to rebuild and restructure many of the nation's inner-city schools that are disheveled. They contend that "re-development of the social fabric of schools, communities, and families in terms of social capital, community partnerships, and parental involvement"

(Goldring et al., 2002, p. 18) is integral to school facility improvement, student outcome gains, resource efficiency, and a rebuilding on neighborhood-school connections (Goldring et al., 2002).

The positive effects of empowering community and school relationships are evidenced by the School Development Program (SDP). Developed by James P. Comer in 1980, SDP is a capacity-building model emphasizing the "total development of all children by creating learning environments that support children's physical, cognitive, psychological, language, social, and ethical development" (Comer School Development Program, 2003, p. 1) while mobilizing the greater school community (Comer School Development Program, 2003). It is currently being implemented in nearly 900 sites across the nation. In a recent meta-analysis performed on the achievement effects of 29 of the most widely implemented comprehensive and whole-school reform models, researchers found that SDP was one of only three school reform models that showed positive effects on academic achievement (Borman, Hewes, Overman, & Brown, 2003).

Crowson (2003) studied four community empowerment models and interprofessional collaboration in terms of their potential for positive impact on the neighborhood school movement. Crowson contended that

> public schools have been in but not of their communities and neighborhoods for a long time. The importance and power of the neighborhood has been rediscovered as a vital complement to the work of the school, and the neighborhood has emerged as an important educator in its own right. (p. 89)

The neighborhood school movement, in this respect, has been presented a valuable asset in the form of the paradigm shift away from cross-town busing and toward unitary norms.

Evidence indicates a disproportionate number of inadequate educational settings are firmly nestled in urban neighborhoods predominantly settled by, and increasingly composed of, minority and low socioeconomic status citizens. Current trends are not devoid of unequal and inadequate educational opportunity. However, if neighborhood school and community empowerment reform models can effectively mobilize public and private entities, rebuild the urban community, enhance the quality of the educational delivery system, and create a shared sense of purpose, there may be a chance to provide adequate educational opportunity in disadvantaged settings (e.g., Henig, Hula, Orr, & Pedescleaux, 2001; Schorr, 1998; Wilson, 1990).

Stage 5: Reconceiving the Issue

Brown *Represents Progress*

Premeditated segregation by race is now unconstitutional. More than a half-century of Jim Crow laws have been overturned. Funding structures have been brought before the courts in 43 states, with more than half resulting in action to remedy fiscal resource disparities. Still, not all that has followed the U.S. Supreme Court's landmark 1954 decision has been favorable.

The defining of *desegregation* as the mixing of Black and White student populations caused de jure barriers to be toppled. However, de facto segregation, as based on residential patterns, has become more exaggerated. This is not a consequence of *Brown*, but it is an everyday reality. Courts, and other actors in the policy system, have been reluctant to tackle de facto segregation issues. Consequently, as large a number of America's schoolchildren as in 1954 now attend racially segregated schools.

The problems inherent in educational racial segregation have been compounded by a set of societal conditions that have evolved subsequent to, and independent of, *Brown*. Today, more so than the 1950s, schooling is critical to economic development. For most of its history, management of the United States' economy, services, military, and businesses depended on the talents of a slender educated elite. However, with the advent of global economic competition, the nation's principal resource has rapidly evolved from what is mined and harvested from the earth to what is reaped from human minds. Human capital is now any nation's most precious commodity. Thus, far more so than was the case in 1954, the divide in academic achievement between Black and White students matters as much for practical economic consequences as for its moral and legal imperatives (Jencks & Phillips, 1998).

In some ways, the policy system's reluctance to deal forcefully with de facto segregation and the judicial system's more frequent granting of unitary status to school districts portends a return to *Plessy*. To be sure, this kind of racial segregation does not carry the imprimatur of law. Still, the net effect is the same. As long as facilities, resources, teacher characteristics, processes, and inputs are equal—and there is no provable intent at racial segregation—then separate and equal is constitutional.

Even if the possible solution is not judicially manageable, or at least is not easily manageable, there is still a problem. A substantial subset of America's citizenry is attending and graduating from schools without the knowledge and skill necessary to succeed in today's marketplace or to participate fully as citizens.

National Assessment of Educational Progress results capture the challenge. In Figure 1, one can see the regrettable disparate pattern of education achievement in reading proficiency by race from 1971 to 1999 (U.S. Department of Education, 2001). This is the legacy of *Plessy* that has not yet been erased.

What to do? The issue of racial segregation has to be reconceptualized. Even if America miraculously succeeded in rendering every school racially integrated, the new problem—the problem of differential academic performance—would not melt away. The most fundamental problem is an achievement gap, not gerrymandered attendance boundaries.

Closing the achievement gap was not a primary policy system challenge in 1954 nor immediately thereafter. Even if had been, however, technology capable of closing the gap was not readily available 50 years ago. Today, social science findings and educational policy inventions can provide a closer approximation to solutions.

Publication in 1983 of a nationally acclaimed report, *A Nation at Risk* (National Commission on Excellence in Education, 1983), triggered a sustained and highly visible national effort to render schools more effective. In this ongoing 2-decade quest for educational productivity, three major strategies intended to close the achievement gap have emerged (Guthrie & Springer, 2004). Two of these strategies directly involve schools. One of these operates on a so-called "systems" approach. Its major components are described below. The other incorporates more of a market mentality

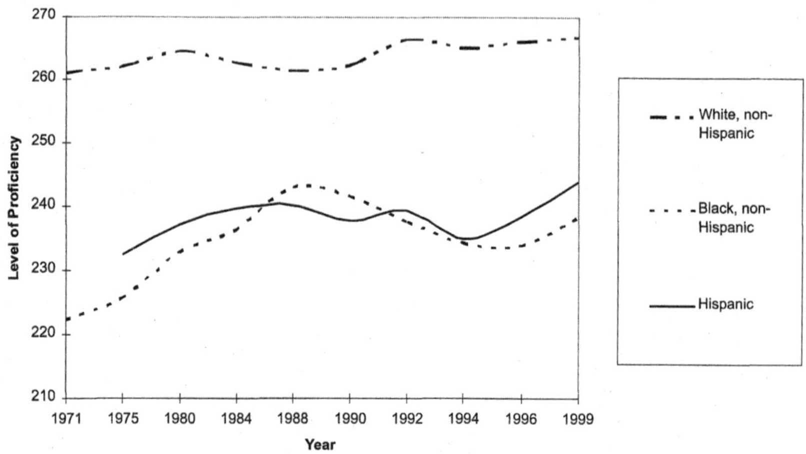

Figure 1. Average level of reading proficiency as scored by the National Assessment of Educational Progress for 13-year-olds by race: 1971 to 1999.

and depends on interschool competition between providers to elevate performance.

Systemic reform, initially explained by Smith and O'Day (1991), depends on a forceful alignment of curriculum objectives, achievement testing, teacher training and licensing, instructional materials, resource allocation, and accountability consequences. These are the kinds of changes that the states of Texas and North Carolina began to implement in the 1990s. If judged by their success in closing the Black–White achievement gap, these are promising practices (Grissmer, Flanagan, Kawata, & Williamson, 2000).

The second, market-oriented strategy asserts that competition between school providers, with losers foregoing resources as with automobile manufacturers, will motivate professional educators sufficiently to boost achievement and close the performance gap. This is a controversial tactic. It has been declared constitutional by the U.S. Supreme Court in the *Zelman v. Simmons-Harris* (2002) case. However, it has not been, at least yet, widely accepted by policymakers.[3] Even vouchers' more timid policy counterpart, charter schools, have met with great opposition from organized education interests.

A third strategy, based on elevating a child's human and social capital through mechanisms operating outside of schools, is complementary to the other two in-school strategies. This out-of-school strategy, advocated by Richard Rothstein and Norman Fruchter, takes into account the effect on student academic achievement of housing, mental health, neighborhood conditions, physical health, parental income levels, and psychological support (e.g., Fruchter, Galletta, & White, 1992; Mediratta, Fruchter, & Lewis, 2002; Rothstein, 2001).

These strategies are not mutually incompatible. Indeed, the No Child Left Behind Act (2001), sponsored by the Bush Administration and enacted by Congress in 2001, blends the first two and easily accommodates the third.

The above-described three-pronged approach accommodates racial integration, when and where it does occur. It also accommodates, in a similar vein, residentially imposed racial segregation of schoolchildren. It enables communities to be restored around their schools and actually depends on strong links between parents and their children's schools. This is the kind of policy alteration that might eventually achieve the broader goal of a racially integrated and color-blind democratic society.

[3]So far, voucher plans have been implemented or authorized only in Milwaukee, Wisconsin; Cleveland, Ohio; and Washington, DC.

References

Alexander v. Holmes County Board of Education, 396 U.S. 19 (1969a).
Alexander v. Holmes County Board of Education, 396 U.S. 1218 (1969b).
Belton v. Gebhart (and Bulah v. Gebhardt), 87 A. 2d 862 (1952).
Bennett, D. A. (1996). Becoming unitary. *American School Board Journal, 183*(8), 25–28.
Board of Education of Oklahoma City Public Schools v. Dowell, 498 U.S. 237 (1991).
Bolling v. Sharpe, 347 U.S. 497 (1954).
Borman, G. D., Hewes, G. M., Overman, L. T., & Brown, S. (2003). Comprehensive school reform and student achievement: A meta-analysis. *Review of Educational Research, 73*(2), 125–230.
Bradley v. School Board, City of Richmond, 382 U.S. 103 (1964).
Briggs v. Elliott, 98 F. Supp. 529 (1951), 103 F. Supp. 920 (1952).
Brown v. Board of Education of Topeka, Kansas, 98 F. Supp. 797 (1951), 347 U.S. 483 (1954), 349 U.S. 294 (1955).
Civil Rights Act of 1964, 42 U.S.C. (1964).
Comer School Development Program. (2003). Comer School Development Program: Yale Child Study Center. Retrieved September 1, 2003, from http://info.med.yale.edu/comer/index.html
Crowson, R. L. (2003). Empowerment models for interprofessional collaboration. In M. M. Brabeck, M. E. Walsh, & R. E. Latta (Eds.), *Meeting at the hyphen: Schools–universities–communities–professions in collaboration for student achievement and well being. 102nd yearbook of the National Society for the Study of Education* (pp. 74–93). Chicago: University of Chicago Press.
Davis v. County School Board of Prince Edward County, 103 F. Supp. 337 (1954).
DeLacy, D. R. (1997). Unitary status. *American School Board Journal, 184*(12), 22–24.
Equal Education Opportunity Act, 20 U.S.C. § 17 (1974).
Fleming, H. C. (1975). *Brown* and the three Rs: Race, residence, and resegregation. *Journal of Law and Education, 4*(1), 8–15.
Forrest, W. R. (1994). "*Brown*" revisited. *Phi Delta Kappan, 76*(1), 12–20.
Freeman v. Pitts, 498 U.S. 1081, 503 U.S. 467 (1992).
Fruchter, N., Galleta, A., & White, J. L. (1992). *New directions in parent involvement*. Washington, DC: Academy for Educational Development.
Goldring, E., Cohen-Vogel, L., & Smrekar, C. (2003, April). *Neighborhood capacity in the post-busing era*. Paper presented at the meeting of the American Educational Research Association, Chicago.
Goldring, E., Crowson, R., Laird, D., & Berk, B. (2002, April). *Unmaking desegregation policy and "going unitary": The loss of a sense of place*. Paper presented at the annual meeting of the American Educational Research Association, New Orleans, LA.
Goldring, E., & Smrekar, C. (2000). Magnet schools and the pursuit of racial balance. *Education and Urban Society, 33*, 17–35.
Gordon, W. M. (1994). The implementation of desegregation plans since *Brown*. *The Journal of Negro Education, 63*, 310–322.
Gordon, W. M., & Bartz, D. E. (1993). Achieving unitary status under the combined standards of "Dowell" and "Pitts." *West's Education Law Quarterly, 2*, 533–539.
Green v. County School Board of New Kent County, 391 U.S. 430 (1968).
Griffin v. County School Board of Prince Edward County, 377 U.S. 218 (1964).
Griggs v. Duke Power Company, 401 U.S. 424 (1971).
Grissmer, D., Flanagan, A., Kawata, J., & Williamson, S. (2000). *Improving student achievement: What state NAEP scores tell us*. Santa Monica, CA: RAND.
Guthrie, J. W., & Springer, M. G. (2004). *A nation at risk* revisted: Did "wrong" reasoning result in "right" results? *Peabody Journal of Education, 79*(1), 7–35.

Halpern, R. (1995). *Rebuilding the inner city: A history of neighborhood initiatives to address poverty in the United States*. New York: Columbia University Press.

Harvard Civil Rights Project. (2002). *Selected unitary status rulings between 1990–2002*. Retrieved August 20, 2003, from http://www.civilrightsproject.harvard.edu/research/reseg03/appendices

Henig, J. R., Hula, R. C., Orr, M., & Pedescleaux, D. S. (2001). *The color of school reform: Race, politics, and the challenge of urban education*. Princeton, NJ: Princeton University Press.

Jencks, C., & Phillips, M. (Eds.). (1998). *The Black–White test score gap*. Washington, DC: Brookings Institution.

Kerner Commission. (1968). *National advisory commission on civil disorders*. Washington, DC: National Advisory Commission on Civil Disorders.

Keyes v. School District No. 1, Denver, Colorado, 413 U.S. 189 (1973).

Kluger, R. (1976). *Simple justice: The history of Brown v. Board of Education and Black America's struggle for equality*. New York: Vintage.

Leeson, J. (1974). What the statistics say … *Race Relations Reporter, 5*(9), 18–36.

Lukas, A. J. (1985). *Common ground: A turbulent decade in the lives of three American families*. New York: Vintage.

Massey, D. S., & Denton, N. A. (1993). *American apartheid: Segregation and the making of the underclass*. Cambridge, MA: Harvard University Press.

McCarthy, M. M. (1991). Elusive "unitary status." *West's Education Law Reporter, 69*, 9–18.

McLaurin v. Oklahoma State Regents for Higher Education, 339 U.S. 637 (1950).

Mediratta, K., Fruchter, N., & Lewis, A. C. (2002). *Organizing for school reform: How communities are finding their voice and reclaiming their public schools*. New York: Institute for Education and Social Policy.

Milliken v. Bradley, 418 U.S. 717 (1974)

Milliken v. Bradley, 433 U.S. 267 (1977).

Missouri v. Jenkins, 495 U.S. 33 (1995).

Murphy, J. T. (1971). Title I of EASEA: The politics of implementing federal education reform. *Harvard Educational Review, 41*(1), 35–63.

National Center for Education Statistics. (2001). *The digest of education statistics, 2001* (NCES 2002-130 by T. D. Synder). Washington, DC: U.S. Department of Education.

National Commission on Excellence in Education. (1983). *A nation at risk: The imperative for educational reform*. Washington, DC: U.S. Department of Education.

No Child Left Behind Act, R.L. No. 107-110 (2001).

Orfield, G. (1978). *Must we bus? Segregated schools and national policy*. Washington, DC: Brookings Institution.

Orfield, G., Bachmeier, M. D., James, D. R., & Eitle, T. (1997). Deepening segregation in American public schools: A special report from the Harvard project on school desegregation. *Equity and Excellence in Education, 30*(2), 5–24.

Orfield, G., & Eaton, S. E. (Eds.). (1996). *Dismantling desegregation: The quiet reversal of Brown v. Board of Education*. New York: New Press.

Orfield, G., & Yun, J. T. (1999). *Resegregating American schools*. Cambridge, MA: Harvard University Civil Rights Project.

Overbea, L. (1982, October 7). In Boston: Busing revolt fades; city learns to adapt. *Christian Science Monitor*, p. 8.

Patterson, J. T. (2001). *Brown v. Board of Education: A civil right milestone and its troubled legacy*. New York: Oxford University Press.

Peeples, E. H., Jr. (1963). *A perspective of the Prince Edward County school issue*. Unpublished master's thesis. University of Pennsylvania.

Plessy v. Ferguson, 163 U.S. 537 (1896).

Roberts v. City of Boston, 59 Mass (5 Cush.) 198 (1850).

Roe v. Wade, 410 U.S. 113 (1973).

Rogers v. Paul, 382 U.S. 171 (1965).

Rothstein, R. (2001). Investing in family capital. *American School Board Journal, 188*(2), 18–21.

Russo, C. J., Harris, J., III, & Sandidge, R. (1994). *Brown v. Board of Education* at 40: A legal history of equal educational opportunity in American public education. *The Journal of Negro Education, 63*, 297–309.

Schmidt, P. (1991, October 9). Blacks divided as court prepared to consider desegregation case. *Education Week*. Retrieved August 8, 2003, from http://www.educationweek.org/ew/ewstory.cfm?slug=06deseg.h11&keywords=Schmidt.P.1-6

Schorr, L. (1998). *Common purpose: Strengthening families and neighborhoods to rebuild America.* New York: Anchor.

Sipuel v. Board of Regents of the University of Oklahoma, 332 U.S. 631 (1948).

Smith, M. S., & O'Day, J. (1991). Systemic school reform. In S. H. Fuhrman & B. Malen (Eds.), *The politics of curriculum and testing: The 1990 yearbook of the politics of education association.* Bristol, PA: Falmer.

Southern Manifesto, 102 Cong. Rec. 4515–4516 (1956).

Swann v. Charlotte–Mecklenburg Board of Education, 402 U.S. 1 (1971).

Sweatt v. Painter, 210 S.W. 2d 442 (1947), 339 U.S. 629 (1950).

U.S. Commission on Civil Rights. (1974). *Milliken v. Bradley: The implications for metropolitan desegregation.* Washington, DC: U.S. Government Printing Office.

U.S. Commission on Civil Rights. (1977). *Reviewing a decade of school desegregation 1966–1975* (Staff Report of a National Survey of School Superintendents). Washington, DC: U.S. Government Printing Office.

U.S. Commission on Civil Rights. (1979). *Desegregation of the nation's public schools: A status report.* Washington, DC: U.S. Government Printing Office.

U.S. Commission on Civil Rights. (1981). *With all deliberate speed: 1954–19??* (Clearinghouse Publication No. 69). Washington, DC: U.S. Government Printing Office.

U.S. Department of Education. (2001). *NAEP trends in academic progress.* Washington, DC: National Center for Education Statistics.

United States v. Jefferson County School Board of Education, 372 F.2d 836 (1966).

Vergon, C. B. (1988). The evolution of the school desegregation movement: Implications for equity and excellence. *Equity and Excellence, 24*(1), 26–35.

Vergon, C. B. (1990). School desegregation: Lessons from three decades of experience. *Educational Policy, 23*(1), 22–49.

Vergon, C. B. (1994). *Brown* at the threshold of the 21st century: Enduring or withering legacy? *Journal of Negro Education, 63*, 482–500.

Walsh, M. (1992, April 8). High court eases federal guidelines for desegregation. *Education Week*. Retrieved August 8, 2003, from http://www.educationweek.org/ew/ewstory.cfm?slug=29scotus.h11&keywords=Walsh.P.1-5

Washington Research Project. (1969). *Title I of ESEA; Is it helping poor children?* (A report by the Washington Research Project of the Southern Center for Studies in Public Policy and the NAACP Legal Defense and Educational Fund, Inc.). Washington, DC: Author.

Weiler, J. (1998). *Recent changes in school desegregation* (ERIC/CUE Digest No. 133). New York: ERIC Clearinghouse on Urban Education. Retrieved August 15, 2003, from http://www.edrs.com/members/sp.cfm?AN=ED419029

Wilson, W. J. (1990). *The truly disadvantaged: The inner city, the underclass, and public policy.* Chicago: University of Chicago Press.

Zelman v. Simmons-Harris, 00–1751, 234 F. 3d 945 (2002).

PEABODY JOURNAL OF EDUCATION, *79*(2), 33–40

A Commentary: Calming *Brown*'s Critics, Still Queasy After All these Years

Rebecca L. Brown
Vanderbilt University Law School

This essay acknowledges some of the disappointing consequences of the *Brown v. Board of Education* (1954) decision. It urges, however, that the strategic choices underlying that decision and the principle it articulates are sound and worthy of celebration 50 years later.

The Supreme Court's dramatic holding 50 years ago that racially separate education is "inherently unequal," left many legal scholars feeling queasy. It was difficult for them to reconcile what seemed the right social message with their belief in a relatively restrained role for unelected courts in the constitutional system.[1] The widespread discomfort led to decades of constitutional theory scholarship devoted to the issue of the so-called "countermajoritarian difficulty."[2] This furor has finally shown signs of

[1]See, for example, Wechsler (1959) for an expression of doubt that *Brown* could be defended on "neutral" grounds, independent of the contingent fact of how a segregated group may be affected by the segregation.

[2]See Friedman (2002) for documentation of Alexander Bickel's coining of the term *countermajoritarian difficulty* to describe the troubling role of the unelected Court in a democracy.

The author served as a law clerk to Associate Justice Thurgood Marshall in the Supreme Court's 1985 Term.

Requests for reprints should be sent to Rebecca L. Brown, Allen Professor of Law, Vanderbilt University Law School, 131 21st Avenue South, Room no. 237, Nashville, TN 37203–1181. E-mail: rebecca.brown@law.vanderbilt.edu

subsiding.[3] Few, if any, scholars today would hold that *Brown v. Board of Education* (1954) was incorrect because it was born of judicial activism.

However, that queasiness has been replaced by another. Looking back on the 50 years since the landmark decision, some observers have concerns regarding the doctrinal legacy left by *Brown*. The case and its progeny have been used to support a view of the Constitution that prevents any consideration of race, even when Congress or a state determines that racial consciousness best promotes equality by ameliorating serious social problems linked to past and present racial inequalities.[4] Surely there is irony in the recognition that the Court's ringing affirmation of the end of discriminatory segregation has led to a doctrine that tells state and federal governments that although they are constitutionally free do whatever they think necessary to help virtually any nonracially defined group to better its lot in society—farmers, athletes, Democrats[5]—they may do nothing to benefit the one group whose continuing disproportionate representation in the lower echelons of society can be traced to treatment they received because of the color of their skin.[6]

Even more frustrating, perhaps, has been the reading of *Brown* that has led some to hold that the Constitution prevents racially separate education even when it is done as a means to rescue young people in crisis, when experts believe there may be some hope for the hopeless in a racially and culturally separate learning environment for improvement of self-esteem and cultural identity. *Brown*, some have said, will not tolerate intentional racial separation when motivated by a desire to raise up the hopeless, any more than it will tolerate intentional racial integration at the more desirable rungs of the social ladder when motivated by commitments of inclusion.[7] Let's get this straight. *Brown*, by any measure one of the greatest cases of

[3]See Brown (1998) for an argument that the concern with countermajoritarian difficulty misunderstands the nature of our constitutional democracy.

[4]See, for example, Sherry (1997; *Brown* implicitly embodied a principle of color blindness), Blumstein (1995; *Brown* contained a "nondiscrimination principle" that forbids race-dependent decisions of any kind), *Adarand v. Pena*, 515 U.S. 200 (1995; holding that all uses of race require compelling state justification), *Shaw v. Reno* (1993; validating White plaintiffs' claimed right to participate in a "color-blind" electoral process).

[5]See *Davis v. Bandemer* (1986; political gerrymandering does not trigger strict scrutiny).

[6]Strictly, this statement should be qualified with the phrase "without a compelling government interest." Race-conscious government actions are subjected to the strictest of judicial scrutiny, requiring the state to demonstrate that its measures are "necessary" to achieve a "compelling government interest" *Adarand v. Pena* (p. 236). Government interests strong enough to count as "compelling" are few, and indeed, for a while were thought to be virtually nonexistent. Recently, however, the Supreme Court identified student-body diversity as a compelling state interest sufficient to permit a narrowly tailored program of race-conscious admissions decisions in state institutions of higher education (*Grutter v. Bollinger*, 2003).

[7]See, for example, Smith (1992) for a response to these arguments.

the 20th century, ended state-sponsored racial discrimination and offered a promise of equality to all. Now, 50 years later, with school integration and race–poverty independence still elusive ideals, its principal contribution is to pluck, from the arsenal of weapons available to governments to combat serious social problems, the one most directly targeted to the evils that *Brown v. Board* identified. Under this view, states cannot intentionally separate or voluntarily integrate to alleviate racial inequities. They must, in effect, leave racial distributions across society where they find them, ignoring the historical, utterly race-conscious path by which those proportions arrived at their regrettable current levels.

This disappointing irony has led some to question *Brown* itself. Would we all have been better off if the Court had simply reaffirmed the "separate but equal" doctrine? Did the National Association for the Advancement of Colored People (NAACP) make a grave mistake in calling for the overruling of *Plessy v. Ferguson* (1896)?[8] I suggest three reasons why the answer to both of these questions should be "No."

The first reason it was not a mistake relates to the decision that the litigation strategists of the NAACP Legal Defense Fund made in the context in which they made it. This was an organization that had set out, starting in the 1930s, with the goal of dismantling racial oppression in this country, and they took their steps one at a time, always with the long view in mind. They had had incremental successes, and perhaps they could continue to achieve incremental successes, one case at a time. One issue that presented these lawyers with continual challenge was the question of whether, and, if so, when, they should attack segregation itself, seeking to overrule *Plessy v. Ferguson*, rather than continue with a more cautious strategy of attacking individual educational opportunities for African Americans as unequal and therefore failing the *Plessy* test.[9] There was a difference of opinion on this important point within the ranks of the Legal Defense Fund itself. Thurgood Marshall, its lead attorney, wrote at the time in favor of the more aggressive approach: "If we had not threatened to challenge the legality of the segregation system and if we do not continue the challenge to segregated schools, we will get the same thing we have been getting all these years—separate but never equal" (Kluger, 1977, p. 524). Much debate among extremely sophisticated strategists ensued on this issue, and in the end, Marshall's view prevailed. His brief to the Supreme Court, asking it to take the *Brown* case, took the more aggressive approach: "Segregation as practiced in America has been universally understood to impose on Ne-

[8] *Plessy v. Ferguson* upheld a state law that required racially separate railroad cars because the state law did not mandate an inequality, giving rise to the doctrine of "separate but equal."

[9] See Kluger (1977).

groes this badge of inferiority, and the contrary dictum in *Plessy v. Ferguson* can no longer stand in the face of a wealth of evidence flatly contradicting it" (Kluger, 1977, p. 538).

In light of the developments over the past 50 years, it may be tempting to say that Marshall made the wrong strategic choice. All of the troublesome disputes and legacies of the "color-blind" approach to racial justice, it is sometimes speculated, could have been avoided if the Supreme Court had simply put some teeth into the "equal" component of the separate but equal doctrine rather than obliterating the "separateness" component.

Many years later, Thurgood Marshall, by then a Supreme Court Justice himself, talked to his clerks about this important strategy choice. He told us, in his inimitable earthy style, that

> you can't have decent education without money. Who had the money? The "white folks." No way were they ever going to give it to the Negroes, no matter what a court told them to do. There are too many ways around that kind of order, to make the schools "equal." The only way to get the white folks to give us decent schools was to make it be their schools too. (personal communication, 1985)[10]

His view, as I understand it, was not that integration was a benefit to African American children in the abstract, a message potentially laden with undertones of racial inferiority that he would never have tolerated. Rather, he saw a world in which racial minorities and poverty were highly correlated, combined with the pervasiveness of overt and vicious racial prejudice, and he quite pragmatically concluded that integration was the only hope for improvement of the quality of the education provided to those children by society at large.

This straightforward, commonsense view, so typical of Justice Marshall, reflects understated sophistication, also typical of him. The idea of tying the interests of those without political power to those who possess it in order to enhance the quality of representation in a democracy is older than the Constitution itself. The lack of universal suffrage in pre–Revolutionary War England, for example, was often justified on the notion of *virtual representation*—that the existence of common interests would permit those who did have a vote to protect the interests of those who did not.[11] This idea was considered one of the most significant pro-

[10]This is a paraphrase of my own memory of the conversation.

[11]See Pitkin (1967; explaining that virtual representation afforded the "substantive content and effect," p. 175, without actual election).

tectors of liberty under British constitutionalism.[12] James Madison (1788/1961) viewed the principle as having important application in the American constitutional structure as well when he described the "communion of interests and sympathy of sentiments of which few governments have furnished examples; but without which every government degenerates into tyranny" (pp. 352–153).

The same insight, indeed, underlies one of the most celebrated constitutional theories of the 20th century, that of representation-reinforcement put forward by Ely (1980), some 30 years after *Brown*. Ely identified the principle of empathy between representatives and their various constituents as essential to democratic functioning (p. 184). In situations in which majorities can effectively sever their interests from those of minority groups, a malfunction of the democratic processes occurs and courts must step in to remedy the problem (p. 181). The idea is that, in a democracy, there is little risk that the elected officials will offend the majority in any serious way, because elections provide an obvious recourse for this kind of act. The more worrisome danger is that representatives will be responsive only to the majority, exporting the costs and burdens of life disproportionately onto those who cannot vote them out of office. Linking the interests of representatives and the majorities that support them with the interests of all invokes a broad principle of equality that responds to this danger of "majority tyranny." Thus, the NAACP Legal Defense Fund's decision to seek to overrule *Plessy*, rather than to apply it in a rigorous way, was profoundly consistent with constitutional tradition and commitment. It echoes the Constitution's treatment of democratic representation.[13] That decision should not lightly be second-guessed.

A second reason that the current anomalies attributable to a principle of color blindness should not present an occasion to reconsider the wisdom of *Brown* is that the invocation of this principle rests on a misreading of *Brown*. Thus, if complaints are to be made, they should be directed not at *Brown* but at those who attribute to that case implications that are utterly inconsistent with its message.

In order to derive from *Brown* a principle requiring states to be neutral with regard to race in all situations, one must isolate it artificially from its historical setting and its own quite clear assumptions. The Court recog-

[12]See Brown (2002).

[13]The Constitution contains some explicit examples of the tying of the powerful with the powerless. The privileges and immunities clause, for example, requires that, whatever benefits they bestow on their own citizens (who have a vote in the state), states must bestow those same benefits on citizens of other states (who do not). See the U.S. Constitution, Article IV, section 2, clause 1.

nized that "intangibles," even in a (highly implausible) hypothetical state of the world in which facilities are posited as equal, would undermine, in fact, the attainment of true equality. Although it did not explicitly rest its holding on the undeniable fact that the segregation laws in place in 1954 had been passed by the politically powerful majority for the purpose of maintaining supremacy of the majority race, the opinion reflects this awareness. The Court acknowledged the constitutional significance of the existence of feelings of inferiority or stigma that are inevitably generated when segregation is accompanied by entrenched racial hierarchy. The Court's reliance on the controversial "doll studies" establishing this point would not have been necessary if the Court had thought it was justified in holding that any use of race is automatically a violation of the equal protection clause. Thus, it is erroneous for later readers of the opinion to suggest that the case makes some abstract claim about race divorced from this context. The Court's opinion cannot reasonably sustain a suggestion that under different societal conditions, motivated by ameliorative rather than invidious aspirations for society, the use of race would necessarily be pernicious.

Finally, the third reason that *Brown* does not deserve condemnation, despite its regrettable legacies, is that even acknowledging that its message of "equality" may have been misapplied in later cases, its message has still contributed to an improved public rhetoric on the issue of race. Had the Court blinked at what everyone knew to be the inevitable inequality in segregated public education in 1954, it would have, at least implicitly, validated the concept of racial subordination.[14] Several societal circumstances were evident at the time. First, no one would have suggested that the laws segregating schools had been passed with full participation of African American voters, for many of whom the right to vote was still elusive due to poll taxes, literacy tests, and other devices intentionally designed to keep them from participating in such policy decisions. Thus, it was clear that the creation of racially separate social institutions was in no way motivated by a desire to help African American children flourish in school and in society. Moreover, whatever state of facts one might hypothesize in order to resolve a constitutional question, there was no realistic expectation that funding for separate African American schools would ever be what it was for the White schools. If the Court either had ignored these realities or had even approved them by suggesting that the existing system of racial segregation could support

[14]Compare Sunga (1997), which suggested that a government's toleration of systemic group discrimination often leads to more serious human rights violations.

an inference of equality, it would have inevitably endorsed the project of racial oppression itself.[15] This would have paved the way for those in the public eye to continue to speak of racial hierarchy and racial subordination as valid topics of debate, rather than as unspeakable and deplorable goals inconsistent with the polity's basic commitments.[16] Thus, I suggest (although there are many who disagree) that it was important for the development of public mores about equality that the Supreme Court inject a dose of candor into the issue by declaring that, under the well-recognized conditions of intentional racial oppression, separate could not reasonably be construed as equal. The fact that it has not led to equality in fact does not compromise the power of that essential belief.

I do see much to celebrate in the 50th anniversary of *Brown*. High on the list is the courage of Thurgood Marshall and the other attorneys involved in making the very daunting decision of whether to take the huge risk of asking the Supreme Court to declare the principle of equality to be the law of the land. Those lawyers knew that this case was a hard beginning and not a triumphant end, but they made the admirable judgment that it was better than crawling to the courts, school by school, pleading for equal funding in an endless battle about facts rather than principle. Integration, for them, was not an end, but a means—employing the ancient device of tying the interests of the powerless with those of the powerful to achieve better laws for all.

Justice Marshall (personal communication, 1986) once told me, perhaps not entirely seriously, that he would like his epitaph to read, "He did what he could with what he had." On the strategy of the *Brown* case, I would suggest that is a true characterization, indeed.

References

Adarand v. Pena, 515 U.S. 200 (1995).

Blumstein, J. F. (1995). Voting rights after Shaw v. Reno: Racial gerrymandering and vote dilution: Shaw in doctrinal context. *Rutgers Law Journal, 26*, 517, 518–529 & nn. 52–56.

Brown, R. L. (1998). Accountability, liberty and the constitution. *Columbia Law Review, 98*, 531–538.

Brown, R. L. (2002). Liberty, the new equality. *New York University Law Review, 77*, 1491, 1513.

[15]Compare Minow (2003), which discussed ways to lessen intergroup prejudices through education, including the building of public institutions and practices dedicated to ideals of equality.

[16]See Eisgruber (1992) for a questioning of the educative value of *Brown* because of its ambivalent appeal to integration as a community ideal) and Rosenberg (1991) for an argument that civil rights progress owed little to the *Brown* decision.

Brown v. Board of Educ., 347 U.S. 483 (1954).
Davis v. Bandemer, 478 U.S. 109 (1986).
Eisgruber, C. L. (1992). Is the Supreme Court an educative institution? *New York University Law Review, 67,* 961, 1022–1028.
Friedman, B. (2002). The birth of an academic obsession: The history 'of the countermajoritarian difficulty, Part Five. *Yale Law Journal 153,* 197–202.
Ely, J. H. (1980). *Democracy and distrust.* Cambridge, MA: Harvard University Press.
Grutter v. Bollinger, 123 S. Ct. 2325 (2003).
Kluger, R. (1977). *Simple justice: The history of* Brown v. Board of Education *and Black America's struggle for equality* (pp. 522–538). New York: Random House.
Madison, J. (1961). The Federalist no. 57. In. C. Rossiter, (Ed.), *The Federalist papers* (pp. 352–353). New York: New American Library. (Original work published 1788)
Minow, M. (2003). Education for co-existence. *Arizona Law Review, 44,* 14–16.
Pitkin, H. F. (1967). *The concept of representation* (pp. 174–176). Berkeley: University of California Press.
Plessy v. Ferguson, 163 U.S. 537 (1896).
Rosenberg, G. N. (1991). *The hollow hope: Can courts bring about social change?* (pp. 157–169). Chicago: University of Chicago Press.
Shaw v. Reno, 509 U.S. 630 (1993).
Sherry, S. (1997). All the Supreme Court really needs to know it learned from the Warren Court. *Vanderbilt Law Review, 50,* 463.
Smith, P. J. (1992). All-Black schools and the equal protection clause: A step forward toward education. *Tulane Law Review, 66,* 2007–2014.
Sunga, L. S. (1997). *The emerging system of international criminal law: Developments in codification and implementation* (p. 150). The Hague: Kluwer Law International.
Wechsler, H. (1959). Toward neutral principles of constitutional law. *Harvard Law Review, 73,* 31–35.

PEABODY JOURNAL OF EDUCATION, *79*(2), 41–50

A Commentary: "*Brown v. Board of Education I*: A Reconsideration"

Lucius T. Outlaw Jr.
Department of Philosophy
Vanderbilt University

This article, a reconsidering of both the benefits and the consequences of the *Brown v. Board of Education* (1954; Davis & Graham, 1995) case, posits determinations as to the historical significance of the U.S. Supreme Court justices' decision. Carefully weighing the words of the justices renders a position that the decision of the Court and the intention of the Court do not fall in alignment with one another. And despite the rightness of the decision and all that has been reaped in the way of its benefits, still, the decision's unarticulated language has rendered a greater significance and has placed enduring consequences on the public education system, as well as in the greater context of race as a whole.

Brown I Almost 50 Years Later ...

There is little doubt that the U.S. Supreme Court's unanimous decision rendered in *Brown I* (*Brown v. Board of Education*, 1954)—that racially segregated schooling was, among other things, unequal and unconstitutional—has been one of profound significance for the organization and pursuit of life projects and well-being in the United States of America. It

Requests for reprints should be sent to Lucius T. Outlaw Jr., Vanderbilt University, Department of Philosophy, 111 Furman Hall, Nashville, TN 37240. E-mail: l.outlawjr@vanderbilt.edu

was, of course, both an immediate strike, and a subsequent weapon, against de jure and de facto invidious racial segregation and continues to be of service in those ways to this day. U.S. citizens continue, then, to reap the benefits, and the consequences otherwise, of the decision.

A great many of the benefits and consequences have been of profound positive significance for Black folks especially, as was the Court's intention—but for White folks, too, though on my reading of the justices' argument in support of their decision, this was not their intention. On the contrary, latent in the Court's decision, in the justices' reasoning, were matters of no less profound significance for folks Black and White that were not so positive in their effects, matters that only recently have received serious critical attention: namely, unarticulated presumptions regarding White folks that served to provide a powerful but silent normative frame for the argument and decision that resulted in a decidedly one-sided weighing of harms and a likewise one-sided posing of remedies.[1]

Flagg (1993/1997) referred to the play of this silent normative frame as "the transparency phenomenon":

> In this society, the white person has an everyday option not to think of herself in racial terms at all. In fact, whites appear to pursue that option so habitually that it may be a defining characteristic of whiteness: to be white is not to think about it. ... Whites' "consciousness" of whiteness is predominantly unconsciousness of whiteness ... whites' social dominance allows us to relegate our own racial specificity to the realm of the subconscious. Whiteness is the racial norm. ... Whiteness, once identified, fades almost instantaneously from white consciousness into transparency. (pp. 220–221)

It is the Court's one-sided weighing and remedying in *Brown*, due, I contend, to the operative force of powerful, unarticulated, "transparent" normative convictions—the normativity of whiteness—that I wish to explore. Hence, my "reconsideration" of *Brown I*: not of the decision against the constitutionality of racially segregated public schools but, rather, a reconsideration of a key aspect of the justices' convictions, important core assumptions, and reasoning, and, as well, those of lawyers for the plaintiffs

[1]An enormous and still growing body of effort has been devoted to exploring and critiquing the presence and influence of racial considerations and valorizations in jurisprudence and constitutes what has come to be recognized as the field of critical race theory, an outgrowth of the field of critical legal theory–studies. A more recent turn in critical race–legal theory has been the emergence of Whiteness studies wherein some persons concern themselves with the normativity of Whiteness in U.S. American culture generally and in jurisprudence in particular.

who prevailed in persuading the justices to come to the decision rendered in the case.

I am confident that via the many events to come leading up to, and on the occasion of, the 50th anniversary of *Brown I* (and that of *Brown II; Brown v. Board of Education*, 1955), when folks will devote time to taking stock of the decisions and developments that followed from them, quite ample attention will be paid to the positive outcomes such that I can focus elsewhere without fear that full appreciation of the historic significance of the cases and decisions will be impaired or miscast by my doing so. However, before I take my tack I must acknowledge that my own life has been profoundly affected by the decisions rendered in the *Brown* cases. Without them I would not likely be where I am today professionally nor have quite the life that I enjoy today. I must give the Court, the plaintiffs, and the latters' lawyers their full props. I do so sincerely and with much gratitude. Still, there is, I believe, more to be noted and appreciated about the decisions that can be disclosed by a close reading and critical consideration of the reasoning supporting the decision in *Brown I*. To an exploratory example of such a reading and critique I now turn.

Profound Outcomes, One-Sided Reasoning …

In 1954, then U.S. Supreme Court Chief Justice Earl Warren, in delivering the opinion of the Court in *Brown I*, recapitulated a focal contention of the plaintiffs' legal team (lawyers from the National Association for the Advancement of Colored People's Legal Defense and Education Fund; LDEF): that "segregated public schools are not 'equal' and cannot be made 'equal,' and … hence they [school-attending Negro children] are deprived of the equal protection of the laws" (Davis & Graham, 1995, p. 164). The LDEF lawyers were taking aim at the constitutionality of *Plessy v. Ferguson* (1896) while pressing the case for the viability of considering the 14th Amendment to the U.S. Constitution as prohibiting invidious racial discrimination against Negroes in public schooling, a matter not addressed explicitly in the amendment. The justices, in their reasoning regarding the equality of segregated schooling, were persuaded that it was not enough to assess comparatively the equality of the "tangible factors" of White and Negro schooling—buildings, curricula, qualifications and salaries of teachers, and so forth—but that it was necessary to "look instead to *the effect of segregation itself on public education* [italics added]" (Davis & Graham, 1995, p. 165). Continuing, the justices reasoned that it was not possible to "turn the clock back" to 1868 when the 14th Amendment was adopted and settle the matter of intended impact on public schooling (because, at the time, there was not much in the way of public schooling) or back to 1896 when *Plessy* was decided. Rather, they concluded as follows:

> We must consider public education in the light of its full development and its present place in American life throughout the Nation. Only in this way can it be determined if segregation in public schools deprives these plaintiffs of the equal protection of the laws. (Davis & Graham, 1995, p. 165)

Setting forth what I think can rightly be regarded as core convictions of the justices, they reasoned that education "is the most important function of state and local governments" and is of recognized importance "to our democratic society. ... It is the very foundation of good citizenship" (Davis & Graham, 1995, p. 165). Success in life is doubtful if a child is denied the opportunity of an education, they argued. Hence, the justices concluded, "Such an opportunity, where the state has undertaken to provide it, is a right which must be made available to all on equal terms" (Davis & Graham, 1995, p. 165). And with this the justices came to the focal question and their answer to it:

> Does segregation of children in public schools solely on the basis of race, even though the physical facilities and other 'tangible' factors may be equal, deprive the children of the *minority* [italics added] group of equal educational opportunities? We believe that it does. (Davis & Graham, 1995, p. 165)

On reconsideration, note the justices' reasoning: The harm—deprivation of "equal" educational opportunity—is thought to be suffered by "children of the minority group," not at all, apparently, by children of the majority group, that is, White children. Schools, the Court had noted in *Sweatt v. Painter* (1950), involve not only "tangible" goods but, as well, "intangible" goods: "those qualities which are incapable of objective measurement but which make for greatness in a law school" (Davis & Graham, 1995, p. 165). Considerations of the important intangibles, the justices reasoned

> apply with added force to children in grade and high schools. To separate them from others of similar age and qualifications solely because of their race generates a feeling of inferiority as to their status in the community that may affect their hearts and minds in a way unlikely ever to be undone. (Davis & Graham, 1995, p. 165)

In coming to this conclusion the justices drew, in part, on a finding of a lower court in the Topeka, Kansas, case that had been consolidated into *Brown I*. Writing for the Court, Chief Justice Warren quoted from the Kansas case:

> Segregation of white and colored children in public schools has a detrimental effect upon the colored children. ... Segregation with the sanction of law, therefore, has a tendency to [retard] the educational and mental development of negro children and to deprive them of some of the benefits they would receive in a racial[ly] integrated school system. (Davis & Graham, 1995, p. 165)

This "finding," the justices were convinced, "is amply supported by modern authority" (Davis & Graham, 1995, p. 165), by which they meant modern social scientific studies conducted by Kenneth and Mamie Clark (1940) that explored and assessed the effects of racial segregation on Negro children through, in part, experiments with Negro child-subjects making choices between White and Colored dolls and giving reasons for their preferences. It was this work by the Clarks, a fundamental resource for the LDEF team's legal strategy, that seemed to provide compelling evidence of the harm of racial segregation experienced by Negro children, harm so great as to affect their hearts and minds "in a way unlikely ever to be undone" and thus impair their development into fully capable citizens in our democracy. Such impairment, the justices reasoned, violated a fundamental right. Thus, they concluded

> in the field of public education the doctrine of "separate but equal" has no place. Separate educational facilities are inherently unequal. Therefore, we hold that the plaintiffs and others similarly situated for whom the actions have been brought are, by reason of the segregation complained of, deprived of the equal protection of the laws guaranteed by the Fourteenth Amendment. (Davis & Graham, 1995, p. 166)

On reconsideration, what judgments were made concerning the effects of racial segregation on White children? Apparently, none—certainly not explicitly. In writing for the Court, Chief Justice Warren's text is seriously ambiguous and thus possibly misleading at critical places. When writing about the necessity to consider the importance of crucial intangibles of schooling, his concluding judgment, affirming the judgment of the lower court's "finding" in the Topeka, Kansas, case, seems not to restrict to a particular race the harm done by racial segregation:

> Such considerations apply with added force to children in grade and high schools. To separate them from others of similar age and qualifications solely because of their race generates a feeling of inferiority as to their status in the community that may affect their hearts and minds in a way unlikely ever to be undone. (Davis & Graham, 1995, p. 165)

However, when read with mindfulness of the context of the paragraph in which this articulation is rendered, of the context constituted by the text of the entire opinion and judgment of the Court, and of the social science–supported arguments advanced by the LDEF lawyers, the only valid conclusion to draw, I am persuaded, is that the justices—and the LDEF lawyers—were convinced that Negro children—but not White children!—were harmed by racially segregated education. The full force of this conclusion is captured, for me, in that especially forceful and most memorable declarative judgment in the Court's opinion: "Separate educational facilities are *inherently* [italics added] unequal" (Davis & Graham, 1995, p. 166).

This has long been an especially arresting and troubling judgment for me because it refers only to the educational facilities and the intangibles of Negro schooling, not to White schools. Understandably so, since while what is at issue explicitly is the play of White racial supremacy in public schooling in the form of racially segregated schools, the concern, nonetheless, is one-sided. In the normative scheme of White racial supremacy, schools for White folks' children are inherently superior because they are by and for White folks and thus are constructed of both tangible and intangible elements and factors normalized on the presumed superior civilizational raciality of White folks. It is this racialized normativity of Whiteness—that is, the collection of ontological and physical and cultural anthropological valorized factors thought to define the "White race" and thereby determine its superiority by virtue of its first-order place among all the races in the "Great Chain of Being" (Lovejoy, 1964)—that is operative, I believe, in the reasoning of the justices. It is operative, even, to some extent, in the reasoning of the LDEF lawyers. In both cases, this normativity of things and matters White was in play as unacknowledged and thus unexplicated and unchallenged convictions functioning as presumptions. The Negro race, in the normative order of White racial supremacy, is inherently inferior. Separate schools for Negroes, then, "inherit," as it were, this inferiority, and hence are "inherently inferior." If one reasoned in accord with the predominate logic of this normativity regarding racialized superiority and inferiority, the only viable remedy by which to benefit Negro schoolchildren was to place them in schools with White children, that is, in White schools.

This is tricky, delicate business, here. One must proceed with care...

Am I decrying the Court's decisions in *Brown I* and *II* and arguing for racially segregated schools? No, not quite. I am concerned, though, first, with the absence of any seeming consideration that racial segregation was harmful to White children, in particular, to White people generally. On my reading, the justices, as did the LDEF team arguing on behalf of the plaintiffs in the cases, presumed the normative superiority of Whiteness. At the very least, there was a strategic concession to such normativity clearly indicated, in my judgment, by the one-sided concern with the harm done by racially segregated schooling: only to Negro children—none at all, apparently, to White children.

One of the near devastating consequences of this line of reasoning and of certain implementations of the Court's judgment has been the widespread underappreciation of the tremendous sociocultural significance of wholly or predominantly Negro, Black, schools as institutional sites of sociocultural production and mediation of much of value to Black folks and to this nation-state, thus to White folks, as well. The production and mediation of sociocultural capital in a number of important forms has been severely disrupted by the profound blanket devaluation of Negro schools as inherently inferior, not, in particular cases, as impaired because lacking, compared to schools serving White folks, both tangibles and intangibles due to the maldistribution of resources and the value of the social capital of Black folks in a society and political economy ordered by the normative logic of capitalist White racial supremacy. To a significant degree, the Court's decision in *Brown I* presumed, and affirmed tacitly, the normativity of White racial supremacy.

To the extent that it did, one consequence was the failure to attack the very notion of White racial supremacy, to identify the normativity of Whiteness and its effects on White children when induced through the tangibles and intangibles of racially segregated schooling. Where was the consideration that White children's prospects as citizens of a multiracial democracy were being impaired by racially segregated schooling—that they might gain substantially from being educated in multiracial schools, that their experiences and associations in such settings would be foundational to their becoming White adults who repudiated all notions and projects of White racial supremacy? Where was the consideration that substantial numbers of Black folks, Black teachers and administrators in particular, were especially well prepared to educate successive generations of White children, with the support of their parents, places of worship, and other associations, away from belief in and adherence to the normativity of White racial supremacy?

Toward a Conclusion

The justices' reasoning in *Brown I* did not pave the way to such radical challenges and possibilities—and could not, in my judgment. For the justices were not yet fully free of entanglements in the normativity of Whiteness as superior even though, nonetheless, they were especially courageous and forthright in rendering a unanimous decision to overturn a previous Court's decision in *Plessy* by declaring racially separate schools unconstitutional. In doing so they cut decidedly against the grain of centuries-old invidious racial segregation under the auspices of White racial supremacy.

I wish the justices had provided more, and less. More in the way of reasoning to support identifying and critiquing White racial supremacy, especially where it resides deeply, but no less influentially, in the taken-for-granted convictions and practices structuring and sustaining the inertia of everyday life. More in the way of reasoning to assist with the important—I would say necessary—work of rehabilitating notions and norms of Whiteness: that is, identifying and cultivating construals of Whiteness without attachments to racial supremacy. I wish they had provided less of a seemingly direct delegitimation and devaluation of Negro schools as crucial sites of the production and mediation of sociocultural, political, and economic capital—and more recognition of them as such. I wish that they had been advised by a Flagg and developed "a deliberate skepticism concerning race neutrality" (Flagg, 1997, p. 221) a stance that, Flagg (1997) wrote, "has the potential to improve the distribution across races of goods and power that whites currently control ... skepticism may help to foster the development of an antiracist white racial identity that does not posit whites as superior to blacks" (p. 222).

Had the justices reasoned from such a stance and made explicit that they were doing so, I believe the today's work of forging a coherent and widely shared and respected notion of democratic pluralism and integration with appropriate practices for a nation-state becoming increasingly varied demographically would be both better grounded epistemologically and legally and otherwise further along. The United States might then have, for example, better resourced, predominantly Black schools, and there might be less of the presumption, among folks White and Black, that such schools are inferior inherently, for, Flagg (1997) counseled, a skeptical stance toward the transparency and supposed neutrality of normative Whiteness "can help develop a relativized white consciousness, in which the white decisionmaker is conscious of the whiteness and contingency of white norms" (p. 223). In this regard I share the sentiment of Justice Clarence Thomas, expressed in a concurring opinion he issued in a more recent school desegregation case, *Missouri, et al., Petitioners v. Kalima Jenkins, et al.* (1995): "It never ceases to amaze me that the courts are so willing to assume that anything that is predominantly black must be inferior" (Thomas, 1995, p. 1). Justices of today's courts are not the only ones making this assumption. On reconsideration, so did the justices deciding *Brown*.

However, these same justices gave all, Black folks especially, much, much more. And folks Black and White, Native American and Hispanic, Latino–Latina, Asian, Asian American—all folks, those subject to, and those practicing, invidious racial and/or ethnic discrimination, have made much, often a great deal more than anticipated, of the justices' courageous decisions. For that, I am, and will always be, profoundly grateful. It is left to antiracists to continue adding to the legacy of their bequest by making apparent and engaging critically the transparent normative framework of Whiteness. For as noted by Hayman and Levit (1997)

> One unfortunate consequence of race-neutral policies may actually be the entrenchment of racists beliefs. ... The set of norms that appears to provide an effective counter to racist tendencies is that which includes principles of fairness and equality. The race-neutral approach of modern racism, in fact, does not so much confront these norms as it does elude them. (p. 246)

Here lies compelling work after *Brown*.

References

Brown v. Board of Education, 347 U.S. 483 (1954).

Brown v. Board of Education, 349 U.S. 294 (1955).

Clark, K. B., & Clark, M. K. (1940). Skin color as a factor in racial identification of Negro preschool children. *Journal of Social Psychology, 11,* 159–169.

Davis, A. L., & Graham, B. L. (Eds.). (1995). *The Supreme Court, race, and civil rights*. Thousand Oaks, CA: Sage.

Flagg, B. (1997). The transparency phenomenon, race-neutral decision making, and the discriminatory intent. In R. Delgado & J. Stefancic (Eds.), *Critical White studies: Looking behind the mirror* (pp. 220–226). Philadelphia: Temple University Press.

Hayman, R. L., & Levit, N. (1993). The constitutional ghetto. In R. Delgado & J. Stefancic (Eds.), *Critical White studies: Looking behind the mirror* (pp. 239–247). Philadelphia: Temple University Press.

Lovejoy, A. (1964). *The great chain of being*. Cambridge, MA: Harvard University Press.

Missouri, et al., Petitioners v. Kalima Jenkins, et al., 93 U.S. 1823 (1995).

Plessy v. Ferguson, 163 U.S. 537 (1896).
Sweatt v. Painter, 339 U.S. 629 (1950).
Thomas, C. (1995). Concurrence. Missouri, et al., Petitioners v. Kalima Jenkins, et al., 93 U.S. (1823).

PEABODY JOURNAL OF EDUCATION, *79*(2), 51–73

Multiple Facets of Inequity in Racial and Ethnic Achievement Gaps

Jaekyung Lee
Graduate School of Education
State University of New York at Buffalo

This article provides a critical look into national trends of the achievement gaps between Whites and Blacks and between Whites and Hispanics over the last 3 decades based on the National Assessment of Educational Progress mathematics assessments. It examines multiple facets of inequity underlying the racial and ethnic achievement gaps from 3 perspectives: equality, adequacy, and reciprocity. Although the Black–White and Hispanic–White mathematics achievement gaps narrowed significantly over the last 3 decades, there was some setback in the national progress during the last decade and the achievement gaps remain substantially large. The study finds that the racial and ethnic achievement gaps are highly inequitable, as it turns out that schools do not measure up to essential conditions of equity: Minority students do not (a) get fairly equal educational opportunities, (b) achieve minimally adequate level of competency, and (c) learn in a racially integrated school. The recent trend of widening racial achievement gaps is also seen as a real setback in equity as there was little systemic improvement in those 3 conditions of equity during the last decade. Implications of the findings for educational policies to enhance broader equity and justice are discussed.

Fifty years have passed since *Brown v. Board of Education* (1954), the landmark decision by the U.S. Supreme Court that launched court-ordered school desegregation. Although this decision and following policy

Requests for reprints should be sent to Jaekyung Lee, 409 Baldy Hall, SUNY at Buffalo, Buffalo, NY 14260–1000. E-mail: JL224@buffalo.edu

interventions made public schools across the nation a less separate and more equal place of learning for minority students, the focus of national concerns about racial equity has shifted from school inputs to student outcomes and from redistribution of social relations and opportunities to redistribution of academic achievement. The culmination of this policy shift may be seen in the most recent federal educational policy initiative, the No Child Left Behind Act of 2001, which is aimed at accomplishing high academic standards for all students and closing the prevailing achievement gaps among students of all racial and ethnic backgrounds.

Since the Coleman report in the 1960s brought attention to racial inequity in student outcomes, the achievement gap between White and minority students has raised a multitude of concerns and resulted in a significant body of empirical research (see Coleman et al., 1966; Jencks & Phillips, 1998; Lee, 2002). Racial and ethnic achievement gaps narrowed substantially in the 1970s and 1980s when Blacks and Hispanics improved their reading and mathematics achievement much more than did their White counterparts. As some of the gaps turned out to widen in the 1990s, a recent study called attention to the phenomenon of reversed achievement gap trends and raised serious concerns about setbacks in the progress the nation had made toward racial and ethnic equity (Lee, 2002).

The conventional research on racial achievement gaps has focused on the issue of equality of educational opportunities and schooling conditions among different racial groups as key determinants of their achievement gaps. However, this approach alone has limitations in enhancing educational equity and social justice. Policymakers need to broaden their perspectives of equity and be more aware of potential biases in their efforts to address the racial achievement gap from a single perspective. Here I raise three questions for evaluating inequity in the past and current racial and ethnic achievement gaps. First, there is an equality issue: How well do minority students fare relative to their White peers in terms of educational resources and opportunities? Second, there is an adequacy issue: How well do minority students perform relative to minimally adequate levels of academic standards? Third, there is a reciprocity issue: How well do minority students learn in racially integrated schools and benefit from the achievement of White students?

This article starts with an overview of national trends of the achievement gaps between Whites and Blacks and between Whites and Hispanics over the last 3 decades based on the National Assessment of Educational Progress (NAEP) mathematics assessments. This analysis of the NAEP, the nation's report card, includes both the long-term trend and the national

NAEP.[1] Then the article examines multiple facets of inequity underlying the achievement gaps among different racial and ethnic groups from conventional and other alternative perspectives, using multiple sets of national data. In this article, I do not seek to explain why the racial achievement gaps exist or why they changed over time but rather attempt to examine how inequitable the racial achievement gaps are and how much progress toward equity was made through changes in the achievement gaps.

Black and Hispanic Achievement Gap Trends

Systematic relations between educationally irrelevant variables (e.g., race and social class) and academic achievement may be regarded as signs of inequity in student outcomes (see Green, 1982). Applying this perspective to the analysis of racial achievement gaps, previous studies often evaluated the degree of racial inequity in academic achievement by measuring the magnitude and significance of differences in standardized test scores between different racial groups of students. In a similar vein, the studies often kept track of changes in achievement gaps as a yardstick of progress toward equity, evaluating how much the racial achievement gap narrowed or widened over time and how significant the trends were (see Grissmer, Kirby, Berends, & Willamson, 1994; Hedges & Nowell, 1998; Lee, 2002).

The long-term NAEP data trend shows a significant narrowing of the Black–White and Hispanic–White achievement gaps in mathematics during the last 3 decades (see Figure 1). The Black–White test score gaps in NAEP mathematics fell by 0.2 to 0.4 in standard deviation units over the 1978–1990 period. The reduction of racial achievement gaps through the 1970s and 1980s revealed great progress on equity. However, setbacks in the last decade occurred when both Black–White and Hispanic–White achievement gaps stabilized or widened (Lee, 2002). The Black–White achievement gap in mathematics increased during the 1990s and reached up to one standard deviation unit, regressing back to the level of achieve-

[1]The NAEP is the only nationally representative and continuing assessment of what America's students know and can do in various subject areas. NAEP long-term trend assessments are designed to give information on the changes in the basic achievement of America's youth. They have measured mathematics achievement at ages 9, 13, and 17 since the early 1970s. This differs from the national NAEP, which is designed to give the most up-to-date information on student achievement. These assessments have measured mathematics achievement at Grades 4, 8, and 12 since 1990. See the NAEP home page on the Web for more information on each of the assessments (http://www.nces.ed.gov/nationsreportcard/).

ment disparity as of the early 1980s. Although the Hispanic–White gap followed a similar pattern, the Hispanic–White achievement gaps were relatively smaller than the Black–White gaps and changed to a lesser extent throughout the period. As of 1999, the overall Black–White and Hispanic–White mathematics achievement gaps remained substantially large, with the ranges of those gaps falling between 0.7 and 1.1 in standard deviation units.

The significance of positive curvilinear racial achievement gap trends in mathematics (i.e., narrowing followed by widening or leveling off) has been tested. Table 1 summarizes the results of time-series regression analyses applying both linear and quadratic growth models to the long-term NAEP math trends data for each age group. For both Black and Hispanic gap trends, there is no clear indication of cohort effect by which change in age 9 is followed by change in age 13 four years later and then change in age 17 eight years later. Rather all significant changes happened at similar periods across three age groups. While a negative linear pattern (i.e., narrowing all the time) was detected for some of the gap trends, the quadratic model was more significant than the linear model. The Black–White achievement gap trend in mathematics switched from a narrowing to a widening or leveling off pattern around 1990 across three age groups. The

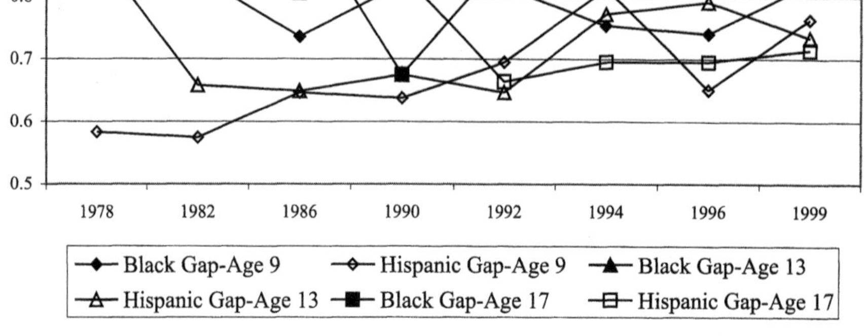

Figure 1. Standardized Black–White and Hispanic–White mathematics test score gaps on the long-term trend National Assessment of Educational Progress for ages 9, 13, and 17: 1978 to 1999. Data sources: See the Appendix.

Table 1

Summary of Regression Analyses of Long-Term National Assessment of Educational Progress Mathematics Achievement Gap Trends

	Linear Trend		*Quadratic Trend*		
Age	*Coefficient*	*Adjusted R^2*	*Coefficient*	*Adjusted R^2*	*Transition Year*
		White–Black Achievement Gap			
9	−.32*	.60	.03*	.86	1992
13	−.61*	.48	.07*	.84	1990
17	−.50*	.47	.05*	.75	1991
		White–Hispanic Achievement Gap			
9	.14	.41	.02	.41	
13	.41	.30	.56*	.68	1989
17	−.46*	.82	.01	.86	

Note. The linear trend coefficient shows the amount of change in test score gap per year: the more negative, the sharper the downward trend. The quadratic trend coefficient shows the extent of curvature in test score gap trend: the more positive, the sharper the transition from downward to upward trend. Transition year is the year when the slope of curve changes and is estimated only for statistically significant quadratic trends.

*$p < .05$.

Hispanic–White achievement gap in mathematics shows the same type of significant curvilinear trends for only 13-year-old students.

The aforementioned trends of racial achievement gap came from the long-term trend NAEP that has more focus on basic skills: The computational focus gives information on how students are performing on traditional procedural skills, and most questions are completed in multiple-choice format without use of a calculator. A question may be raised: Is the recent trend of a widening Black–White or Hispanic–White gap also evident on the national NAEP, which reflects more recent math standards and thus can be more consistent with current teaching and learning practices? Table 2 shows national standardized Black–White and Hispanic–White test score gaps in both long-term trend and main NAEP mathematics during the period of the 1990s. Although the two assessments are not directly comparable because of their differences in student samples as well as test content–format, both the long-term trend and the national NAEP results show that the test score gaps were consistently large. Both assessment results also demonstrate that the racial achievement gaps in mathematics increased from 1990 to 2000: Estimated increases in the size of the gaps from the national NAEP appear to be slightly larger than estimates from the long-term NAEP.

Table 2

Comparison of Standardized White–Black and White–Hispanic Mathematics Achievement Gaps for Age 13 in Long-Term Trend NAEP and for 8th Graders in National NAEP

	White–Black Gap		*White–Hispanic Gap*	
Year	*National NAEP*	*Long-Term NAEP*	*National NAEP*	*Long-Term NAEP*
1990	0.89	0.87	0.75	0.68
1992	1.09	0.93	0.86	0.64
1996	1.07	0.93	0.85	0.80
1999–2000[a]	1.07	0.98	0.91	0.73

Note. NAEP = National Assessment of Educational Progress. Standardized gaps for both NAEP assessments were computed by dividing the average test score differences by the pooled standard deviations of all students' test scores. While most of the 13-year-olds are eighth graders, the age-based student sample for the long-term trend NAEP is not equivalent to the grade-based student sample for the national NAEP.

[a]The results from the 2000 national NAEP and the 1999 long-term trend NAEP are shown in the same row.

Multiple Facets of Inequity in the Achievement Gaps

Does the evidence of a racial–ethnic achievement gap directly tell us about the degree of inequity in student outcomes? Does the evidence of the widening racial gap trend directly indicate setback in progress toward equity? Answers to these kinds of questions are hard to directly obtain with the NAEP test score results alone and require other evidence on the racial gap in key factors related to the test score gap. Indeed, it is wrong to say that the racial gap in achievement outcome in itself implies substantial breach of the principles of educational equity and social justice.

How does an ability factor play a role in the racial achievement gap? While there are controversies about whether differences in academic achievement between racial groups as measured by standardized tests are due in part to differences in ability, no one has found genetic evidence indicating that one racial group has less innate intellectual ability than others (see Flynn, 1999; Herrnstein & Murray, 1994; Neisser, 1998). Rather, there is a powerful piece of evidence in favor of genetic equality among racial groups (Flynn, 1999; Jencks & Phillips, 1998; Neisser, 1997). Although some have reported that Blacks have gained more in IQ than have Whites recently and the Black–White IQ score gap narrowed (Flynn, 1999; Vincent, 1991), the evidence is not strong. Indeed, the narrowing of the Black–White gap was much more evident on achievement tests than on intelligence tests. IQ score trends do not match the NAEP test score trends, and this discrepancy may imply that there are unique factors influencing achievement trends beyond IQ.

When we focus on environmental factors to determine the causes of the achievement gap among different racial and ethnic groups of students, we find that academic achievement is influenced by many interrelated factors simultaneously, and it is almost impossible to disentangle the effect of one factor from another (e.g., school facilities vs. teacher quality). Nevertheless, I suggest establishing some major criteria for evaluating the degree of inequity in the racial achievement gap and planning interventions according to the evaluation results. The achievement gap may be viewed as a more serious breach of the principle of equity and justice to the extent that the following conditions are not satisfactorily met:

1. Minority students are given equal educational opportunity to learn (*equality*).
2. Minority students achieve a minimally adequate level of competency (*adequacy*).
3. Minority students learn in a racially integrated school and benefit from the achievement of White students (*reciprocity*).

The same size of racial achievement gap could be disguising quite different levels of inequity and injustice. When the issue is viewed in this way, questions are raised: When does the racial achievement gap pose a serious threat to society and thus need immediate remedy? Or, when should the achievement of minority students be treated as intolerable and, therefore, as requiring a policy intervention?

Equality of Educational Opportunity

Conventional research on the racial achievement gap has focused on the equality of educational opportunity. The most influential research done in this area was the Coleman report (Coleman et al., 1966). This report was a product of the Civil Rights Act of 1964, which provided that a survey be conducted to ascertain the lack of equal educational opportunities for individuals by reason of race and other educationally irrelevant factors. Whereas the act presupposed the study's findings on racial inequalities but left undefined what counts as equal educational opportunities, the study examined various measures of educational opportunities in relation to student achievement. Findings from the Coleman report have been often misinterpreted as evidencing that money does not matter in education or that schools have no effect on student achievement (Haller & Klein, 2001).

Although researchers disagree on the best measure of school quality and the significance of school effects, a great deal of evidence suggests that instructional resources and teacher quality affect student achievement (Darling-Hammond, 2000; Ferguson, 1991; Hedges, Laine, & Greenwald, 1994). Studies have found racial inequality of student access to qualified teachers. The more impoverished and racially isolated the school, the greater the likelihood that students in the school are taught by inexperienced teachers, uncertified teachers, and out-of-field teachers (see Darling-Hammond & Post, 2000; Hanushek, Kain, & Rivkin, 2001; Ingersoll, 1996; Lankford, Loeb, & Wyckoff, 2002; Prince, 2002). Research related to the recent emphasis on challenging content and performance standards has also found instructional resources in predominantly minority, high-poverty schools to be less than adequate (Berne, 1994; Haycock et al., 2001).

To examine the racial gap in students' access to qualified teachers, I compared high school mathematics teachers' qualifications by their schools' racial composition of students in the 1987–88 and 1999–2000 Schools and Staffing Survey (SASS) public school data. Figure 2 shows that math teachers in predominantly Black or Hispanic high schools are less likely to teach in their field of study and certification than their counterparts in predominantly White schools.[2] The opportunity of being taught by qualified teachers did not improve for predominantly minority schools, and both Black and Hispanic gaps in in-field teaching remained unchanged between 1988 and 2000.

To examine the racial gap in school spending, I also compared per pupil current education expenditures by school districts' racial composition of children in the 1990 and 1998 Common Core of Data (CCD) and F-33 data. Figure 2 also shows that predominantly Black or Hispanic school districts generally tend to spend less on education than their predominantly White counterparts. The racial disparity in the level of district spending on education is statistically significant with the exception that predominantly Hispanic school districts were on a par with their predominantly White

[2]In 1987–88, the in-field teaching rate was 86% for predominantly White schools, 72% for predominantly Black schools, and 70% for predominantly Hispanic schools. However, the Black–White and Hispanic–White gaps did not turn out to be statistically significant because of very small sample sizes for teachers in those predominantly minority schools (less than 200) and the resulting large standard errors of the percentage estimates. Jackknife replicate weights were used to estimate the error variance given the complex multistage sampling method used by the SASS.

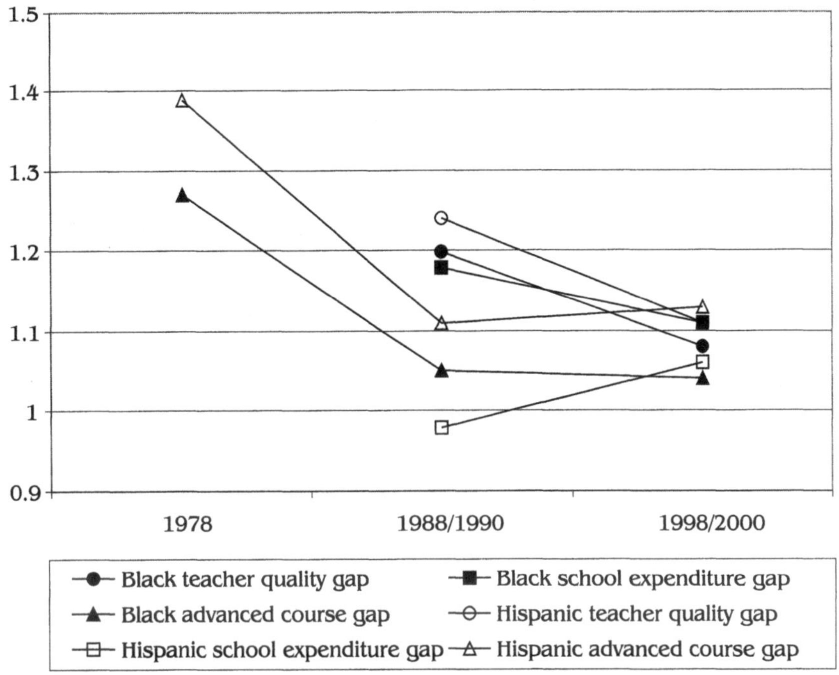

Figure 2. Black–White and Hispanic–White gap (in ratio) trends in selected measures of school educational conditions and opportunities: 1978 to 1998/2000. Data sources: See the Appendix.

counterparts in 1990. The Black–White spending gap did not change significantly from 1990 to 1998.

According to the NAEP student survey results, classroom opportunity to learn, as indicated by students' access to advanced courses, appears to have significantly improved for Black and Hispanic 17-year-olds during the last 2 decades. The Black–White and Hispanic–White gap in the ratio of taking advanced mathematics courses narrowed mostly between 1978 and 1990, implying that minority students' access to advanced courses became more equitable. However, no further progress in narrowing the gap was made between 1990 and 1999.

Examination of educational opportunity for different racial and ethnic groups requires looking at inequalities at home as well as in schools. Trends of the gap between Blacks and Whites across a variety of family educational conditions show substantial progress toward the greater equalization of educational opportunity at home throughout the last 3 decades (see Figure 3). The Black–White gaps in educational attainment,

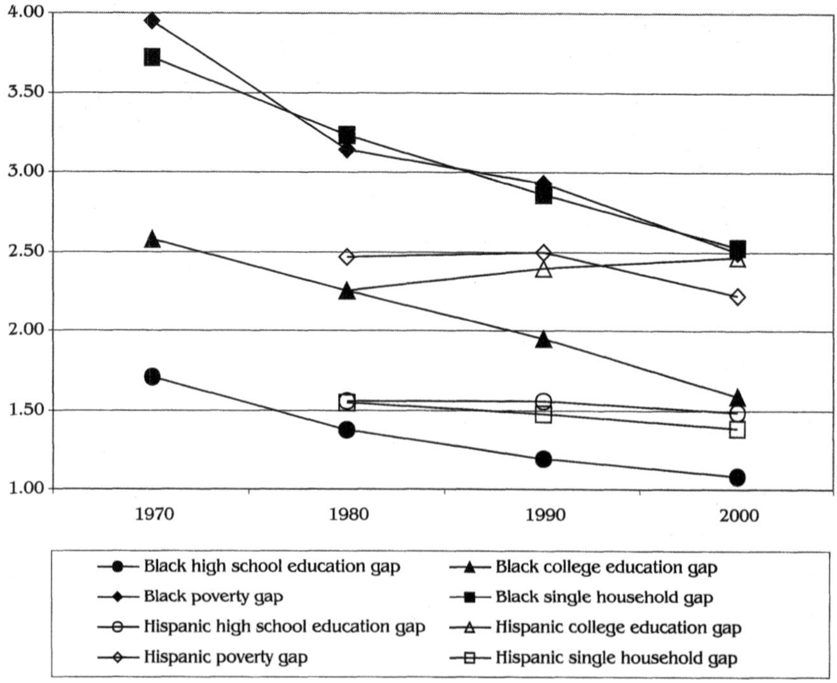

Figure 3. Black–White and Hispanic–White gap (in ratio) trends in selected measures of family educational conditions and opportunities: 1970 to 2000. Data sources: See the Appendix.

poverty, and single-parent households narrowed continuously throughout the last 3 decades. Despite this continuous progress, Black students still remain more likely to live in poverty, with parents who have a lower level of education, and in a single-parent family. Figure 3 also shows corresponding trends of the Hispanic–White gap in family educational conditions. Although the Hispanic–White gap was originally smaller than the Black–White gap, it hardly narrowed over the past 2 decades, and thus Hispanics' gap relative to Whites is no longer smaller than that of Blacks.

By and large, the aforementioned comparisons indicate that Black and Hispanic students are doubly bound by lack of educational opportunities that they face both at home and at school. The problems with less adequate instructional resources and less qualified teachers in predominantly minority schools are no less significant than the challenges posed by minority students' relatively disadvantaged family learning environment. Although there has been significant national progress toward narrowing many of the racial gaps in the past 2 or 3 decades, the progress was not sufficient to eradicate all inequalities.

Adequacy

Adequacy concerns primarily how well students perform against a certain level of achievement deemed adequate. This perspective might help address problems with an approach focusing on equality of educational opportunity. No matter how much the relative achievement gap among different racial and social groups has been narrowed, some disadvantaged minority students' performance level still may not be acceptable. This adds a new dimension of gap relative to adequate performance, thereby removing the possibility of lowering the achievement of the higher performing group in order to close the relative gap.

If all students can be brought to at least a minimally adequate achievement level, then their achievement outcome may be declared to be equitable somehow. However, setting minimally adequate learning standards and assessing students with minimum competency tests may risk lowering academic expectation and discouraging teachers from pursuing academic excellence beyond the required minimum level. The standards-based education reform movement since *A Nation at Risk* (National Commission on Excellence in Education, 1983) addressed this problem by adopting high standards for all students and using high proficiency tests aligned with the standards. This perspective also had implications for school finance reform where the focus has shifted from equality to adequacy (Clune, 1994; Ladd, Chalk, & Hansen, 1999).

Murnane and Levy (1996) pointed out that 17-year-olds should score 300 or more on the NAEP reading and mathematics tests in order to meet the New Basic Skills, the minimum skills people now need to get a middle-class job. If we accept level 300 as the minimally adequate level of achievement for high school graduates, Black and Hispanic students did make significant progress toward that goal over the last 2 decades (see Figure 4). Nevertheless, the progress almost stalled during the 1990s, and the gap of Blacks and Hispanics in basic knowledge and skills still remains very large. As of 1999, 27% of Black and 38% of Hispanic 17-year-olds performed at or above Level 300 in mathematics. The corresponding figure for their White peers was 70%.

The inadequacy of Black and Hispanic students' achievement is also evident on the national NAEP. *Basic* denotes partial mastery of prerequisite knowledge and skills for proficient work at each grade and thus may be regarded as a minimally adequate level of achievement on the national NAEP.

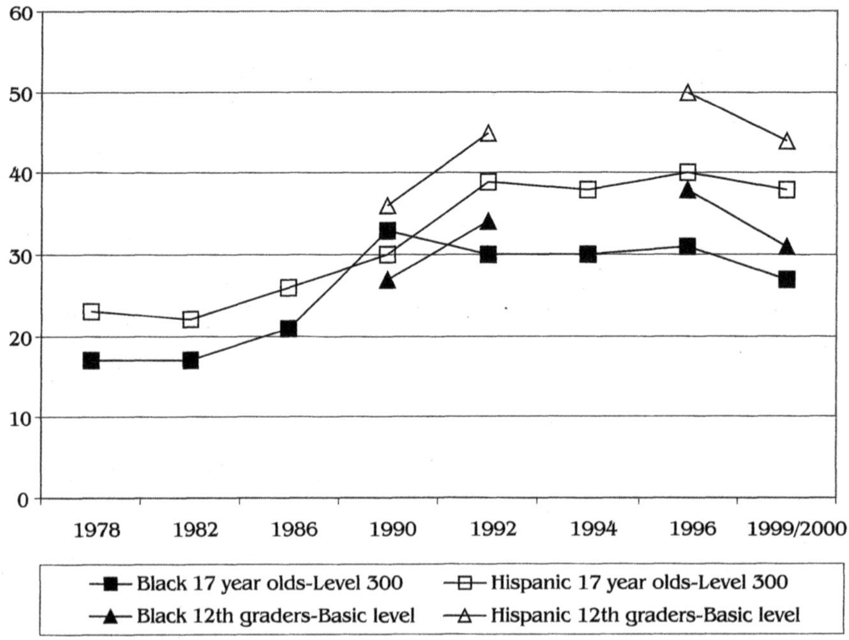

Figure 4. Trends of percentages of Black and Hispanic 17-year-olds at or above long-term National Assessment of Educational Progress (NAEP) math Level 300 (1978 to 1999) and trends of percentages of Black and Hispanic 12th graders at or above national NAEP math Basic level (1990 to 2000).

The percentage of Black and Hispanic 12th graders at or above the Basic achievement level hardly increased from 1990 through 2000. As of 2000, a majority of Black and Hispanic 12th graders still remained below the minimally adequate achievement level in mathematics (see Figure 4). The percentage of 12th-grade Black students performing below the Basic proficiency level in mathematics is about 3 times larger than that of their White peers (20% for Whites vs. 61% for Blacks at Grade 4; 23% for Whites vs. 68% for Blacks at Grade 8; 26% for Whites vs. 69% for Blacks at Grade 12). The long-term NAEP and the national NAEP concur that a majority of students in both Black and Hispanic groups have not reached an adequate achievement level yet and there was little or no progress made during the 1990s.

The NAEP results on Black and Hispanic high school students' achievement level would appear to be more inadequate if one takes into account students who dropped out of schools and did not take the test. The trend of Black and Hispanic high school dropout rates shows that the Hispanic dropout rate has been twice as high as Black's (see Figure 5): The Black

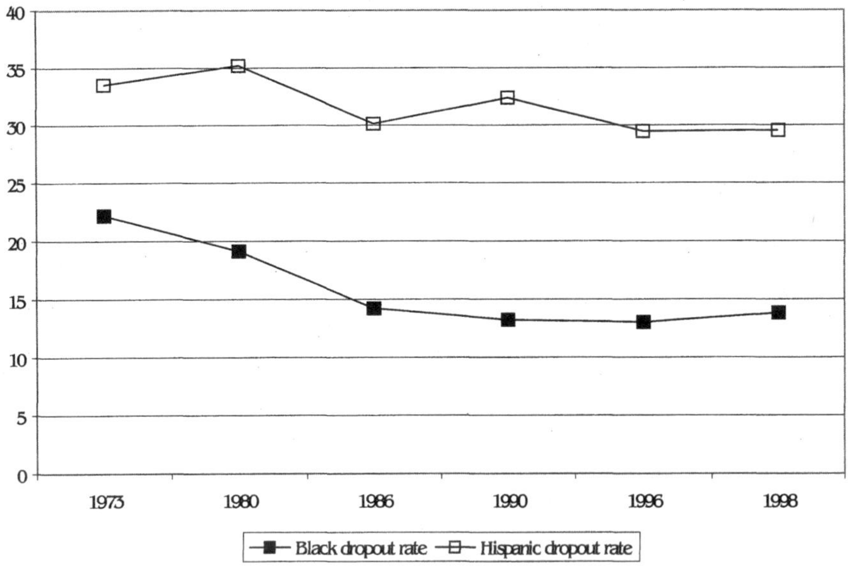

Figure 5. Percentage of Black and Hispanic high school dropouts among persons 16 to 24 years old: 1973 to 1998. Data sources: Table A11 in Kaufman, Kwon, Klein, and Chapman (2000).

dropout rate was around 15% to 20%, whereas the Hispanic dropout rate was in the range of 30% to 35%. Both Black and Hispanic dropout rates fell somewhat until the mid 1980s, but no further progress has been made since then. Therefore, the achievement of Black and Hispanic high school students did not improve during the 1990s when their dropout rates stayed the same.

Reciprocity

Reciprocity concerns the extent to which different racial and ethnic groups share common learning experiences and benefit each other with shared knowledge and skills. In reporting and comparing the academic achievement of different racial groups in the past, race–ethnicity was seen as a static, categorical variable rather than as a dynamic, relational variable. The focus of policy concern was primarily how well Blacks as one of several racial categories perform relative to Whites as its reference category. This focus left unanswered the question of how much the academic achievement of students from one racial group affects the achievement of students from the other groups and how this peer group effect has any bearing on equity. From this perspective, achievement is seen as a public good rather than a private good, and the racial achievement gap may be considered more tolerable to the extent that the higher achieving racial group's achievement helps improve the achievement of the lower achieving racial group.[3]

Given the fact that the national Black–White and Hispanic–White achievement gaps are very large, one may argue that this approach can benefit only those minority groups and thus it is not reciprocal. However, making a generalization based on the average racial achievement gaps can be misleading, as within-group variability in achievement is much greater than between-groups variability. According to the 1999 long-term trend NAEP math results, the average national Black–White gap is about 31 points, whereas the gap between high-performing (2 standard deviations above the mean) and low-performing (2 standard deviations below the mean) students of the same race (both Blacks and Whites) amount to 112 points. About 15% of Black students perform better than an average White student.

Reciprocity among racial groups may be enhanced through racial integration between and within schools, as students can benefit more from each other (i.e., peer group effect) in a racially integrated school that realizes the goal of reciprocity with cooperative learning. Although studies on the effect of racial desegregation on student achievement have shown mixed results, most relevant studies have found that Black students' test scores increased and Whites' scores did not decline (see Armor, 1995; Crain & Mahard, 1982; Orfield, 1978; St. John, 1975). Also there is a great deal of research showing that there are many long-term benefits of racial integration for all racial groups and the larger society with respect to going to integrated colleges, living in integrated neighborhoods as adults, and building social capital (see Briggs, 2003; Kahlenberg, 2001).

Although school segregation for Blacks has significantly dropped in the past, the more recent trend is toward increased segregation (see Fig-

[3]Transfer of educational benefits as public goods may happen spontaneously when the externality of education is assumed. The conventional view of externality as proposed by economists focuses on future social benefits of education realized in the labor market or community (e.g., increasing productivity of coworkers in a firm, living in an educated, literate society; see McMahon, 1998; Psacharopoulos, 1996). In contrast, the concept of reciprocity as discussed in this article assumes more proactive efforts to promote educational integration among different racial groups of students and facilitate their sharing of knowledge and skills in school settings.

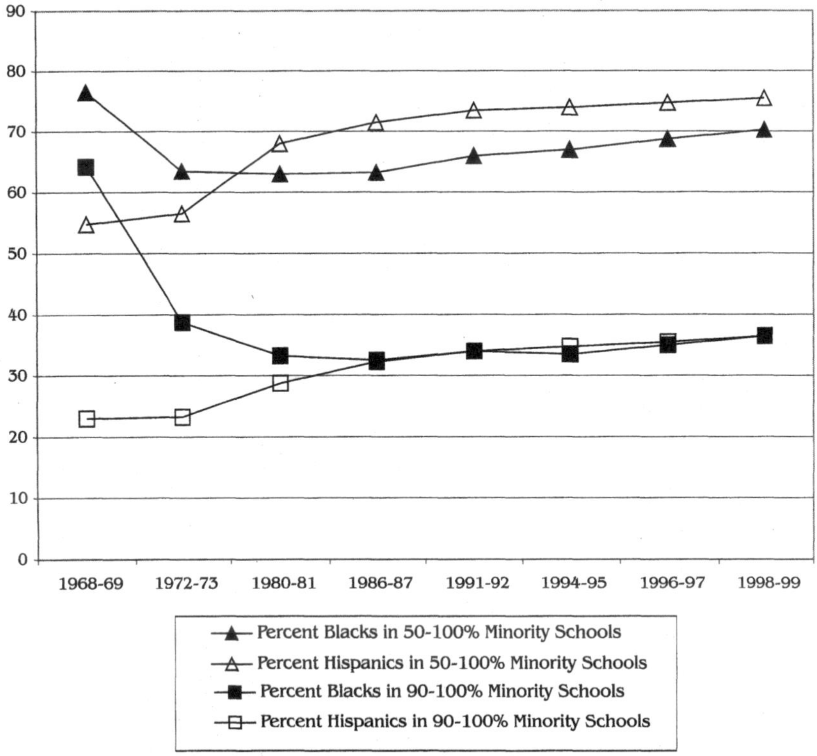

Figure 6. Black and Hispanic school segregation trends by the percentage of minority students (50%–100% and 90%–100%) in school: 1968 to 1998. Adapted from "Schools More Separate: Consequences of a Decade of Resegregation" by G. Orfield, 2001, Table 9. Retrieved August 11, 2003, from http://www.civilrightsproject.harvard.edu/research/deseg/Schools_More_Separate.pdf. Adapted with permission of the author.

ure 6). The percentage of Black students in predominantly minority schools (50%–100% minority) dropped from 77% in 1969 to 63% in 1987 but increased to 70% by 1999 (Orfield, 2001). Conversely, Hispanic segregation grew steadily throughout the last 3 decades, surpassing the level of Black segregation in predominantly non-White schools (Orfield & Yun, 1999). Increasing racial segregation implies that the chance for both Black and Hispanic students to benefit from learning with White peers may have decreased. Table 3 shows the trends of Blacks' and Hispanics' access to the higher achievement of White students, which has been restricted by their limited exposure to Whites in segregated schools.

Table 3

Trends of Exposure Index, Math Achievement Gap, and Exposure to Math Achievement Gap Index for Black and Hispanic Students

	Black			Hispanic		
Year	Exposure Index (A)	Black–White Math Gap (B)	Exposure to Gap Index (A×B/100)	Exposure Index (C)	Hispanic–White Math Gap (D)	Exposure to Gap Index (C×D/100)
1970–73[a]	32.0	40	12.8	43.8	30	13.1
1980–82[b]	36.2	37	13.4	35.5	28	9.9
1986	36.0	26	9.4	32.9	21	6.9
1990–91[c]	34.4	25	8.6	31.1	23	7.2
1994	33.9	27	9.2	30.6	25	7.7
1996	32.7	27	8.8	29.9	23	6.9
1999	31.7	30	9.5	29.1	24	7.0

Note. The exposure index is the percentage of White students in school attended by typical Black or Hispanic students as obtained from Table 10 in Orfield (2001). The math gap is the national average National Assessment of Educational Progress math test score gap combined across three age groups (ages 9, 13, and 17). The gap exposure index is computed by multiplying the exposure index by math gap and dividing by 100. It is a proxy measure of minority students' exposure to the portion of White students' achievement exceeding minority students' achievement.

[a]The year of exposure index is 1970, and the year of math gap is 1973. [b]The year of exposure index is 1980, and the year of math gap is 1982. [c]The year of exposure index is 1991, and the year of math gap is 1990.

Summary and Conclusion

Table 4 summarizes the findings of this article with regard to the trends and status of inequity in racial–ethnic achievement gaps from each one of the aforementioned three perspectives, and it lists policy strategies used in the past to address these issues. How inequitable are current racial and ethnic achievement gaps? This question can be answered by looking at how well the aforementioned three conditions are being met. The current racial achievement gap is highly unacceptable from the standpoint of equity and justice, as any one of the three conditions are not being met. How much setback in equity does the recent trend of the widening racial achievement gap show? In a similar vein, this question may be answered by evaluating changes in the aforementioned three conditions. For example, the widening Black–White achievement gap might have been seen differently if Black students had made significant progress toward an adequate achievement level; however, their achievement level remained flat.

One may think it is very unrealistic for schools to measure up to all of the three conditions of educational equity and justice that I have proposed in this article. Indeed, there are some obstacles to accomplishing these conditions. First of all, there are home-related factors such as parents' education and income that are beyond schools' control. Making educational opportunities equal in schools may not be sufficient for minority students who have socioeconomically disadvantaged family backgrounds that negatively affect their achievement. One may even argue that to ensure fair educational opportunity for disadvantaged minority students, schools must allocate resources to them until there is no achievement gap left. However, there are some difficulties with this perspective of equity, as not only is it implausible to find a sufficient pool of school resources to remove any racial achievement gaps but also there is no guarantee that the reallocation of school resources alone would close the achievement gap.

A major concern with efforts to equalize educational opportunity and, ultimately, student achievement is that it might harm Whites by negatively affecting their opportunity to learn and lowering their achievement. Adequacy perspective may lesson this problem by paying more attention to improving the absolute level rather than reducing the relative gap. However, it is very difficult to achieve social consensus on an adequate level of student achievement and required resources. Moreover, when the minimally adequate achievement level rises along with rapid social changes and increasing expectations, it becomes difficult for schools to catch up with the standards as a moving target. It may be no less unrealistic to at-

Table 4

Summary of Educational Conditions and Policies for Improving the Justice of Racial–Ethnic Achievement Gaps

Condition	*Past Trend and Current Status*	*Educational Policy*
Equality	Home: Black and Hispanic gaps in family educational conditions (parental education, poverty, single household) narrowed significantly over the past 3 decades, but the size of gaps remains substantial.	State aid to equalize disparities in local school funding Incentives to attract more qualified teachers to predominantly minority schools
	School: Black and Hispanic gaps in key schooling conditions (teacher qualifications, school resources, advanced courses) also narrowed. The inequalities were relatively smaller at school than at home. The gaps remain unchanged in the 1990s and still exist.	Raising of standards for teacher certification and student course work Provision of compensatory education services (e.g., Head Start, Title I) to disadvantaged minority students
Adequacy	Blacks and Hispanics have made substantial progress toward minimally adequate achievement (e.g., Level 300 on the long-term NAEP for 17-year-olds or Basic on the national NAEP) over the last 2 decades. However, the progress slowed down in the 1990s, and a majority of Blacks and Hispanics still do not meet the minimum competency level.	High school exit exams (minimum competency test or end-of-course exams) Setting of performance standards that ensure minimally adequate level of achievement for minority students Guaranteeing minimally adequate level of school resources in low-income, predominantly minority schools
	Black and Hispanic high school dropout rates dropped until the mid-1980s but stayed the same since then.	Provision of remediation to students who fail to meet desired performance standards
Reciprocity	School segregation for Blacks decreased significantly until the mid-1980s but increased since then. School segregation for Hispanics increased continuously, surpassing the level of segregation for Blacks. Blacks and Hispanics remain highly segregated from Whites and the probability of shared learning and achievement among different racial groups in mutually beneficial ways is very low.	Racial integration (busing, magnet schools) Detracking, cooperative learning, peer tutoring

Note. NAEP = National Assessment of Educational Progress.

tempt to have all students perform at or above the same academic standards than to eradicate any achievement gap among racial and ethnic groups.

Problems with both equality and adequacy perspectives might be the implicit treatment of academic achievement as a private good as opposed to a public good that can be shared among groups. Here the reciprocity perspective helps focus attention on the hidden side of the achievement gap, that is, how much White students' achievement contributes to minority students' achievement or vice versa, rather than how well minority students perform relative to White students or against certain performance standards. It also acknowledges the reality of the achievement gap and attempts to use existing gaps to the advantage of the disadvantaged. However, reciprocity is relatively more difficult to measure and thus may be ignored by policymakers: School desegregation does not guarantee reciprocal education.

Despite the obstacles and challenges, there have been policy attempts in the past to realize the ideals of educational equity and social justice from each one of the three perspectives. Although these three lines of policies may all contribute to narrowing the racial and ethnic achievement gaps, the past policies tended to be fragmented and pursued at the expense of each other. What educational policymakers must be concerned about is not simply the fact that relative achievement gaps are large and the gaps have widened recently but also the fact that a majority of minority students do not meet minimally adequate achievement levels and they hardly made progress toward the standards. They also have to be concerned about the possibility that increasing school segregation may worsen racial inequalities in schooling conditions and outcomes. Now it is time for the entire nation to tackle multiple facets of inequity underlying the achievement gap, asking why there was little progress and there were even some setbacks toward racial and ethnic equity during the last decade.

References

Armor, D. J. (1995). *Forced justice: School desegregation and the law.* New York: Oxford University Press.

Berne, R. (1994). Educational input and outcome inequities in New York state. In R. Berne & L. O. Picus (Eds.), *Outcome equity in education* (pp. 1–23). Thousand Oaks, CA: Corwin.

Briggs, X. S. (2003). *Social capital and segregation: Race, connections, and inequality in America* (KSG Working Paper No. RWP02-011). Retrieved August 10, 2003, from http://ssrn.com/abstract=320243

Brown v. Board of Educ., 347 U.S. 483 (1954).

Clune, W. H. (1994). The shift from equity to adequacy in school finance. *Educational Policy, 8,* 376–394.

Coleman, J. S., Campbell, E. Q., Hobson, C. J., McPartland, J., Mood, A. M., Weinfeld, A. D., & York, R. L. (1966). *Equality of educational opportunity.* Washington, DC: U.S. Government Printing Office.

Crain, R. L., & Mahard, R. E. (1982). *Desegregation plans that raise Black achievement: A review of the research.* Santa Monica, CA: Rand.

Darling-Hammond, L. (2000). Teacher quality and student achievement: A review of state policy evidence. *Education Policy Analysis Archives, 8*(1). Retrieved August 5, 2003, from http://epaa.asu.edu/epaa/v8n1/

Darling-Hammond, L., & Post, L. (2000). Inequality in teaching and schooling: Supporting high-quality teaching and leadership in low-income schools. In R. D. Kahlenberg (Ed.), *A notion at risk: Preserving public education as an engine for social mobility* (pp. 127–167). New York: Century Foundation.

Ferguson, R. (1991). Paying for public education: New evidence on how and why money matters. *Harvard Journal of Legislation, 28,* 465–498.

Flynn, J. R. (1999). Searching for justice: The discovery of IQ gains over time. *American Psychologist, 54,* 5–20.

Green, T. F. (1982). Excellence, equity, and equality. In L. S. Shulman & G. Sykes (Eds.), *The handbook of teaching and policy* (pp. 318–341). New York: Longman.

Grissmer, D., Kirby, S. N., Berends, M., & Willamson, S. (1994). *Student achievement and the changing American family.* Santa Monica, CA: Rand.

Haller, E. J., & Klein, P. F. (2001). *Using educational research: A school administrator's guide.* New York: Longman.

Hanushek, E. A., Kain, J. F., & Rivkin, S. G. (2001). *Why public schools lose teachers* (Working Paper No. 8599). Cambridge, MA: National Bureau of Economic Research.

Haycock, K., Gerald, C., & Huang, S. (2001, Spring). Closing the gap: Done in a decade. *Thinking K–16, 2,* 3–21.

Hedges, L. V., Laine, R. D., & Greenwald, R. (1994). Does money matter? A meta-analysis of studies of the effects of differential school inputs on student outcomes. *Educational Researcher, 23,* 5–14.

Hedges, L. V., & Nowell, A. (1998). Black–White test score convergence since 1965. In C. Jencks & M. Phillips (Eds.), *The Black–White test score gap* (pp. 149–181). Washington, DC: Brookings Institution.

Herrnstein, R. J., & Murray, C. (1994). *The bell curve: Intelligence and class structure in American life.* New York: Free Press.

Ingersoll, R. (1996). The problem of under-qualified teachers in American secondary schools. *Educational Researcher, 28,* 26–37.

Jencks, C., & Phillips, M. (Eds.). (1998). *The Black–White test score gap.* Washington, DC: Brookings Institution.

Kahlenberg, R. D. (2001). *All together now: Creating middle-class schools through public school choice.* New York: Century Foundation.

Kaufman, P., Kwon, J. Y., Klein, S., & Chapman, C. D. (2000). *Dropout rates in the United States: 1999* (NCES Publication No. 2001-022). Washington, DC: U.S. Department of Education.

Ladd, H. F., Chalk, R., & Hansen, J. S. (Eds.). (1999). *Equity and adequacy in education finance: Issues and perspectives.* Washington, DC: National Academy Press.

Lankford, H., Loeb, S., & Wyckoff, J. (2002). Teacher sorting and the plight of urban schools. A descriptive analysis. *Educational Evaluation and Policy Analysis, 24,* 37–62.

Lee, J. (2002). Racial and ethnic achievement gap trends: Reversing the progress toward equity? *Educational Researcher, 31,* 3–12.

McMahon, W. W. (1998). Conceptual framework for the analysis of the social benefits of lifelong learning. *Education Economics, 6*, 309–346.
Murnane, R., & Levy, R. J. (1996). *Teaching the new basic skills.* New York: Free Press.
National Commission on Excellence in Education. (1983). *A nation at risk: The imperative for education reform.* Washington, DC: U.S. Department of Education.
Neisser, U. (1997). Never a dull moment. *American Psychologist, 52*, 79–81.
Neisser, U. (Ed.). (1998). *The rising curve: Long-term gains in IQ and related measures.* Washington, DC: American Psychological Association.
Orfield, G. (1978). *Must we bus? Segregated schools and national policy.* Washington, DC: Brookings Institution.
Orfield, G. (2001). *Schools more separate: Consequences of a decade of resegregation.* Retrieved August 11, 2003, from http://www.civilrightsproject.harvard.edu/research/deseg/Schools_More_Separate.pdf
Orfield, G., & Yun, J. T. (1999). *Resegregation in American Schools.* Camsbridge, MA: Harvard University, Civil Rights Project.
Psacharopoulos, G. (1996). Economics of education: A research agenda. *Economics of Education Review, 15*, 339–344.
Prince, C. D. (2002, Winter). Attracting well-qualified teachers to struggling schools. *American Educator*, 16–21.
Smith, M. S., & O'Day, J. A. (1991). Educational equality: 1966 and now. In D. Verstegen & J. Ward (Eds.), *Spheres of justice in education* (pp. 53–100). New York: Harper Business.
St. John, N. H. (1975). *School desegregation outcomes for children.* New York: Wiley.
Vincent, K. R. (1991). Black/White IQ differences: Does age make a difference? *Journal of Clinical Psychology, 47*, 266–270.

Appendix
Descriptions of Racial and Ethnic Gap Variables

Diverse kinds of racial and ethnic gap variables were used in this article. The definition and data sources of gap measures (as shown in Figures 1–3) are described here in order of presentation.

NAEP math achievement gap. Standardized average mathematics test score differences between Blacks–Hispanics and Whites. The data came from the long-term trend NAEP 1978–1999 Web site (http://www.nces.ed.gov/nationsreportcard/tables/Ltt1999).

High school education gap. Ratio of White high school education rate to corresponding Black and Hispanic rates. High school education rate is the percentage of people 25 years old and older who have completed high school. The data came from the U.S. Bureau of the Census, 1970–1998 Current Population Survey.

College education gap. Ratio of White college education rate to corresponding Black and Hispanic rates. Education rate is the percentage of people 25 years old and older over who have completed college. The data came from the U.S. Bureau of the Census, 1970–1998 Current Population Survey.

Poverty gap. Ratio of Black and Hispanic poverty rates to corresponding White rate. Poverty rate is the percentage of children under 18 below the poverty level. The data came from the U.S. Bureau of the Census, 1970–1998 Current Population Survey.

Single household gap. Ratio of Black and Hispanic single household rates to corresponding White rate. The single household rate is the percentage of one-parent family households with own children under 18. The data came from the U.S. Bureau of the Census, 1970–1998 Current Population Survey.

Advanced course gap. Ratio of White advanced mathematics course-taking rate to corresponding Black and Hispanic rates. The advanced mathematics course-taking rate is the percentage of 17-year-olds who report having taken any one of the following courses: Algebra I, Geometry, Algebra II, Precalculus, or Calculus. The data came from the National Center for Education Statistics (NCES), 1978–1999 Long-term Trend NAEP Mathematics Student Survey.

Teacher quality gap. Ratio of predominantly White high schools' in-field mathematics teacher rate to corresponding rates for predominantly Black and Hispanic schools. In-field math teaching rate is the percentage of public school mathematics teachers who taught high school grades (9–12) with an undergraduate major and a certificate in their main assignment field. The math teachers were classified as having a college major in the field if they reported having a college degree in any one of these fields: mathematics, math education, physics, engineering, and statistics. This rate was calculated for each group of schools with 50%–100% of their students classified as White, Black, or Hispanic (i.e., predominantly White schools, predominantly Black schools, predominantly Hispanic schools). The data came from 1987–88 and 1999–2000 Schools and Staffing Survey.

School expenditure gap. Ratio of predominantly White school districts' per pupil educational spending to corresponding measures for predominantly Black and Hispanic districts. Per pupil educational spending is current expenditure on education per pupil with the following adjustments: (a) adjusting each district's per-pupil current expenditure for regional cost differences using "geographic cost-of-education index" retrieved from the NCES Web site (http://www.nces.ed.gov/edfin/prodsurv/data.asp); (b) estimating the number of poor students by multiplying the child-poverty rate by its fall enrollment; (c) adjusting its fall enrollment by multiplying the estimated number of poor students by 1.2 and the number of special education students by 2.3; and (d) calculating the district's adjusted per pupil expenditure by dividing its adjusted current spending by its adjusted enrollment. The average amount of spending was calculated for each group of school districts with 50%–100% of children classified as White, Black, or Hispanic (i.e., predominantly White districts, predominantly Black districts, predominantly Hispanic districts). The data came from 1989–90 and 1997–98 Common Core of Data and F-33. The districts' racial composition of children in both 1989–90 and 1997–98 years was based on the 1990 Census and thus did not reflect any changes between 1990 and 1998.

PEABODY JOURNAL OF EDUCATION, *79*(2), 74–97

Private Schools, Segregation, and the Southern States

Charles T. Clotfelter
Sanford Institute of Public Policy
Duke University

This article considers the role of private schools in an assessment of segregation in K–12 schools, with special reference to the South. It presents evidence to support two main conclusions. First, private schools have grown in importance in the South since 1960, in contrast to their declining importance in the rest of the country. This contrary trend can be attributed to the region's small proportion of Catholics, to its rising affluence, and to school desegregation. Because of the typically large areas covered by school districts in the South, private schools have offered White families an especially effective means of avoiding exposure to non-Whites in schools, particularly in counties with very high minority concentrations. In those counties the rate at which Whites enrolled in private schools tended to rise with the percentage of all students who were non-White, increasing sharply in counties about 55% non-White.

A previous version of this article was presented at a conference on the Resegregation of Southern Schools, held at the University of North Carolina, Chapel Hill, August 30, 2002, and sponsored by the Civil Rights Project of Harvard University and the University of North Carolina School of Law. Substantial portions of this article will appear in *After* Brown*: The Rise and Retreat of School Desegregation* (Princeton University Press, in press). Permission has been granted by Princeton University Press. I am grateful to Robert Malme and Abiskar Mitra for research assistance and to the Spencer Foundation and Duke University for research support. The views expressed are those of the author and do not necessarily reflect those of any organization.

Requests for reprints should be sent to Charles T. Clotfelter, Duke University, Sanford Institute of Public Policy, Box 90245, Durham, NC 27708. E-mail: charles.clotfelter @duke.edu

Second, the article presents measures of the extent to which private schools contribute to segregation in schools in all regions. Using data on public and private enrollments in 1999–2000, the article shows that private schools accounted for only about 16% of such segregation in the nation's metropolitan areas, with the bulk of segregation attributed to racial disparities between public school districts. For the nation, segregation increased between 1995–1996 and 1999–2000, and a rise in White private enrollments had a role in this increase.

Although *Brown v. Board of Education* (1954) was its necessary precursor, substantial desegregation did not arrive in much of the South until shortly before 1970. Not until the Supreme Court's decisions in *Green v. County School Board of New Kent County* (1968) and *Alexander v. Holmes County Board of Education* (1969) did the regime of segregated schools in the South finally come to an end. As Orfield (1983) showed, the effect of enforcement efforts following those decisions transformed the public schools in the South from the least to the most integrated in any region in the country. However, as in other regions of the country, not all Whites stood by in idle acceptance of this astonishing change. In communities across the South, especially where suburban alternatives did not exist, many White families turned to private schools, swelling the enrollments of existing schools and causing hundreds of new schools to be established. Still, it was not clear at the time how many of these hastily founded schools would survive.

Now is a propitious time to reexamine the role that private schools are playing with respect to school desegregation and segregation.[1] Especially in light of the growth in incomes and urbanization in the South over this period, it is pertinent to ask whether patterns of private school enrollment in the South have become more similar to those historically observed in the Northeast and the Midwest. Among the reasons why it is important to learn about patterns of private enrollment is that they almost certainly affect the overall segregation of schools. By providing places of enrollment that are quite obviously separate from those provided by the public schools, private schools contribute to the overall segregation of students, where *segregation* is taken to mean the uneven distribution of students of different racial groups across schools. Were private schools not to exist, in other words, students might experience higher levels of interracial contact than they do in fact. In addition, the rising affluence of the South, com-

[1]In this article, *segregation* is used primarily in the sense that social scientists have come to use it, as the extent to which students of different racial groups attend separate schools, rather than as the name of the policy used to keep races separated. See Massey and Denton (1988) for an assessment of various measures of segregation. In the present article, *race* is understood to include ethnicity, so that non-Whites include Hispanic or Latino students.

bined with the unusually rapid rise in incomes of households in the upper half of the income distribution occurring nationwide, makes private schools a particularly important topic to investigate, because those rising incomes make private schools financially feasible for more families.

This article has two main aims: to examine the trend in private school enrollment in the South since the advent of school desegregation and to highlight the contribution of private schools to overall segregation, both in the South and elsewhere. By way of preview, the article establishes two findings. First, private schools in the South have grown in importance, in contrast to their gradual decline in the rest of the country. School desegregation appears to be one major reason for this growth. Second, private schools contribute to racial segregation in the schools of all regions, although they are usually less important than racial disparities that exist between and within public school districts.

The article is organized as follows. First, the Desegregation and the Growth of Private Schools in the South section reviews some previous research on private schools in the South, focusing in particular on the emergence of private schools in counties with high percentages of Black students, and reviews broad trends in private school enrollment by region. It shows that private school enrollment has steadily grown in importance since the advent of desegregation at the same time that private schools have become less prominent elsewhere. Next, the Data and Measures section describes the data used in the present study. The Measuring Segregation and the Role Played by Private Schools section presents measures of the contribution of private schools to segregation in the South as compared to other regions. It shows that private schools account for a portion of overall segregation, but much less than is attributed to racial disparities between and within public school districts. The contribution of private schools to segregation is greatest in nonmetropolitan areas in the South. The next section, Private Schools Outside Metropolitan Areas and Tipping, thus focuses on nonmetropolitan areas and the existence of tipping points in patterns of private school enrollment. The Recent Trends in Private School Enrollment and Segregation section then provides documentation of trends. There is a brief concluding section.

Desegregation and the Growth of Private Schools in the South

Private schooling has a long and honored role in American education. Not only did private schools predate public ones but they have retained a small but significant share of elementary and secondary school enrollment. Historically, private schools have claimed a larger share of enrollments in the Northeast and Midwest than in the relatively impoverished South and the newer West. Yet, in the wake of desegregation orders following the *Brown* decision, households in numerous Southern communities turned to private schools as never before. Virginia's massive resistance to desegregation in the 1950s featured the closing of schools in several districts. In Prince Edward County, private schools for Whites were organized, obtaining financial support from public funds as well as nonprofit organizations (Patterson, 2001, p. 99).

Again in the late 1960s, all-White segregation academies sprang up in the largely Black cotton belt of Mississippi, Alabama, and Georgia, following the Supreme Court's decisions in *Green* and *Alexander*, cases that effectively eliminated dual school systems. Many of these hastily organized private schools offered modest facilities, as this description of Americus, Georgia, in 1970 illustrates:

> Private schools multiplied over the area like an overnight backyard visitation of mushrooms. Generally dingy, dubious, makeshift affairs, one of them operates in the facilities of the Brooklyn Heights Baptist Church, another in a vacated squat mortar building near the center of town, where one finds oddly quiet children with pale blank gazes in its dim cramped corridors, empty RC Cola crates stacked in corners, and a vague sour rankness enclosed within its walls like the effluvium of a fox den. (Frady, 1971/2003, pp. 860–861)

To be sure, these episodes of White resistance were extraordinary, even for the region or the period. Yet it may fairly be said that private schools flourished throughout the South during the period of desegregation. Over the period 1960 to 2000, whereas the share of all students attending private schools in the United States dropped by more than 3 percentage points, the share in the South increased by 4 percentage points. As shown in Table 1, the South in 1960 had by far the lowest share of students in private schools of any region in the country. Owing in part to its relatively small proportion of Catholics, whose parochial schools made up a large share of private schools in the country, the South had only 5% of its elementary and secondary students in private schools, less than a quarter the comparable share in the Northeast. Over the decade of the 1960s, when most of the desegregation of the Southern public schools took place, the private enrollment rate in that region increased slightly but did so while rates declined in every other region of the country. Indeed, the South's private enrollment share has risen rather steadily until, by 1999–2000, it was only about 1 percentage point below the national average.

Table 1

Percentage in Private School, Grades 1–12, by Region, 1960 to 2000

Region	*1960*	*1970*	*1980*	*1990*	*2000*
Northeast	21.8	17.9	14.6	14.1	13.1
Border	12.1	9.7	9.9	10.1	11.3
South	5.0	5.2	7.8	7.5	9.1
Midwest	17.9	13.3	11.6	11.1	11.7
West	9.1	7.1	8.2	7.8	8.3
United States	13.6	11.0	10.5	9.8	10.3

Notes. Data are from *After* Brown: *The Rise and Retreat of School Segregation,* by C. T. Clotfelter, in press, Princeton, NJ: Princeton University Press, copyright by Princeton University Press, reprinted with permission, and from U.S. Census Bureau (1964, Tables 105, 114, and 275; 1973, Table 154; 1983, Table 239; 1993, Table 147; 2000).

In some parts of the South, private enrollments spiked markedly in the wake of thoroughgoing school desegregation orders as in the case of Mississippi noted earlier. That state's private enrollment tripled between 1967 and 1972, as shown in Table 2, raising the private share from 3.5% to 10.6% of all students. Nor was this merely a temporary blip. By 1980, most of this increase had been solidified into a significantly higher share of students in private schools, a share that continued into 1997.

One noteworthy aspect of private enrollment in Mississippi was the phenomenon of massive exodus of White students out of the public schools in some districts. As detailed in Clotfelter (1976), the rate of exit from the public schools in 1968 and 1969 was especially high in districts in which the school-age population was majority Black. Indeed, the evidence

Table 2

Public and Private K–12 Enrollment in Mississippi, Fall of Selected Years

Year	*Private*	*Public*	*Total*	*% Private*
1967	21,817	599,891	621,708	3.5
1972	62,366	526,366	588,732	10.6
1980	50,116	471,615	521,731	9.6
1997	54,529	504,792	559,321	9.7

Note. For 1980, public enrollment is based on Fall 1981 enrollment. Data are from the following sources. Private enrollment: Clotfelter (1976, Table 1, p. 30), *Digest of Education Statistics 1989* (1989, Table 37, p. 48), *2000* (2001, Table 64, p. 73). Public enrollment: *Digest of Education Statistics 1970* (1970, Table 37, p. 48), *1973* (1974, Table 29, p. 30);, 1989 (1989, Table 54, p. 67), *2000* (U.S. Department of Education, National center for Education Statistics, 2001, Table 39, pp. 50–51).

from that period is consistent with the existence of a tipping point just over 50% in the proportion of a county's school population that was Black.

Yet, as Table 1 makes clear, the expansion of private schools was by no means confined to Mississippi. Private enrollment in North Carolina, for example, increased by one third between 1970 and 1971 in the wake of desegregation orders. And in the metropolitan area of Memphis, private enrollment increased from 13,000 to 33,000 between 1970 and 1973, following a court order involving busing for desegregation (Clotfelter, 1976, p. 29). The question for today is whether these early jumps in enrollment have been sustained in the form of continuing higher levels with their consequent effect on racial segregation in schools.

Data and Measures

The present study makes use of detailed enrollment data available for public and private schools for the 1999–2000 year. Information on public schools comes from the Common Core of Data, which is based on data reported by state departments of education.[2] Data on private schools are taken from the U.S. Department of Education, National Center for Education Statistics Private School Universe Survey, a periodic survey most recently undertaken for the 1999–2000 year.[3] To assess recent trends in enrollments and other measures, comparable data from both sources were collected for the 1995–1996 school year as well. Because the focus of this article is on private enrollments and segregation in the regions of the country whose schools were segregated by law before 1954, most of the tables in the article present comparisons at the regional level.[4] School districts are

[2]Data for two states, Idaho and Tennessee, were not included in the 1999–2000 Common Core. Thus public school enrollment data for the 1998–1999 year were used for Tennessee, and data for 2000–2001 were used for Idaho.

[3]Private school enrollment data exclude special education schools, include kindergartens in schools whose highest grade was kindergarten, and were weighted to reflect nonresponses using the weight variable SFNLWT. In a few counties, weighting increased private enrollment significantly, although it made little difference in regional segregation calculations.

[4]Regions are, as defined by Orfield and Monfort (1992), as follows. The South includes of Alabama, Arkansas, Florida, Georgia, Louisiana, Mississippi, North Carolina, South Carolina, Tennessee, Texas, and Virginia. Border states include Delaware, District of Columbia, Kentucky, Maryland, Missouri, Oklahoma, and West Virginia. The Northeast includes Connecticut, Maine, Massachusetts, New Hampshire, New Jersey, New York, Pennsylvania, Rhode Island, and Vermont. The Midwest includes Illinois, Indiana, Iowa, Kansas, Michigan, Minnesota, Nebraska, North Dakota, South Dakota, Ohio, and Wisconsin. The West includes Arizona, California, Colorado, Idaho, Montana, Nevada, New Mexico, Oregon, Utah, Washington, and Wyoming.

grouped by metropolitan area, using the same 1990 geographic boundaries for both years of data.[5] Because patterns are likely to differ between large and small metropolitan areas, calculations based on metropolitan areas with total school enrollments of 200,000 or more are shown separately from smaller areas. Nonmetropolitan counties are analyzed separately and, for tabular purposes, summarized by region.

Table 3 summarizes the data on enrollments from the combined sources for the 1999–2000 year. Among the five regions, private enrollment was most common in the Northeast and Midwest and lowest in the South and West, patterns roughly consistent with the rates presented in Table 1.[6] The largest metropolitan areas in each region showed the highest rates of private enrollment, followed by the smaller metropolitan areas, with the lowest rates in counties outside of metropolitan areas. The percentage of students attending private schools was more than twice that of nonmetropolitan areas in every region. A principal advantage of the Private School Universe Survey is its detailed enrollment information by race. Among the calculations these data allow is the percentage of Whites who attended private school, which is shown by region in the last column of Table 3. A striking aspect of this column is the similarity across regions it reveals. Except for the Northeast, whose rate of private school enrollment for Whites was almost 20%, Whites in the rest of the country enrolled at rates very close to 15%. In fact, the rate for Whites in the South was at least comparable to those in all regions except the Northeast.

Measuring Segregation and the Role Played by Private Schools

The basic measure of segregation used in this article begins with the exposure rate, which measures the racial composition of the school attended by the average student of a given group.

[5]Metropolitan Statistical Areas (MSAs) and Primary Metropolitan Statistical Areas (PMSAs) were used. Those that had components in more than one region were assigned to the region containing the larger enrollment.

[6]By way of comparison, the U.S. Department of Education, National Center for Education Statistics (2001, Tables 40, 59), gives estimates that total 51,269,000 for total Fall 1999 K–12 enrollment, 10.1% of which was in private schools. The totals implied in Table 3 understate the published numbers for public enrollment by 2.1% and private enrollment by 0.1%. Using comparable data for public and private schools for 1997–1998, Reardon and Yun (2000, Table 1, p. 16) understated private enrollment by 4.1% compared to the published figures for that year. They calculated the private enrollment share for the nation as 9.7%, somewhat smaller than the 10.0% share implied by the published figures.

Table 3

Percentage of K–12 Students in Private School by Region and Metropolitan Status and Percentage of Whites in Private School by Region, 1999–2000

		Percentage of Students in Private Schools				
Region	*School Enrollment (000s)*	*Large Metro Areas*	*Small Metro Areas*	*Nonmetro Counties*	*All*	*Percentage of Whites in Private Schools*
Northeast	9,169	17.4	11.7	7.9	13.8	19.9
Border	4,354	14.4	11.6	4.5	11.1	16.5
South	14,773	10.3	9.0	4.8	8.4	14.3
Midwest	10,491	14.7	11.7	6.7	11.3	13.8
West	11,265	9.7	6.7	3.9	8.1	12.5
United States	50,052	12.6	10.0	5.4	10.1	15.0

Note. Large metropolitan areas are defined as those with K–12 enrollments of 200,000 or more in 1999–2000. Alaska and Hawaii are not included in West and U.S. totals. Metro area is assigned to region on the basis of the largest county within the area. Data are from *After* Brown: *The Rise and Retreat of School Segregation,* by C. T. Clotfelter, in press, Princeton, NJ: Princeton University Press, copyright by Princeton University Press, reprinted with permission; from U.S. Department of Education, National Center for Education Statistics, (2001a, 2001b); and from author's calculations.

For example, the exposure rate of White to non-White students in a metropolitan area, interpreted as the percentage non-White in the average White student's school, is $E = (W_j n_j)/W_j$, where W_j is the number of Whites and n_j is the non-White percentage in school j. To the extent that schools in the metropolitan area differ in their racial compositions, this exposure rate will fall below its maximum possible value, the percentage of all students in the metropolitan area who are non-White. The gap between the actual exposure and this maximum is a measure of unevenness, or segregation, and when expressed as a percentage yields a widely used index of segregation: $S = (n - E)/n$, where n is the percentage non-White of all students in the metropolitan area. The index's minimum value, $S = 0$, indicates racially balanced schools (no segregation), whereas its maximum, $S = 1$, indicates that Whites and non-Whites attend entirely separate schools.[7]

In Clotfelter (1999), I showed how this measure can be decomposed to distinguish segregation in public schools attributable to racial disparities between school districts from those within school districts.[8] In the current article, I extend that logic to include segregation arising from the existence of private schools. To see how this can be done, consider how the actual exposure rate calculated for a metropolitan area would compare to the exposure rates (shown in parentheses) that would apply to four hypothetical scenarios, each one less segregated than the last: (a) each district racially balances its schools (E^*); (b) all public schools in the metropolitan area are balanced at the same racial composition (E^{**}); (c) in addition, all private schools are racially balanced within the private sector (E^{***}); and (d) all schools, public and private, are racially balanced at the same racial composition, which is the racial composition of all students in the area (n).

Because $E \leq E^* \leq E^{**} \leq E^{***} \leq n$, the total segregation index can be partitioned to yield four components, representing the portion due to racial disparities in the composition of schools:

1. Within public school districts $(E^* - E)/n$.
2. Between public school districts $(E^{**} - E^*)/n$.
3. Among private schools $(E^{***} - E^{**})/n$.
4. Between public and private schools $(n - E^{***})/n$.

[7]Reardon and Yun (2002) referred to this measure as the *normalized exposure index*.

[8]Although it is grammatically incorrect for cases involving more than two districts, I retain the term *between* in referring to differences among public school districts because the *within–between* dichotomy is familiar terminology to decompositions in statistics and economics. In referring to differences among private schools, however, I use the term *among* because there is no similar dichotomy for private schools and because the number in any area is almost always greater than two.

Data on the racial composition of individual public and private schools were used to calculate the various exposure rates necessary to perform this decomposition for 332 metropolitan areas.[9] The decomposition can easily be illustrated using the case of Atlanta, Georgia. In 1999–2000, the exposure rate of Whites to non-Whites in all schools (public and private) in the Atlanta metropolitan area was 23.2%, whereas the percentage of non-Whites in the school population was 44.8%, yielding a relatively high segregation index of .483.[10] If, however, every school district had balanced its schools so that all the schools in a district had the same racial composition, the exposure rate would have been higher, 30.0%, and so on with each of the hypothetical policies listed above. Calculations of E^* (30.0%), E^{**} (42.7%), and E^{***} (44.0%) can be used to partition the total segregation index of .483 into a portion due to imbalance within districts (.152), that due to disparities between districts (.285), that due to racial disparities among private schools (.030), and that due to the overall racial disparity between public and private schools (.017). The details of these calculations are spelled out in the Appendix. Typical of the large metropolitan areas I examined in Clotfelter (1999), the largest part of Atlanta's segregation in 1999–2000 can be attributed to the differences in racial composition between public school districts—in Atlanta's case, between the largely Black Atlanta and DeKalb County districts and a host of predominantly White districts—whereas the contributions of the other three factors are each much smaller in magnitude.

Similar calculations were made for nonmetropolitan counties as well, where measured segregation is based on gaps within each county rather than within each metropolitan area. The calculations for nonmetropolitan counties were then aggregated to the state level by taking averages weighted by enrollment.[11] Because the notion of segregation itself is rooted in the existence of racial disparities among individual schools, the diversity, and therefore usually the size, of the geographical unit of observation will influence the degree of measured segregation.

Thus large, diverse metropolitan areas will tend to have more segregation than smaller, more homogeneous ones. By the same token, less segre-

[9]All MSAs and PMSAs, for those metropolitan areas that are part of Consolidated Metropolitan Statistical Areas, using 1990 definitions of components, were included. Excluded were metropolitan areas in Idaho, for which no data were available in the CCD, as well as Alaska and Hawaii.

[10]The index of .483 was calculated as $S = (44.8 - 23.2)/44.8$, where the result may not be exact due to rounding.

[11]In New England, metropolitan areas are defined as aggregations of towns and cities rather than counties, so nonmetropolitan counties in New England were defined as the remaining portions of counties not part of metropolitan areas.

gation is apt to be measured in individual counties than in metropolitan areas, which are usually composed of more than one county. But counties are the best and most natural unit for assessing segregation outside metropolitan areas; the next logical unit, the state, is clearly too large, because racial balance at the state level is an unrealistic and rather unappealing standard of comparison.[12] Because counties thus tend to cover smaller and less diverse geographical areas than metropolitan areas, one expects that between-districts disparities will be less important in the nonmetropolitan counties.

To give a sense of the levels and decomposition of segregation in metropolitan areas, Table 4 presents calculated segregation indices for the Southern metropolitan areas that ranked highest and lowest in overall segregation. Among the largest metropolitan areas shown, the most segregated ones were Memphis, Tennessee, and New Orleans, Louisiana, each having an index of .580. In each case, disparities among their public school districts was the biggest contributor to overall segregation, adding .329 and .285, respectively. Among the region's smaller metropolitan areas, the most segregated were Birmingham, Alabama, and Monroe, Louisiana, with indices of .625 and .591, respectively. By comparison, the nation's most segregated metropolitan area in 1999–2000 was Detroit, where racial disparities among its 109 school districts accounted for .599 of its total .684 segregation index (see Clotfelter, in press, chapter 4). At the other end of the spectrum, Tampa, Florida, and Miami, Florida, were the least segregated of the largest metropolitan areas in the region, with indices of .215 and .242, respectively. By virtue of the large size of school districts in Florida, neither of these areas had many districts, leaving little room for interdistrict racial disparities. Among the region's smaller metropolitan areas, the least segregated areas actually came close to achieving overall racial balance. Fort Walton Beach, Florida, served by a single district, had an index of .051. Laredo, Texas, with a school population almost entirely non-White, had an index of .062.

The importance of private schools in explaining overall school segregation differed among these eight illustrative metropolitan areas. When the two components related to private schools are added together, private schools accounted for at least half of total segregation in two of the least segregated areas, Miami and Laredo. In New Orleans, private schools accounted for about two-fifths of the total (.235 out of .580). In the remaining areas shown in the table, however, private schools accounted for a fifth or less of the total.

[12]Even less appealing is the nation, which was the implicit unit of comparison used by Coleman, Hoffer, and Kilgore (1982).

Table 4

Metropolitan Areas in South With Highest and Lowest Indices of Segregation, 1999–2000

					Components of Segregation				
Area	*No. of Districts*	*Enrollment*	*% Non-White*	*% Whites in Private Schools*	*Between Districts*	*Within Districts*	*Among Private Schools*	*Between Public and Private Schools*	*Total*
Large metro areas									
Most segregated									
Memphis, TN	10	229,669	56.5	23.9	.131	.329	.040	.081	.580
New Orleans, LA	6	245,231	54.7	41.1	.070	.285	.120	.115	.580
Least segregated									
Tampa–St. Petersburg, FL	4	367,637	31.0	14.6	.108	.075	.021	.013	.215
Miami, FL	2	399,299	85.6	26.9	.122	.000	.092	.028	.242
Small metro areas									
Most segregated									
Birmingham, AL	17	174,435	38.6	10.1	.055	.523	.043	.004	.625
Monroe, LA	2	29,409	45.8	15.3	.200	.326	.000	.064	.591
Least segregated									
Fort Walton Beach, FL	1	30,533	19.0	3.9	.048	.000	.003	.000	.051
Laredo, TX	4	47,943	97.2	16.1	.019	.005	.030	.009	.062

Notes. Large metropolitan areas are defined as those with K–12 enrollments of 200,000 or more. Metropolitan areas are defined as of 1990. Total segregation values may not equal the sum of segregation components because of rounding. Data are from U.S. Department of Education, National Center for Education Statistics (2001a, 2001b), and from author's calculations.

To obtain a more general assessment of segregation patterns and particularly the contribution of private schools, Table 5 summarizes school segregation for the nation by region and metropolitan status. Where segregation applies to racial disparities among all schools—both public and private—and where metropolitan areas are used as geographical units of comparison, the average segregation index in metropolitan areas was .362, of which .226, or 62%, can be attributed to disparities among public school districts. Second in importance, accounting for 0.079, or about 22% of the total, were disparities between the schools within public school districts. Private school enrollment was relatively less important in contributing to racial segregation: Taken together, the disparity in average racial composition of public and private schools and differences among private schools accounted for about 16% of total segregation. For nonmetropolitan areas, where the county is taken as the unit of comparison, the average segregation index was .096, with district segregation accounting for 40% of the total.

Comparisons by region in Table 5 present an interesting contrast to previous regional comparisons. Although the South shows less than average segregation when comparing metropolitan areas, its segregation in nonmetropolitan areas was higher than that in the rest of the United States. It is worth emphasizing that the segregation indices calculated in the present article differ in two significant respects from conventional calculations based on segregation within districts: They include private schools, and they examine disparities within metropolitan areas or nonmetropolitan counties rather than just within school districts. How important were private schools in contributing to segregation in the South? In nonmetropolitan areas, they were very important indeed, accounting for .057, or 42%, of total segregation. In the South's metropolitan areas, private schools were a factor more in line with private schools in the rest of the nation, accounting for 16% of total metropolitan segregation there.

Private Schools Outside Metropolitan Areas and Tipping

As the previous discussion makes clear, private schools tend to exacerbate racial segregation in schools, but in most communities they contribute less to segregation than aspects of the public schools do. However, the history of desegregation in the United States does offer some examples of communities for which the private schools have represented the major device for Whites to avoid some of the effects of school desegregation. As illustrated by the case of Mississippi in the period 1968 to 1972, some districts with very high proportions of Black students saw a huge exodus of

Table 5

Components of Segregation by Region, Metropolitan and Nonmetropolitan Areas, 1999–2000

	Metropolitan Areas' Components of Segregation					*Nonmetropolitan Counties' Components of Segregation*				
Region	*Within Districts*	*Between Districts*	*Among Private Schools*	*Public–Private Disparity*	*Total*	*Within Districts*	*Between Districts*	*Among Private Schools*	*Public–Private Disparity*	*Total*
Northeast	.055	.294	.057	.028	.434	.011	.041	.019	.009	.081
Border	.076	.240	.031	.020	.366	.022	.023	.004	.009	.058
South	.117	.158	.025	.028	.328	.051	.029	.004	.053	.135
Midwest	.057	.329	.039	.012	.436	.014	.035	.006	.003	.058
West	.074	.159	.028	.019	.280	.025	.075	.005	.006	.111
United States	.079	.226	.036	.022	.362	.030	.038	.006	.023	.096

Note. For definition of components of segregation, see Appendix A. Data are from *After* Brown: *The Rise and Retreat of School Segregation,* by C. T. Clotfelter, in press, Princeton, NJ: Princeton University Press, copyright by Princeton University Press, reprinted with permission; from U.S. Department of Education, National Center for Education Statistics, (2001a, 2001b); and from the author's calculations.

White students to private schools. An obvious question to pose today is whether such patterns have been sustained over time. For the case of Mississippi, the aggregate data in Table 2 suggest that much of the increase in private enrollments was sustained, in that those enrollments did decline after their peak, but not to predesegregation levels. However, I know of no follow-up research to explore whether the patterns observed in the enrollments of the early 1970s have continued, in particular the tendency for White departures from the public schools to "tip" at some point. Nor has there been research to see whether such patterns are evident outside of Mississippi.

As a way of assessing current patterns of private enrollment in nonmetropolitan areas, Table 6 shows the percentage of Whites who were enrolled in private schools, by the proportion of non-Whites in the county.

Table 6

Nonmetropolitan Private School Enrollment and County Racial Composition, Border, South and Other Regions, Grades K–12, 1999–2000

	Number of Counties and % Whites Enrolled in Private Schools					
	Border		*South*		*Rest of United States*	
% Non-White in County	N	%	N	%	N	%
0 to under 5	233	2.2	388	0.4	820	3.6
5 to under 10	31	7.5	36	4.7	165	7.1
10 to under 15	17	7.8	28	3.4	68	6.5
15 to under 20	7	5.7	31	4.1	46	6.3
20 to under 25	7	10.7	30	8.7	22	5.4
25 to under 30	5	7.6	30	5.4	16	6.2
30 to under 35	6	5.1	19	9.5	12	5.1
35 to under 40	5	7.1	41	7.7	9	6.0
40 to under 45	3	9.9	44	8.9	8	3.3
45 to under 50	1	3.3	37	12.5	7	4.1
50 to under 55	2	1.9	30	12.2	8	4.0
55 to under 60	0	—	39	19.0	11	4.7
60 to under 65	1	2.3	21	28.6	8	3.6
65 to under 70	0	—	17	38.7	3	19.7
70 to under 75	0	—	13	35.9	1	0.0
75 to under 80	0	—	14	35.5	1	1.2
80 to under 85	0	—	12	60.6	1	17.5
85 to under 90	0	—	9	72.4	3	10.4
90 to under 95	0	—	5	76.5	3	13.9
95 to 100	0	—	4	5.8	2	32.5

These rates are tabulated separately for Border, South, and the remaining regions. For the South, but only for the South, the private enrollment share clearly tended to rise with the percentage non-White in the county over most of the range of racial compositions. Furthermore, there was a perceptible jump in the private share above 55%, followed by large increases at 65% and 80%, so that the share of Whites attending private school in counties over 80% non-White was at least triple the rate for counties below 55%. Outside the South, however, the private enrollment share among Whites showed little relationship to the county racial composition. As the columns under *N* indicate, there were relatively few nonmetropolitan counties outside the South that were predominantly non-White. For the few that did have high non-White percentages, African Americans were not the major non-White racial group.

Private schools served most clearly as a vehicle for White flight in largely Black nonmetropolitan counties in the South. In 1999–2000, private schools enrolled over half of all White students in 41 nonmetropolitan counties, 29 of which are in Mississippi, Alabama, or Georgia (Appendix B lists these counties). The vast majority of these counties had very high percentages of non-White students. Many of them lie in the South's Black belt counties that once used slave labor to cultivate cotton and that were among the counties with the largest disparities in funding between schools for Whites and Blacks in the days of de jure segregation (Bond, 1934).

They were also the counties where social divisions in the Jim Crow era were most rigid and severely enforced. Sunflower County, Mississippi, the location of Dollard's classic *Caste and Class in a Southern Town* (1937/1957), in 1999–2000 continued to operate largely separate schools for Whites and Blacks, wherein 73% of all Whites attended private schools. A similar story applies to nearby Washington County, where 58% of the Whites were in private schools in 1999–2000.

Blackmon (1992) described that county's major town, Leland, as largely segregated 20 years after the advent of school desegregation. In these Deep South counties with high proportions of Blacks, where relations between the races historically were marked by separation and inequality, private schools became—and continue to be—the primary means of maintaining segregation in K–12 schooling.

Combined with the general stability or growth of private enrollments in the South after 1970, these findings suggest that private schools were playing much the same role in nonmetropolitan counties of the South in 1999–2000 as they were shortly after desegregation. In the relatively few predominantly Black counties, Whites seeking to avoid being in the minority in schools opted for private schools, thus further exacerbating the racial disparity between public and private schools. In those counties, this tipping phenomenon obviously made significant racial integration in the schools virtually impossible to achieve.

Recent Trends in Private School Enrollment and Segregation

It was possible to track recent trends in private school enrollment and segregation by using comparable data on public and private schools in 1995–1996 and using them to make comparisons to 1999–2000. Table 7 presents calculations of both using the previous categories defined by regions and metropolitan status. The table suggests that the rate of private enrollment among Whites increased across the board, rising from 12.9% to 13.9% for the nation. These increases were especially large in the South and in the Border region.[13] Segregation also increased, except in the largest metropolitan areas in the Border region. For the nation, the average index rose from .288 to .301.

Conclusion

The empirical analysis presented in this article shows clearly that private schools have a role in the racial segregation of students in K–12 schools, and this finding has special force in parts of the South. The article examines the role of private school enrollment in contributing to segregation in elementary and secondary schools, with special attention to that region. To do so, it extends the measurement of school segregation so as to include private schools as well as public schools. It uses a measure of segregation that allows for decomposition into a part attributable to racial disparities within school districts, a part due to disparities between districts, and two additional parts associated with disparities associated with private schools. Using data on public and private enrollments in 1999–2000, the article shows that most of the segregation in U.S metropolitan areas and almost half in Southern metropolitan areas was due to racial

[13]A note of caution may be indicated by the presence of some very large values in the weighting variable applied to enrollments in the 1999–2000 survey. An extreme example is Simpson County, Kentucky, where the weighted total private enrollment for the county exceeds the unweighted total by a factor of 15, and so that county was omitted from the Table A1 in the Appendix. In any case, it is well to recall that the private enrollment figures for both years were derived using weights provided in the data set.

Table 7

Recent Trends in Private School Enrollment and Segregation, 1995/1996–1999/2000

Region	*% Whites in Private Schools* 1995–1996	*% Whites in Private Schools* 1999–2000	*Overall Segregation* 1995–1996	*Overall Segregation* 1999–2000
Border				
Large metro	17.1	18.3	.467	.465
Small metro	11.5	13.8	.162	.174
Nonmetro	3.9	4.9	.053	.058
South				
Large metro	13.8	15.6	.361	.363
Small metro	11.6	13.2	.278	.291
Nonmetro	8.7	9.6	.121	.135
Rest of United States				
Large metro	18.5	19.1	.421	.433
Small metro	12.2	12.0	.270	.291
Nonmetro	6.0	6.3	.063	.078
United States	12.9	13.9	.288	.301

Note. Large metropolitan areas are defined as those with K–12 enrollments of 200,000 or more in 1999–2000. Metropolitan areas are defined as of 1990. Data are from U.S. Department of Education, National Center for Education Statistics (2001a, 2001b), and from author's calculations.

disparities between public school districts. By contrast, private schools accounted for only about 16% of such segregation for metro areas in both the nation and the South. Nationwide, the percentage of Whites enrolled in private schools increased between 1995–1996 and 1999–2000, as did school segregation.

In the South, private schools have tended to play a larger role. In the 3 decades following the advent of serious school desegregation in the late 1960s, private school enrollment in the South grew in importance, whereas it generally declined elsewhere. Three factors would appear to explain this divergent Southern trend in private school enrollment. The first is clearly school desegregation itself. Both the timing and location of the growth in private schools strongly suggest that the surge in demand was motivated by a desire among Whites to avoid public schools with sizable proportions of Black students. However, the aspect of the South that transformed this desire into a demand for private schools was the geographically large size of public school districts throughout most of the region. Unlike the metropolitan areas of the North and Midwest, those in the South have far fewer districts. It may even be the case that the existence of de jure segregation in public schools encouraged Southern states to use counties, rather than towns and cities, as the basic organizing unit for public school administration, because Whites needed no separate districts to achieve racially separate schools. For whatever reason, the large size of the districts in the South meant that, when desegregation came, Whites seeking to avoid its effects typically did not have the option so widely available in the North and West, to move to a nearby predominantly White enclave. Thus private schools became the most ready avenue for exit. And in most districts outside metropolitan areas, private schools were the only alternative. The clearest indication of the link between desegregation and private enrollment in these nonmetropolitan areas is the finding that the rate at which Whites enrolled in private schools tended to rise with the non-White percentage in the county, increasing markedly in counties with percentages of non-White students over 55%.[14]

The second factor contributing to the South's divergent trend in private enrollment is the region's low proportion of Catholics. For reasons wholly unrelated to school desegregation, Catholic parochial school enrollment in the country has been declining since about 1960 (U.S. Department of Education, National Center for Education Statistics, 2001, Table 63, p. 72), so that in regions of the country where those schools were the predominant form of private schools, private enrollments faced a declining trend to start with, a trend that affected the South to a much lesser extent.

A third reason for the South's increase in private enrollment is its economic integration into the national economy, bringing with it rising personal income and an influx of migrants from other regions. These changes in turn led to an increase in demand for schooling and, specifically, private schooling. The South, in short, became more like the rest of the country. Middle-class Whites, like their counterparts in other regions, demanded good schools, and they often associated that demand with schools having comparatively small shares of non-Whites.

[14]Reardon and Yun (2002, pp. 7–8) offered evidence they said undermines the notion that private enrollments are motivated by the desire to avoid desegregated public schools: the historically higher private enrollment rates in regions with lower rates of interracial contact in public schools (the Northeast and Midwest) and the stability of private enrollment during the 1970s, the period of the most intense desegregation activity. In fact, these observations simply confirm that avoidance of desegregation is not the exclusive or primary motivation for private enrollment. The dominance of Catholic parochial schools in some regions and their decline everywhere largely explain these observations. Abundant evidence supports the importance of avoidance motives in private enrollment, including the explanatory power of the percentage Black in Reardon and Yun's regressions explaining White private enrollment rates (Table D1).

References

Alexander v. Holmes County Board of Education, 396 U.S. 19 (1969).

Blackmon, D. A. (1992, September). The resegregation of a southern school. *Harper's Magazine*, 14–21.

Bond, H. M. (1934). *The education of the Negro in the American social order.* New York: Prentice Hall.

Brown v. Board of Educ., 347 U.S. 483 (1954).

Coleman, J. S., Hoffer, T., & Kilgore, S. (1982). *High school achievement: Public, Catholic, and private schools compared.* New York: Basic Books.

Clotfelter, C. T. (1976, Winter). School desegregation, tipping, and private school enrollment. *Journal of Human Resources, 22,* 29–50.

Clotfelter, C. T. (1999, November). Public school segregation in metropolitan areas. *Land Economics, 75,* 487–504.

Clotfelter, C. T. (in press). *After* Brown*: The rise and retreat of school segregation.* Princeton, NJ: Princeton University Press.

Dollard, J. (1957). *Caste and class in a southern town.* Garden City, NY: Doubleday Anchor. (Original work published 1937)

Frady, M. (2003). Discovering one another in a Georgia town. In *Reporting civil rights: Vol. 2. American journalism 1963–1973.* New York: Library of America. (Reprinted from *Life,* February 12, 1971)

Green v. County school Board of New Kent County, 430 U.S. 391 (1968).

Massey, D. S., & Denton, N. A. (1988, December). The dimensions of residential segregation. *Social Forces, 67,* 281–315.

Orfield, G. (1983). *Public school desegregation in the United States, 1968–1980.* Washington, DC: Joint Center for Political Studies.

Orfield, G., & Monfort, F. (1992, March). *Status of school desegregation: The next generation.* Cambridge, MA: Harvard University, Metropolitan Opportunity Project.

Patterson, J. T. (2001). *Brown v. Board of Education: A civil rights milestone and its troubled legacy.* New York: Oxford University Press.

Reardon, S. F., & Yun, J. T. (2002, June 26). Private school racial enrollments and segregation (unpublished paper). Cambridge, MA: Harvard University, Civil Rights Project.

U.S. Census Bureau. (1964): *Characteristics of the population, United States summary, 1960.* Washington, DC: U.S. Government Printing Office.

U.S. Census Bureau. (1973): *Characteristics of the population, United States summary, 1970.* Washington, DC: U.S. Government Printing Office.

U.S. Census Bureau. (1983): *Characteristics of the population, United States summary, 1980.* Washington, DC: U.S. Government Printing Office.

U.S. Census Bureau. (1993): *Characteristics of the population, United States summary, 1990.* Washington, DC: U.S. Government Printing Office.

U.S. Census Bureau. (2000): *American Fact Finder.* Retrieved July 18, 2003, from http://factfinder.census.gov/servlet/BasicFactsServlet

U.S. Department of Education, National Center for Education Statistics. (2001a). *Common core of data, 1999/2000.* Retrieved from http://nces.ed.gov/ecd/pubschuniv.asp

U.S. Department of Education, National Center for Education Statistics. (2001b). *Private school universe, 1999/2000.* CD-ROM.

U.S. Department of Education, National Center for Education Statistics. (1970, 1974, 1989, 2001). *Digest of education statistics, 1970, 1973, 1989, 2000.* Washington, DC: U.S. Government Printing Office.

Appendix A
Actual and Hypothetical Exposure Rates for a Metropolitan Area

Exposure Rate for the Metropolitan Area

Actual. Weighted average of exposure rates of public and private schools:

$$E = (E_1 W_1 + E_2 W_2)/(W_1 + W_2).$$

Hypothetical Cases

Case 1: Racially balanced public school districts. Every public school in each district has the same racial composition. Thus the exposure rate for public schools is raised to E_1^*, which is a weighted average of district racial compositions:

$$E^* = (E_1^* W_1 + E_2 W_2)/(W_1 + W_2).$$

Case 2: Metropolitan-wide racial balance in public schools. Every public school throughout the metropolitan area has the same racial composition. Thus the exposure rate for public schools is raised to n_1:

$$E^{**} = (n_1 W_1 + E_2 W_2)/(W_1 + W_2).$$

Case 3: Racial balance in private schools, racial balance in public schools, existing racial disparity in overall racial composition between public and private schools. Although public and private schools may have different overall racial compositions, all private schools have the same racial composition, and all public schools have the same racial composition. Thus the exposure rate for private schools is raised to n_2:

$$E^{***} = (n_1 W_1 + n_2 W_2)/(W_1 + W_2).$$

Case 4. Racial balance with a common racial composition in all schools, public and private. Every school throughout the metropolitan area has the same racial composition. Thus the exposure rate for all schools is raised to n.

Components of School Segregation

Portion due to differences within districts: $(E^* - E)/n$.
Portion due to differences between districts: $(E^{**} - E^*)/n$.
Portion due to segregation among private schools: $(E^{***} - E^{**})/n$.
Portion due public–private racial disparity: $(n - E^{***})/n$.
Total segregation: $(n - E)/n$.

Definitions

W_1, W_2 = White students in public, private schools, respectively.

E_1, E_2 = exposure rate of Whites to non-Whites in public and private schools, respectively. This is a weighted average of individual school racial compositions, where the weights are the number of White students in each school. Where W_i and N_i are the number of Whites and non-Whites, respectively, in school i in either sector and W and N are their totals for the district, either exposure rate is calculated as:

$$E = (1/W)\ W_i\ [N_i/(\ W_i + N_i)],$$

n_1, n_2 = proportion non-White enrollment in public, private schools, respectively.

Appendix B

Nonmetropolitan Counties With More Than Half of White Students in Private Schools, 1999–2000

					Segregation				
State	*County*	*Districts*	*% Non-White in County*	*% White in Private Schools*	*Within District*	*Between Districts*	*Among Private Schools*	*Between Public and Private Schools*	*Total*
MS	Noxubee	1	88.2	100.0	.000	.000	.000	.977	.977
AL	Sumter	1	89.6	99.4	.000	.000	.000	.993	.993
MS	Wilkinson	1	65.2	98.5	.000	.000	.000	.970	.970
MS	Claiborne	1	90.4	98.1	.000	.000	.000	.944	.944
AL	Wilcox	1	82.1	97.3	.000	.000	.042	.918	.960
AL	Greene	1	93.3	97.1	.000	.000	.000	.915	.915
AL	Bullock	1	92.5	95.0	.001	.000	.000	.914	.915
AL	Loundes	1	89.0	94.6	.000	.000	.000	.939	.940
AL	Perry	1	86.3	93.4	.001	.000	.003	.825	.829
MS	Holmes	2	81.7	90.1	.001	.018	.000	.854	.873
GA	Warren	1	69.2	86.9	.000	.000	.000	.814	.814
MS	Quitman	1	83.5	86.2	.001	.000	.000	.809	.810
MS	Kemper	1	78.1	85.2	.002	.000	.000	.817	.819
MS	Tunica	1	89.5	84.3	.000	.000	.000	.817	.818
SC	Lee	1	72.8	83.2	.006	.000	.000	.770	.776
GA	Terrell	1	82.3	82.1	.001	.000	.000	.791	.791
MS	Humphreys	1	86.3	81.5	.001	.000	.000	.778	.779

GA	Hancock	1	92.6	79.0	.001	.000	.000	.777	.777
MS	Sunflower	3	81.8	72.9	.069	.008	.000	.671	.748
AR	Lee	1	80.6	67.2	.003	.000	.000	.617	.620
MS	Adams	1	63.8	65.0	.002	.000	.047	.435	.485
MS	Amite	1	65.9	64.1	.006	.000	.000	.538	.544
MS	Leflore	2	82.6	62.0	.155	.014	.121	.438	.728
GA	Randolph	1	74.0	61.3	.001	.000	.000	.530	.532
SD	Shannon	1	99.6	60.0	.006	.000	.002	.007	.016
GA	Dooly	1	67.4	59.4	.012	.000	.083	.389	.485
TN	Fayette	2	55.2	58.5	.090	.000	.000	.421	.511
MS	Washington	4	75.4	58.2	.106	.110	.004	.456	.677
MS	Yazoo	2	68.5	58.0	.078	.109	.000	.481	.668
MS	Clay	2	64.0	57.8	.002	.004	.000	.439	.445
LA	East Carroll	1	82.9	57.2	.237	.000	.000	.475	.712
VA	Fredericksburg City	1	50.2	56.9	.013	.000	.007	.182	.203
LA	Plaquemines	1	36.5	56.2	.264	.000	.002	.324	.591
LA	Madison	1	76.4	55.9	.103	.000	.000	.479	.583
MS	Coahoma	3	79.3	55.8	.151	.025	.004	.461	.640
MS	Carroll	1	56.3	54.0	.027	.000	.000	.395	.423
NE	Antelope	5	1.4	53.5	.003	.004	.000	.002	.009
LA	East Feliciana	1	64.1	53.3	.103	.000	.000	.414	.517
AL	Choctaw	1	55.5	51.8	.094	.000	.000	.369	.464
SC	Fairfield	1	76.4	51.2	.020	.000	.000	.443	.463
SC	Calhoun	1	64.3	50.6	.122	.000	.000	.388	.510

Note. Alaska boroughs and Simpson County, Nebraska, were excluded. Data are from U.S. Department of Education, National Center for Education Statistics (2001a, 2001b), and from author's calculations.

PEABODY JOURNAL OF EDUCATION, 79(2), 98–121

Reconstructing Los Angeles Magnet Schools: Representations in Newspapers

Ryane McAuliffe Straus
Department of Political Science
University of California, Irvine

This article is a study of the social construction of school desegregation in Los Angeles, California. Particular emphasis is placed on how magnet schools were presented to area residents in the local press over a period of 3 decades. I use quantitative and qualitative techniques with 355 newspaper articles. I find that magnet schools were originally discussed as part of a larger desegregation program, but that references to desegregation declined steadily. Magnet schools are now discussed as providers of academic excellence, and desegregation issues are largely ignored. This follows the current trend in political and academic circles, in which the rhetoric surrounding education is increasingly focused on standards and accountability rather than equality and access.

The last 3 decades have seen an important shift in the national discussion about education. For a generation after *Brown v. Board of Education* (*Brown I*, 1954), government agencies tried to fulfill court mandates to desegregate public schools (at least, they claimed to make this attempt). Poli-

An earlier version of this paper was presented at the meetings of the American Political Science Association, Philadelphia, August 28–31, 2003.

Requests for reprints should be sent to Ryane McAuliffe Straus, Department of Political Science, University of California, Irvine, 3151 Social Science Plaza, Irvine, CA 92697. E-mail: rmstraus@uci.edu

ticians and educators developed a wide variety of policies designed to desegregate schools. The most controversial of these were mandatory reassignment and busing plans, in which students were transported to schools outside their neighborhoods to promote racial balance. Other districts, and even some of those that engaged in busing, developed magnet schools that allowed students to transfer to a different school for academic reasons. These schools were designed to attract students of all backgrounds and were to be placed in locations easily reached by all.

The use of mandatory busing policies has now declined throughout the nation (Orfield & Eaton, 1996). Magnet schools, however, are still used in districts around the country. However, although they were originally designed to promote voluntary desegregation (Metz, 1992; Rossell, 1990), they are now known more for their academic programs than as methods to obtain racial balance. Some districts have even ended their attempts to maintain racially balanced magnet schools, often because racial balance is seen as a type of quota. The San Francisco Unified School District, for example, agreed in 1999 to consider economic background rather than race when admitting students to its prestigious Lowell High School.

Despite (or perhaps because of) the fact that the national discourse has turned away from the importance of providing every child with a quality, integrated education, our public schools remain extremely segregated (Civil Rights Project, 2002a, 2002b; Frankenberg & Lee, 2002; Orfield & Eaton, 1996; Orfield, Schley, Glass, & Reardon, 1993; Orfield & Yun, 1999). Magnet schools often fail at their original goal of integrating students (Straus, 2003), even while students, parents, and community members laud their academic excellence.

Theoretical Framework

This article uses the policy design framework developed by Schneider and Ingram (1997) to study the changing social construction of magnet schools in the Los Angeles Unified School District (LAUSD). Policy design, developed in response to shortcomings of other policy theories, combines elements of pluralism, policy sciences, public choice, and critical theory. Policy design, however, emphasizes the study of the content of policy rather than the politics surrounding its development, the values that provide its framework, and the relationship between social construction and power. The relationship between policy design and social construction is dynamic and runs in both directions; during the design phase, a policy is dependent on various social constructions. During and after implementation, policy becomes an independent factor that influences social construction and other facets of political power. These social constructions then become part of the social fabric, with the power to influence later policy designs.

I tackle part of this complex process in this article with a focus on the second half of the relationship between social construction and policy. Here, in other words, policy is taken as an independent variable, and I study the changing social construction of the policy itself. This is important because our understanding of policy is influenced by social values, and policy, in turn, affects the values of society. Thus, the way in which policy is understood has consequences for how it is implemented.

The question addressed by this article is as follows: Did the social construction of LAUSD magnet schools change between 1976 and 1999? I measured social construction by analyzing articles from the *Los Angeles Times* (the region's primary newspaper)[1] in three time periods: the beginning of the busing controversy (1976 to 1979), a period about 10 years later (1985 to 1987), and a recent period (1996 to 1999). I used newspapers to find out how people in the region were exposed to the desegregation process and the development of magnet schools; these articles are not meant to be understood as evidence of the district's interpretation of these events.[2] Although the media cannot mandate what people think about specific issues, it does have influence (Gamson, 1992; Wong & Jain, 1999).

Finding that this change did occur would place discussions of education, and magnet schools in particular, within a broader context. Discussions of race in America have changed significantly since the Civil Rights Movement and the concurrent movement to desegregate schools. Rather than striving to ensure that all students have access to an equal education, political rhetoric surrounding public schools now focuses on standards, accountability, and how to make students excel. Although quality and achievement are certainly important goals for education, schools are capable of more than that. As a public institution that directly affects about 90% of Americans, schools provide a large part of a citizen's social and political development. As noted by Earl Warren in the *Brown* case, segregated schools are "inherently unequal." Kenneth Clark, the sociologist who testified in *Brown*, argued (as cited in Schlesinger, 1991) that segregation is harmful even when it is not forced upon the powerless by the powerful.

This article adds several unique aspects to the study of school desegregation. First, no major study of school desegregation has used Los Angeles

[1]Although other newspapers exist, they have neither the circulation nor the respect of the *Times*. *La Opinion* reigns among the Spanish-speaking population, but linguistic barriers prevent me from using it here.

[2]Although this article does not claim that LAUSD viewed magnet schools under a changing framework, it is likely that this occurred, as well. Newspaper articles are heavily based on official reports (Page, 1996), suggesting that articles reflect press releases offered by the district.

as a case study. LAUSD provides a good case for several reasons: It is the nation's second-largest school district, it is located in a major urban area, and it is composed of several major racial and ethnic groups. With a district that is about 70% Latino, 12% Black, 10% White, and 5% Asian (LAUSD, 2002), LAUSD is faced with unique desegregation problems.

Second, Los Angeles has significant experience with magnet schools; the district has relied on them for desegregation since 1978. Magnet schools provide the backbone of the district's voluntary integration plan, which, with over 150 magnet programs, is "the largest such effort in the nation" (LAUSD, 2000). The entire district now enrolls nearly 750,000 students, about 50,000 of whom attend magnet programs (LAUSD, 2000). These factors—the district's size, its long history with magnet programs, and its diversity—make it a prime candidate to study whether the social construction of magnet schools has changed.

Third, few studies of desegregation have used a social construction framework. Although race is often discussed as a social construction (Omi & Winant, 1994; Yanow, 2003), policies themselves generally are not (for an exception, see Schneider & Ingram, 1997). Works may discuss the development of policies and the controversies surrounding them (see especially Hochschild, 1984; Orfield, 1978), but there is a dearth of work examining how citizens understand various aspects of school desegregation. That is the goal of this article: to identify how citizens were exposed to magnet schools and whether and how this has changed since their original implementation.

Historical Context

In spite of conventional wisdom, many non-Southern school districts engaged in segregative school enrollment policies, though they ended before the decision in *Brown v. Board of Education* (*Brown I*, 1954). California, for example, permitted the exclusion of Black students from public schools until 1880, and other discriminatory laws against Asians, Blacks, and Latinos were in place until 1947 (Almaguer, 1994; Savage, 1985b). Many schools remained segregated, however, in part because of attendance boundaries, faculty assignments,[3] and sites chosen for new schools that reinforced residential segregation.

The California State Supreme Court ruled in *Jackson v. Pasadena City School District* (1963) that segregated schools violated the equal protection clause of the state constitution. Federal courts had decided long before that

[3]Before and during much of the desegregation of Los Angeles students, the district was also under a federal Office of Civil Rights order to integrate faculty.

segregation violated the federal constitution, but the state explicitly went further than the federal courts. Whereas the federal courts have limited their desegregation remedies to areas that were engaged in at least some form of de jure segregation, or segregation based on government actions, the state court ruled that "residential segregation is in itself an evil which tends to frustrate the youth in the area and to cause antisocial attitudes and behavior" (*Jackson v. Pasadena City School District*, 1963, p. 881). The state supreme court was clear that de facto segregation, which occurs due to "natural" residential patterns without any official state actions, was as much a violation of the state constitution's equal protection clause as was de jure segregation, saying in part, "The right to an equal opportunity for education and harmful consequences of segregation require that school boards take steps, insofar as reasonably feasible, to alleviate racial imbalance in schools *regardless of its cause* [italics added]" (*Jackson v. Pasadena City School District*, 1963, p. 881).

In *Crawford v. Board of Education of the City of Los Angeles* (1976), the court applied the *Jackson* doctrine to LAUSD. In *Crawford*, the court claimed that "[School] boards in this state bear a constitutional obligation to attempt to alleviate school segregation, *regardless of its cause* [italics added]" (*Crawford v. Board of Education of the City of Los Angeles*, 1976, p. 293).

One of the board's first moves in response to the *Crawford* decision was to create a committee of community leaders, parents, and teachers. The 100-plus members of the Citizens Advisory Council on School (sometimes Student) Integration (CACSI) worked for 9 months to develop a plan that would actively integrate Los Angeles schools. The committee recommended sweeping reforms to meet the court's order, including what was considered to be "massive" cross-town busing for students at all grade levels.

However, because the CACSI plan was so ambitious, it was almost completely ignored by the board. Only one member supported it; the remaining six members began to put together a plan piece by piece. The board's plans, which developed over several years, were primarily voluntary. Their first attempt at mandatory desegregation was to establish "integrated learning centers," to be attended by all fourth through sixth grade students for 9 weeks each year. When the court overruled this plan for insufficiency, the board gradually added more mandatory components until about 50,000 students in Grades 4 to 8 were bused to create integrated environments.[4]

[4]Even this did not solve the problem; as many as 250,000 minority students remained in racially isolated schools at the height of busing for desegregation.

Mandatory busing policies never went beyond Grades 4 through 8; it was thought that students in the lower grades were too young to be bused and that they did not yet have racial awareness. The board also believed that busing too many students too soon would create too many problems, both logistically and politically. Later grades were to be added one year at a time. As is often the case when districts undergo very slow processes of busing for desegregation (Hochschild, 1984), the piecemeal, incremental busing policy chosen here proved ineffectual. It lasted only 3 years.

The most popular policy developed by the district, and the only one still in place, is magnet schools,[5] or schools that offer a specific academic or pedagogical focus. Although many magnet schools provide the type of education found in private schools, they are public and therefore free. They are also voluntary; students are not placed in magnet programs unless they request it and complete an application. It is the voluntary nature of magnet schools, combined with their additional academic resources, that made them so popular among the antibusing parts of LAUSD in the late 1970s.

The first magnet schools in the district opened in 1978, the same year the district began mandatory busing. The first magnet schools were for elementary students, because the district's integration plan focused only on Grades 4 through 6, and then (after the court ruled this insufficient) only Grades 4 through 8. Los Angeles magnet schools in this time period were explicitly for integration purposes; the *Times* defined them as schools "with instructional programs so attractive and unusual that they will lure students of all races from all over the city" (Trombley, 1977, p. 1).

Data and Methods

The data for this analysis are 355 articles from the *Los Angeles Times*. Articles are from three time periods, 1976 to 1979, 1985 to 1987, and 1996 to 1999. The starting point is 1976 because that is when the California State Supreme Court made its decision in *Crawford v. Los Angeles Board of Education*. Thus, starting here permits an examination of the district's immediate responses to the court order. Including 4 sequential years (1976, 1977, 1978, and 1979) of data ensures coverage of the earliest discussions of busing in LAUSD through the establishment of magnet schools.

The primary question, however, is whether and how the social construction of magnet schools has changed since their establishment. I have included more recent years (1996 to 1999) in order to examine how magnets

[5]Another voluntary option, Permits with Transportation, is also still used. However, this one had been in use since before *Crawford*; it was not a response to it.

are discussed now. I use a 4-year time period to make it comparable with the first group. However, because studying the beginning and ending points only would do little to illuminate the process of change, I also selected a 3-year period in the middle: Three years from the 1980s (1985, 1986, and 1987) are also included in the analysis.

Articles originally published in the 1970s were selected using the *Bell and Howell Index to the Los Angeles Times*. I examined articles indexed under the following sections: Los Angeles Schools, School Segregation, and School Discrimination. I selected only those articles that were directly relevant to the desegregation process and the development of magnet schools within LAUSD; articles about the district but on a different topic (such as curriculum or athletic programs) were not included. Similarly, articles indexed under these topics that were primarily about desegregation programs in other cities were omitted, whereas those about statewide desegregation issues that had a direct impact on LAUSD were included.

School desegregation was a topic of significant interest in Los Angeles in the 1970s. Of the 628 articles that fit my selection criteria from 1976 to 1979, I analyzed 157, or 25%. To select these articles, I placed all of them in date order and chose every fourth article. This process ensures that articles from all dates, of all lengths, and of all foci had an equal chance of being included in the analysis. Thus, the sample is random and can be used to analyze the group as a whole.

Articles from 1985 to 1987 and 1996 to 1999 were available in online databases. In addition, the *Bell and Howell* index now used different keywords, making it impossible to conduct these searches the same way as the first one. Instead, I used the search engine provided by Newsbank. I conducted several searches, many of which provided overlapping articles. All articles selected for these time periods were found by using combinations of the following keywords: *desegregation*, *education*, *integration*, *magnet school*, *school*, and *segregation*. Because the *Bell and Howell* index included only articles in the home edition, I limited these searches to home edition articles. These searches provided 112 relevant articles for 1985 to 1987 and 87 for 1996 to1999. Because these groups had a much lower total number of articles than the first, I included all relevant articles for analysis rather than selecting a sample.

Articles were then coded to conduct a content analysis. To code articles, I read them and counted the number of times specific terms were used in each article. I counted terms only once per paragraph to control for repetitive writing. Thus, an article that is primarily about desegregation will have a much higher count than one that does not because it would be discussed in more paragraphs, but a journalist that repeated words unnecessarily would not affect my data. These were then entered into a spreadsheet, organized by article. Each cell in the spreadsheet shows how many times a particular article mentioned a specific term.

In addition to quantitative data, I also conducted qualitative analyses of individual articles. Although the quantitative data provide excellent tools for examining trends and comparing emphases on different topics, the way in which this occurs can be examined only by looking at the articles themselves. Thus, I selected representative articles from each decade and analyzed how magnet schools are presented. I compared these constructions within and across decades.

Quantitative Analysis

Using newspapers as a measure of social construction leads one to expect certain trends and relationships. For example, because the busing and desegregation controversies were at their highest in the 1970s, one should expect a newspaper to report on these issues more often than they would in later years. This is especially true for busing, the mandatory portion of which ended in 1980; after that, there was simply no longer any news to report. Similarly, it is logical to expect greater coverage of magnet schools in more recent time periods than in the 1970s, as the policies were only in development then but are now deeply ingrained. One may also expect early discussions of magnet schools to place greater emphasis on their role in a desegregation plan, because the court was actively demanding desegregation at that time.

I also expected to find significant discussions of race and racial issues. Desegregation policies, in Los Angeles and elsewhere, are based on the Supreme Court's enunciation in *Brown* that keeping students separate by race places psychological hardships on minorities and that these hardships are likely never to diminish. In addition, *Crawford* was brought by a Black family who felt their schools were inferior to the White schools less than 1 mile (1.6 km) away. The Los Angeles case and others are explicitly based on racial issues, and one should expect to find discussions of these issues in the local press.

Certain facts about Los Angeles, however, cause us to expect changes in racial discussions. Although *Crawford* (like most desegregation cases) was originally defined as a Black–White issue, Latinos had eclipsed Blacks as the largest minority group in the district by 1976, were the largest group by 1980, and became the majority of the district by 1985 (Orfield, 1988). Because the district is predominantly Latino, one should expect the local press to discuss Latinos at least as much as Blacks or Whites over the 3-decade period.

I conducted quantitative analyses in two ways. First, I calculated the mean number of times a topic was discussed during each decade.[6] This information indicates how prevalent a topic was at each time period. To compute the mean, I summed the number of uses of a specific term during the decade and divided it by the total number of articles. Thus, a mean of 1.0 shows that a term was mentioned, on average, once per article during a specific time period. A mean below 1.0 shows that a term was used less than once per article, and a mean higher than that shows that a term was used more than once per article. Mean scores show the importance of a topic when evaluated relative to the mean scores of other issues.

Second, I determined the percentage of articles in which each term was used for each decade.[7] When evaluated in relation to other percentage scores and with the mean scores, these data indicate how frequently a topic was discussed. I computed this number by finding the total number of articles that referred to a specific topic during the decade and dividing that by the total number of articles. Percentage scores show the frequency of the appearance of a topic and should be considered in relation to other percentage scores.

Overall Trends

Many of my expectations were validated by the data, though not always with the predicted relationships. I discuss topics of interest in two categories: Desegregation-related issues (including *busing*, *desegregation*, *integration*, *segregation*, and *magnet schools*) and race-related terms (including *race*, *minority*, *black*, *white*,[8] *Latino*, and *Asian*).[9] I examine mean and percentage scores for both of these groups.

Desegregation-related topics. Except for magnet schools, discussions of desegregation and desegregation-related policies have declined steadily

[6]I also calculated this figure for each year. I do not discuss individual years in this article, but details can be obtained by contacting me.

[7]These figures by year can also be obtained by contacting me.

[8]In my own writing I follow the convention of capitalizing such terms as *Black* and *White* when discussing racial groups. The *Los Angeles Times* does not do this, so I do not capitalize when discussing terms that come from the newspaper.

[9]Each of these terms, except *race*, is actually a collapsed category including the term discussed and other related terms. *Minority* includes *non-White*; *Black* includes references to *Negro* and *African American*; *White* includes *Anglo*, *Caucasian*, *majority*, and *nonminority*; *Latino* includes *brown*, *Chicano*, *Hispanic*, *Latin*, *Mexican American*, *Spanish surname*, and *Spanish speaking*; and *Asian* includes *Asian American*, *Oriental*, *Chinese*, *Japanese*, and several other Asian nationalities.

since they were implemented by LAUSD. Mean scores of issues strictly related to desegregation all declined to an average of fewer than two mentions per article in the 1980s, and fewer than one mention per article in the 1990s. In other words, topics that were discussed much more forcefully in the 1970s were not even found an average of once per article by the 1990s. Discussion of magnet schools, however, showed a marked increase over the period in question. They were mentioned fewer than once per article in the 1970s, once per article in the 1980s, and more than three times per article in the 1990s (see Figure 1).

The most common term found in the first group of articles was *desegregation,* which made sense given the selection criteria and the nature of the study. Also as expected, *desegregation* is much less commonly used in more recent articles. This is because LAUSD, like other districts, had moved away from desegregation efforts well before this period. In fact, in the few times in which the term was mentioned in 1996 to 1999, it was used to explain the development of magnet schools or to describe past district policies. Articles in the late 1990s never discussed a need for desegregation or current attempts to desegregate schools.

Comparing trend lines within Figure 1 also yields interesting results. *Desegregation* was mentioned an average of about six times per article in the 1970s but declined to just over once per article in the 1980s and only half of that in the 1990s. *Integration* and *segregation* were never discussed nearly as much as *desegregation,* but all had declined to similar levels by

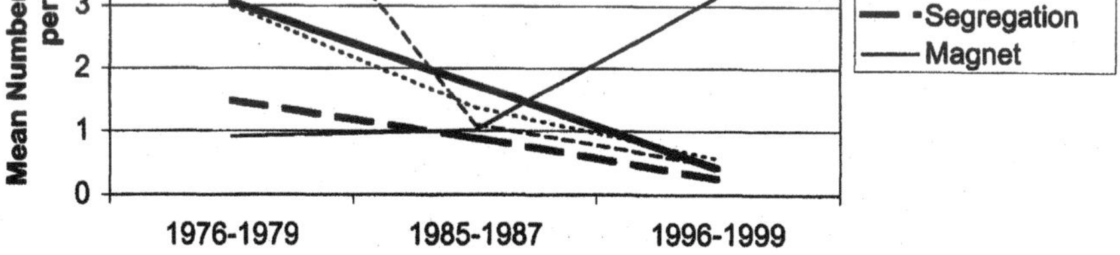

Figure 1. Desegregation trend lines by mean.

the 1990s. The same is true for *busing*, the most controversial of the several plans designed to desegregate LAUSD schools. Thus, the decline of discussion of desegregation is not due simply to a different way of talking about the issue. Rather, all discussions of this nature declined significantly and were rather unlikely to be mentioned at all in the local press by the 1990s.

Similar relationships are found when considering the percentage scores rather than the mean scores (see Figure 2). Whereas mean scores indicate strength, percentage scores show the frequency of a discussion. Like mean scores, percentage scores for all issues strictly related to desegregation declined steadily from 1976 to 1999. Note that the percentage scores for all five terms were more evenly distributed in the 1970s than were the mean scores. This indicates that, even when articles discussed more than one of the five topics included in Figures 1 and 2, *desegregation* was more important in these articles.

Magnets were discussed as much as desegregation by the 1980s and have now eclipsed desegregation as the most common topic in desegregation-related articles. This is to be expected; upon the court's decision in 1976, the district's first response was to discuss the possibility of busing students for integration. However, as it became clear that middle-class Los Angelenos would not be persuaded to include their children in busing programs, the district began considering other options to comply with the court order. One of these was magnet schools, whose growing popularity is clearly shown in Figures 1 and 2.

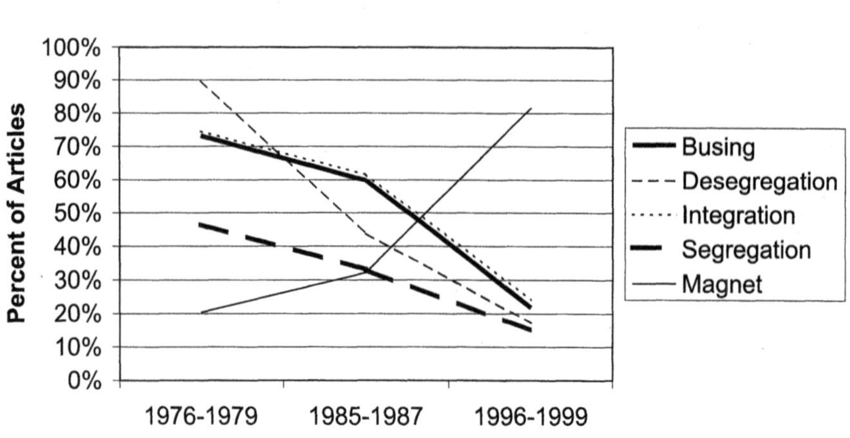

Figure 2. Desegregation trend lines by percentage.

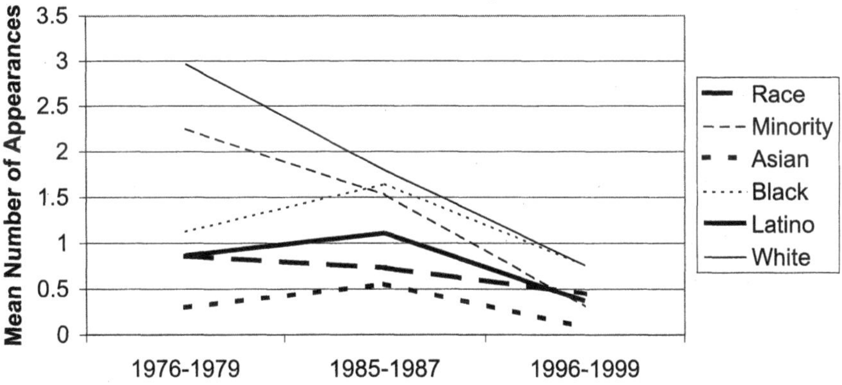

Figure 3. Racial trend lines by mean.

Race-related topics. Discussions of race within articles on education also declined during this period (see Figure 3). Although some topics show a mild peak in the 1980s, the mean scores for all race-related topics declined overall from 1976 to 1999. Although some trend lines in this figure are steeper than others, none of these topics was discussed more than once per article by the 1990s.

Even more interesting, however, is to compare the mean scores among racial topics. The highest mean score for the 1970s was *white,* at nearly three mentions per article. No other single group came even close to this. The second most common racial group mentioned in the 1970s was *black,* but Whites were discussed more than 2½ times as often. And, although nearly three fourths of LAUSD students are now Latino, they are still not discussed as much as Blacks. (Asians, a smaller group, are discussed less than the other three.) In spite of the fact that the *Crawford* suit was brought by a Black family for the benefit of themselves and other minority students, Whites were nearly always discussed more often than any other group. Whites appear to be a more important group—they at least receive more attention—than any other in each of the 3 decades. This points to the way in which the social construction of magnet schools has changed; they are now more about providing White children with a quality education than providing voluntary integration to all.

Percentage scores are similar, though not identical (see Figure 4). For all categories, the percentage scores for the 1990s were lower than the percentage scores for the 1970s. Here, however, the relationships are slightly different. Whereas the mean scores showed a significantly greater emphasis

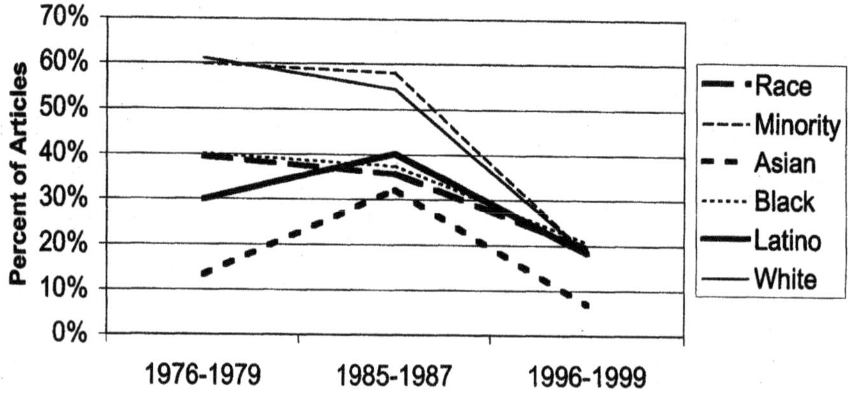

Figure 4. Racial trend lines by percentage.

on Whites than any other group, the percentage scores show that Whites and minorities are discussed almost in tandem. This suggests that articles are likely to discuss both groups (shown by percentage scores) but to concentrate more on Whites (shown by mean scores).[10]

Qualitative Analysis

However, numbers such as these, showing the mean number of times terms are used per article, or showing how many of these articles they are found in, can only tell half the story. Now that certain trends have been confirmed—that discussions of desegregation declined over a 3-decade period, that Whites were almost always discussed more than other groups, and that magnets were discussed much more often in more recent times, for example—it is also important to see how these terms were discussed and whether the way in which they were constructed changed significantly over this period.

I find that this did occur. Magnet schools were almost always discussed within a larger desegregation context when they were developed in Los

[10]The greater emphasis on White students and tendency to discuss minorities as a group is evidence that Los Angeles residents were exposed to a dichotomous understanding of racial integration, rather than a multiracial understanding that would be more appropriate for the area. The propensity to discuss desegregation in terms of Whites and minorities comes from the historical focus on desegregating Black and White students in the South.

Angeles, but discussions of this type declined significantly over the 3-decade period. Articles in the 1990s discussed magnet schools as academic alternatives within a decaying urban school system. My analysis of the *Los Angeles Times* shows that residents of the area were exposed to two predominant constructions: First, that magnet schools are just one part of a larger effort to achieve greater racial and ethnic integration and, second, that magnet schools provide quality public education (see Figure 5).

Of the 32 articles from 1977 to 1979 (there were none in 1976) that included any mention of magnet schools, 31 of them discussed the programs as part of a larger desegregation plan. Although their definition usually included a brief mention of the academic program they provide, the article as a whole was about the district's struggle to devise a desegregation plan that would be acceptable to the court.

Most of these articles were about the development of the desegregation plan for LAUSD. A typical example is provided by the article published on January 19, 1977 (Trombley, 1977), the first in the sample to discuss magnet schools. This article, headlined "Integration Plan Leans on Voluntary Approach," discussed the district's mostly voluntary plan to desegregate schools in order to comply with the *Crawford* mandate. Like most articles of the time, magnets were only a small fraction of the total article; this article focused primarily on integration, race, and busing. The context of the discussion of magnets makes it clear that they are meant to be part of a racial desegregation program. In explaining the various parts of the program, the article says:

> The district also will develop "magnet schools" for students in the first three grades, as well as for older students. These would be schools with

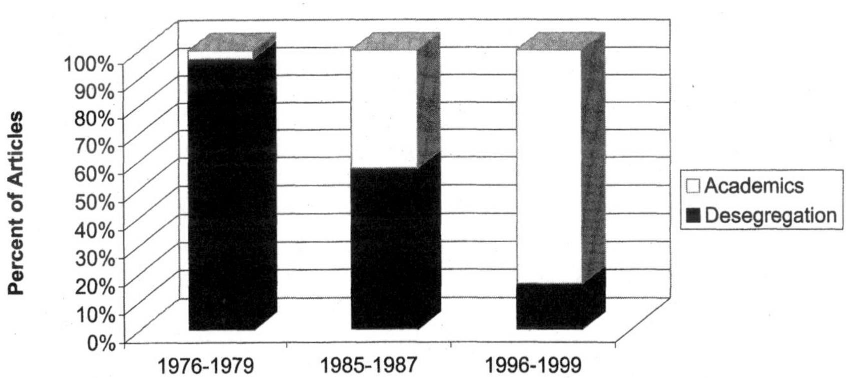

Figure 5. Social construction of magnet schools.

> instructional programs so attractive and unusual that they will lure students of all races from all over the city. ... Magnet schools will be developed for the fourth, fifth, and sixth grades, too, under the board guidelines, along with the specialized integrated learning centers [and there] will also be magnet schools at the senior high level. (Trombley, 1977, p. 1)

Also consider an article published on January 14, 1978 (Boyarsky, 1978). This one is the first to have a clear focus on magnet schools, with the headline "On Magnet Preferences: Survey To Be First Step in L.A. School Integration." The article located magnet schools within the larger desegregation plan, in which students may choose to attend a magnet school voluntarily before being subject to mandatory methods of integration; the district distributed brochures of the developing program and asked parents to respond with their preferences for an academic focus. This article, for the first time, used the term "magnet" more than any other term included in the analysis. However, although magnet schools are now the focus of the article, they remain within a larger context of desegregating the district. Consider the following passage:

> [The] Board President ... said that if all the parents and children in the affected ... grades volunteer for the magnet schools, there will be no need for mandatory busing. ...
>
> It is likely, however, that some children will decline the magnet schools. That will mean that in a few short weeks ... the district will have to set up groupings of schools ... in which various Anglo and minority schools will be paired for integration.
>
> But until parents and children make their choices on the magnet schools, the district will not have much of an idea as to how to organize these leagues. (Boyarsky, 1978, p. A20)

Also consider an article from the beginning of the second school year of desegregation in LAUSD. In "Busing Odyssey Far From Over," published on September 18, 1978 (Trombley, 1978), shortcomings of the district's plan were discussed. For example, although nearly 1,300 buses were used and about 50,000 students were transported at the start of the 1978–1979 school year, "there were still at least 250,000 minority youngsters in segregated schools" (Trombley, 1978, p. A1). In addition to the persistence of racial isolation, this article discussed the usage rates of each approach to integration. Magnet schools and the voluntary busing program Permits with Transportation (PWT), in which students in crowded schools volunteer to transfer to less crowded schools to promote racial balance, hit their expected enrollment figures. Mandatory approaches, however, did not. The four mentions of magnet schools are fairly innocuous; their enrollment figures are given, and logistical problems with bus routes are discussed. This article placed magnet schools on an equal footing with the district's PWT program, making it clear that they are both part of the desegregation program.

During this early period, only one article that discussed magnets placed a greater focus on their academic potential than on their use for desegregation. On January 10, 1978, "Would Open in September: Business 'Magnet School' at Downtown Site Urged" (McCurdy, 1978) was the first article to discuss the district's secondary magnet schools. The short article explained the possible academic offerings of a proposed business magnet school, discussed where it might be located, and stated that the choice of this focus was influenced by desires of local leaders in business and industry.

Even with a clear focus on the more academic nature of the school, however, issues of racial integration remain important. For example, the article provided brief statements about the integration purposes of magnet schools, saying: "Four elementary magnet schools already have been approved by the board as part of the voluntary phase of its desegregation plan" and "The racial composition of the [business magnet] school would be kept between 56% and 76% minority" (McCurdy, 1978, p. B1). Thus, even though the school's academic promise was the focus of this article, it was made clear that the program is part of a larger desegregation plan and that the district would mandate an integrated student body.

These four examples show that early discussions of magnet schools were firmly based on their use for integration within a larger district approach to comply with the court mandate in *Crawford*. Only one article placed a greater emphasis on the academic offerings of a magnet school than its possibilities for desegregation, and even that one also discussed the district's racial composition target for the school. In addition, this article was about the district's first magnet high school. The plan submitted to the court by the board was based on desegregating parts of Grades 4 through 8 only, not secondary schools. Thus, the prominence of the discussion here of the curriculum of the proposed magnet school was likely due to the fact that this specific school would not formally fit within the proposed desegregation plan.

Although discussions of magnet schools in the 1970s were nearly always in the context of a larger integration plan, this was less true in the 1980s. Of the 30 articles from 1985 to 1987, only 13 were clearly based on integration whereas 10 had a distinct focus on academics. (An additional 7 articles were neutral.)

Not only did the total, aggregate emphasis begin to shift from integration to academics in this decade, but even articles that discussed magnet schools as part of an integration program did so differently. Whereas articles in the 1970s focused predominantly on the district's response to *Crawford*, articles in the 1980s rarely mentioned any type of desegregation program except to note that the schools were established as part of desegregation in the 1970s. This is not surprising, as mandatory busing and, with it, the concerns of many area residents ended in 1980. What is interesting, however, is that racial issues were still mentioned when magnet schools were discussed; there simply was no implication that segregation is a problem. Race was now a hindrance to more important goals, such as small school districts and neighborhood schools. Magnets were also discussed as a method that could help combat the district's primary problems of the decade, overcrowding and a subsequent move to year-round schools.

Consider, for example, an article published on October 9, 1986 (Nall, 1986), which discussed a small city, Lomita, whose schools are part of LAUSD. Lomita parents and city leaders wanted to secede from LAUSD, arguing that a smaller district would allow them to provide better education to their students. Race was discussed in this article, but only as a problem keeping Lomita from seceding and creating its own school district. The nature of this article and the differences it poses from earlier pieces make it worth offering a lengthy quotation:

> The Los Angeles district opposes secession, in part because it would require the relocation of about 1,500 students who attend Lomita schools but live just outside the city or are bused in from more distant areas. … The Los Angeles district's manager of contractual relations … said students are bused to Lomita Magnet School from … more than 20 miles [about 32 km] away.
>
> In addition … secession would result in [a] higher concentration of minorities in Los Angeles schools. … "Right now, the white population at Lomita Magnet is 38%. … If Lomita were to withdraw and busing were to stop, the white population would rise to 68%." (Nall, 1986, sec. 9, p. 9)

This article blamed the district's opposition to Lomita's secession plans squarely on the racial composition of the area. In addition to two mentions of the magnet school above, the article also provided a brief definition of magnets. However, whereas previous definitions of magnet schools gave them a positive construction as methods of voluntary integration, this one is negative:

> The magnet school, which offers special programs to attract distant students and improve racial and ethnic balance in the district, was a sore point with some residents. …They complained that several Lomita chil-

> dren, including minority students, had been denied admission to the magnet school and had to attend schools outside their neighborhood. (Nall, 1986, sec. 9, p. 9)

Not only did the district oppose Lomita's secession on the basis of how it would affect racial balance, but the most popular development of the desegregation case was presented here as a policy that forces children to travel far from home. The article suggested that parents understand the reason behind magnet schools by inserting the phrase "including minority students," implying that local minorities ought to be able to attend the magnet school (even if local White students cannot).

Also consider a follow-up article on the same subject, published on April 16, 1987 (Gladstone, 1987), when the State Board of Education rejected Lomita's request for secession. In this article, as in the one discussed earlier, LAUSD's continuing voluntary desegregation program was blamed for Lomita's inability to enact local control:

> The key issue for the state board was whether forming a Lomita district would promote racial and ethnic segregation and discrimination. In a report to the board, Bill Honig, state superintendent of public instruction, said the proposed Lomita secession "would adversely affect existing desegregation programs" and urged that it be denied. (Gladstone, 1987, sec. 9, p. 1)

A Lomita city council member, however, argued that secession from LAUSD would reduce Lomita minority enrollment "by only a few percentage points" and would have virtually no effect on the mammoth district as a whole. In arguing that this issue should not prevent Lomita from seceding, the council member said

> We would have an excellent racial balance on our own. ... It's crazy to say that our enrollment, which is only a fraction of a percent of the total L.A. school population, could have any significant impact on desegregation problems in Los Angeles. (Hargrave, quoted in Gladstone, 1987, sec. 9, p. 1)

However, in addition to the changed nature of discussions of desegregation in the 1980s, many more of these articles focused on the academic qualities of magnet schools than did articles from the 1970s. Typical of articles in this period, the one published on January 16, 1985 (Savage, 1985a), mentioned magnets only to describe something else; there was no discussion of race or integration. This article was about 13 California high school students who won honors in a national science contest. In describing LAUSD's sole winner, the article said that the student lives in Northridge "but attends the math and science 'magnet school' at Van Nuys High" (Savage, 1985a, p. A3). The article also quoted the administrator of the magnet program at Van Nuys High School, who said that "[He] is a dynamite student who has taken advantage of every opportunity" (Spence, quoted in Savage, 1985a, p. A3).

This article is a good example of the newer construction of magnet schools. No longer is the program placed within a larger context. Instead, magnets here provided a background for describing an excellent student who won honors in a national competition. The implication was that magnet schools are for students who are as motivated as this one, who was presented as a representative of the ideal magnet school student. Although the student's name suggests an Asian background, race was never explicitly discussed. Magnets were similarly discussed in articles about academic decathlons and schools that won money for improving their standardized test scores; they were mentioned by name as schools with high achievement levels. These articles, however, almost never defined magnet schools or discussed their previous incarnation as vehicles for voluntary integration.

Another article, from June 23, 1985 (Mitchell, 1985), provides similar evidence of the changing nature of the construction of magnet schools. When the desegregation plan was first established, segregated White schools had the option of "pairing" with a segregated minority school to avoid mandatory busing. One of the first pairs was between Canfield and Crescent Heights elementary schools, which were only 1 mile (1.6 km) apart but had distinctly different racial enrollments. The two schools united to promote integration; students attended Canfield in an affluent White neighborhood for kindergarten through Grade 3, and Crescent Heights in a middle-class Black neighborhood for Grades 4 through 6. By 1985, however, the pair was losing both White and high-achieving Black students when they were due to enroll for Grade 4 at Crescent Heights. As the article explains:

> The problem has been that many white families send their children to Canfield, in their neighborhood, but refuse to send them to Crescent Heights. Instead, when they are ready for the fourth grade at Crescent Heights, students are put in private schools or sent to district magnets or other schools on the Westside. Many black parents also avoid Crescent Heights. (Mitchell, 1985, sec. 9, p. 9)

At first glance, this article might seem to be more about integration than academics. Race was a clear theme in the article. The single mention of magnet schools, however, is in the selection above, in which they were discussed as an alternative to integration rather than a method of obtaining integration. This is evidence of the changing construction of magnets as they became a benefit for the (predominantly White) middle class rather than for racial minorities.

Articles from the 1990s show that the trend continued, and discussions of desegregation became even more rare. Of the 56 articles from 1996 to 1999 that discussed LAUSD magnet schools, 38 focused predominantly on academics rather than integration. Only 7 articles concentrated primarily on desegregation. (An additional 13 articles were neutral.)

By this time, magnet schools had been part of LAUSD's approach to education for nearly 2 decades. Although the total number of references to race and desegregation remains somewhat high, most of these were in the context of a program originally designed for that purpose. Articles that defined magnets as schools to create voluntary integration typically made that objective seem outdated, as though integration were a problem for a previous generation. Often, however, articles in the 1990s did not define magnets at all. This is likely because the schools had been around for so long that *Times* journalists assumed (and rightly so) that most people were already familiar with the concept of a magnet school. However, because they no longer made the connection between magnets and race, the local interpretation of magnet schools was also allowed to change.

Consider, for example, an article published on April 5, 1996 (Cardenas, 1996). Not once did this article mention any racial issues or the district's history with desegregation. The story is about a deaf teacher at the math and science magnet program at Granada Hills/Cal State Northridge Science Math Technology High School, one of the few deaf teachers in the district who teaches hearing students. Although this is one of the articles that did not define magnet schools at all, it is clear that this is a school designed for bright, motivated students. Note, first, the name of the high school; it is immediately linked to a large local university. In addition, the article described the "rigorous magnet school curriculum" (Cardenas, 1996, p. B4).

Another article, published on May 21, 1996 (Pyle, 1996), did continue to make the link between magnets and desegregation. This article was about the King/Drew Medical Magnet, a school in South-Central Los Angeles near the University of Southern California. The school had long been housed in portable classrooms on the campus of a medical school, and the district decided to provide the school with a permanent structure and to enlarge it significantly. Again, this article did not explain what a magnet school is; it is assumed that the reader already knows this. However, race was not left out of the picture. The school was described as follows:

> Unlike most other Los Angeles Unified magnets, which have lower minority student bodies than the district average, the medical magnet is about three-quarters African American students. It is a non-selective magnet, open to any students interested in the health professions, and has attracted nationwide attention for its relationships with the university and with adjacent Martin Luther King Hospital. (Pyle, 1996, p. B3)

Note that this passage made an explicit comparison between the racial compositions of most magnet schools and of the district as a whole. The article did not, however, explain their history as a desegregation policy. This article also presented a negative construction of the capabilities of its students; immediately after claiming that it is predominantly African American, it stated that the school is nonselective. This implies that students in this high school would not be accepted at more competitive magnets and that non-Black students are talented enough that they are accepted at other schools. Along with contributing to the changing social construction of magnet schools, this article went even further to imply that integrated schools are less competitive than, and therefore inferior to, others.

Conclusions

This study of 3 decades' worth of newspaper articles regarding Los Angeles desegregation policies has shown that the way in which desegregation and magnet schools are discussed has changed significantly. This change in social construction is evident in articles published in the *Los Angeles Times* from 1976 to 1999. Early discussions of magnet schools explicitly placed them within a broader desegregation context. Although their academic programs were discussed as well, greater importance was placed on their role in the district's approach to meeting the *Crawford* mandate. This began to change in the 1980s, and by the 1990s articles were more likely to focus on a school's standards, curriculum, and honors-winning students. Whether one considers a purely quantitative analysis of word counts or a deeper textual study of how words are used, articles went through a gradual shift from emphasizing the importance of magnet schools in the integration process to the academic benefits they provide. This means that residents in the area were exposed to different understandings of the policy over this period. Other scholars have established that, although the press cannot dictate what people think, it does influence their beliefs and understandings of complex issues (Gamson, 1992).

The power of this change in social construction is illustrated by other work showing that racial balance declined during the same period. Schools nationwide are becoming more segregated (Civil Rights Project, 2002a, 2002b; Frankenberg & Lee, 2002; Orfield & Eaton, 1996; Orfield et al., 1993; Orfield & Yun, 1999). Los Angeles schools, including magnets, are also segregated (Straus, 2003). As these schools became more segregated, their social construction also changed. They were no longer discussed as methods of integration but as beacons of academic excellence in an otherwise deteriorating urban school system.

The reason for this is not hard to find. LAUSD was released from its desegregation order in 1989. Thus, there was simply no longer a court-ordered desegregation plan in which to place these schools. Those articles that did discuss desegregation either implied that this was a problem dealt with by the district long ago or they briefly mentioned that magnets are part of a voluntary integration plan.

This analysis is not meant as an indictment against the *Los Angeles Times*. The *Times* reported the news, as newspapers are expected to do. However, although there was reason for the changed nature in which magnets were discussed, this does not alter the importance of the fact that this change did occur. Residents of the greater Los Angeles area who read these articles in the 1970s were exposed to magnet schools as part of an important effort to desegregate schools. Those same residents are now exposed to magnets as a way to avoid otherwise poor schools. Magnet schools are now a benefit for members of the middle class, who receive a quality education without the expense of a private school.

This trend, away from integration and toward a nebulous discussion of quality, is not limited to Los Angeles or California. Districts nationwide have been released from their desegregation plans, sometimes while they still had quite high levels of segregation (Orfield & Eaton, 1996). Districts have argued that they have tried to desegregate but have failed, or that transportation is too expensive and takes away from other resources, or that there is simply no need to educate students of different races together. As members of the education community make this argument, similar trends are visible in national political debates. The Civil Rights Movement is long over, and a backlash against affirmative action programs is evident. Some argue that the American polity is dividing into several ethnocentric groups whose only concern is themselves (Schlesinger, 1991).

Although outright discrimination is certainly lower now than it was decades ago, vast differences remain in the wealth and income of Americans (Oliver & Shapiro, 1995; Wilson, 1987). Neighborhoods remain racially segregated, and this residential segregation causes our schools to be segregated, as well (Kozol, 1991; Massey & Denton, 1993; Reardon, Yun, & Eitle,

2000; Rivkin, 1994). Without policies to prevent segregation in schools, American children will grow up not knowing how to interact with people different from them, perpetuating a divided social structure and the very inequality that schools could otherwise abolish.

References

Almaguer, T. (1994). *Racial fault lines: The historical origins of White supremacy in California.* Berkeley: University of California Press.

Boyarsky, B. (1978, January 14). On magnet preferences: Survey to be first step in L.A. school integration. *Los Angeles Times,* pp. A1, A20.

Brown v. Board of Education of Topeka, Kansas (Brown I), 347 U.S. 483 (1954).

Cardenas, J. (1996, April 5). A higher education for deaf students: Mainstreaming at Granada Hills math and science magnet school offers a more challenging opportunity for college-bound. *Los Angeles Times,* p. B4. Retrieved May 14, 2003, from Newsbank database.

Civil Rights Project. (2002a, January). *The impact of racial and ethnic diversity on educational outcomes: Cambridge, MA school district.* Cambridge, MA: Harvard University, Civil Rights Project. Retrieved August 1, 2003, from http://www.civilrightsproject.harvard.edu

Civil Rights Project. (2002b, February). *The impact of racial and ethnic diversity of educational outcomes: Lynn, MA school district.* Cambridge, MA: Harvard University, Civil Rights Project. Retrieved August 1, 2003, from http://www.civilrightsproject.harvard.edu

Crawford v. Board of Education of the City of Los Angeles, 17 Cal. 3d 28., 551 P.2d 28, 1976 Cal. LEXIS 294, 130 Cal. Rptr. 724 (1976).

Frankenberg, E., & Lee, C. (2002). *Race in American public schools: Rapidly resegregating school districts.* Cambridge, MA: Harvard University, Civil Rights Project.

Gamson, W. A. (1992). *Talking politics.* New York: Cambridge University Press.

Gladstone, M. (1987, April 16). State rejects secession of Lomita schools. *Los Angeles Times,* sec. 9, p. 1. Retrieved August 3, 2003, from Newsbank database.

Hochschild, J. (1984). *The new American dilemma: Liberal democracy and school desegregation.* New Haven, CT: Yale University Press.

Jackson v. Pasadena City School District, 59 Cal. 2d 876; 382 P.2d 878; 31 Cal. Rptr. 606; 1963 Cal. LEXIS 221 (1963).

Kozol, J. (1991). *Savage inequalities: Children in America's schools.* New York: Crown.

Los Angeles Unified School District. (2000). *Parents will get new magnet/PWT brochures by mail to apply for Los Angeles school programs in 2001–02.* Los Angeles: Author.

Los Angeles Unified School District. (2002). *5 year review LAUSD ethnic survey.* Retrieved January 20, 2002, from http://www.lausd.net

Massey, D. S., & Denton, N. A. (1993). *American apartheid: Segregation and the making of the underclass.* Cambridge, MA: Harvard University Press.

McCurdy, J. (1978, January 10). Would open in September: Business "magnet school" at downtown site urged. *Los Angeles Times,* pp. B1–B2.

Metz, M. H. (1992). *Different by design: The context and character of three magnet schools* (2nd ed.). New York: Routledge.

Mitchell, J. L. (1985, June 23). Integration passing test at paired schools. *Los Angeles Times,* sec. 9, p. 1. Retrieved August 3, 2003, from Newsbank database.

Nall, C. (1986, October 9). County panel hears school sesession bid. *Los Angeles Times,* sec. 9, p. 9. Retrieved August 3, 2003, from Newsbank database.

Oliver, M. L., & Shapiro, T. M. (1995). *Black wealth/White wealth: A new perspective on racial inequality.* New York: Routledge.

Omi, M., & Winant, H. (1994). *Racial formation in the United States: From the 1960s to the 1990s* (2nd ed.). New York: Routledge.

Orfield, G. (1978). *Must we bus? Segregated schools and national policy.* Washington, DC: The Brookings Institution.

Orfield, G. (1988). *Exclusion of the majority: Shrinking college access and public policy in metropolitan Los Angeles.* Unpublished manuscript.

Orfield, G., & Eaton, S. E. (Eds.). (1996). *Dismantling desegregation: The quiet reversal of Brown v. Board of Education.* New York: Free Press.

Orfield, G., Schley, S., Glass, D., & Reardon, S. (1993). *The growth of segregation in American schools: Changing patterns of separation and poverty since 1968.* Cambridge, MA: Harvard University, Harvard Project on School Desegration.

Orfield, G., & Yun, J. T. (1999). *Resegregation in American schools.* Cambridge, MA: Harvard University, Civil Rights Project.

Page, B. (1996). *Who deliberates?* Chicago: University of Chicago Press.

Pyle, A. (1996, May 21). Medical magnet school will get permanent home. *Los Angeles Times,* p. B3. Retrieved May 14, 2003, from Newsbank database.

Reardon, S. F., Yun, J. T., & Eitle, T. M. (2000). The changing structure of school segregation: Measurement and evidence of multiracial metropolitan-area school segregation. *Demography, 37,* 351–364.

Rivkin, S. G. (1994). Residential segregation and school integration. *Sociology of Education, 67,* 279–292.

Rossell, C. H. (1990). *The carrot or the stick for school desegregation policy: Magnet schools or forced busing.* Philadelphia: Temple University Press.

Savage, D. G. (1985a, January 16). 13 Californians win honors in science contest. *Los Angeles Times,* p. A3. Retrieved August 3, 2003, from Newsbank database.

Savage, D. G. (1985b, December 1). NAACP's latest suit revives issue of "metro" busing. *Los Angeles Times,* p. B1.

Schlesinger, A. M., Jr. (1991). *The disuniting of America: Reflections on a multicultural society.* New York: Norton.

Schneider, A., & Ingram, H. (1997). *Policy design for democracy.* Lawrence: University Press of Kansas.

Straus, R. M. (2003, March). *(De)Segregation in Los Angeles magnet schools.* Paper presented at the meeting of the Western Political Science Association, Denver, CO.

Trombley, W. (1977, January 19). Integration plan leans on voluntary approach. *Los Angeles Times,* p. 1.

Trombley, W. (1978, September 18). Busing odyssey far from over. *Los Angeles Times,* pp. A1, A26–A27.

Wilson, W. J. (1987). *The truly disadvantaged: The inner city, the underclass, and public policy.* Chicago: University of Chicago Press.

Wong, K. K., & Jain, P. (1999). Newspapers as policy actors in urban school systems: The Chicago story. *Urban Affairs Review, 35,* 210–246.

Yanow, D. (2003). *Constructing "race" and "ethnicity" in America: Category-making in public policy and administration.* Armonk, NY: Sharpe.

PEABODY JOURNAL OF EDUCATION, *79*(2), 122–135

Brown v. Board of Education and the Coleman Report: Social Science Research and the Debate on Educational Equality

Kenneth K. Wong and Anna C. Nicotera
Department of Leadership, Policy, and Organizations
Peabody College of Vanderbilt University

In light of the 50th anniversary of the *Brown v. Board of Education* (1954) ruling, this article focuses on how the majority opinion in *Brown* set a precedent for the use of social science research in defining and examining inequity in education. This article argues that following *Brown*, social science research has gained prominence in its social function in shaping the debate in equal educational opportunity. Whereas *Brown* introduced racial desegregation in the governmental agenda, social science research since the 1960s has sustained the societal concerns on the challenge of inequality. This article examines how the use of social science research in Equality of Educational Opportunity (J. S. Coleman et al., 1966), an extensive study of schools and schooling under the direction of James Coleman of Johns Hopkins University and Ernest Campbell of Vanderbilt University during the mid 1960s, shaped the course of education research and policy toward the notion of equal educational opportunities. Further, this article discusses the more recent work of William Julius Wilson (1987) that shifts the equality of opportunity debate out of the courts and from individual and group opportunities to the equality of life chances.

Requests for reprints should be sent to Kenneth K. Wong, Peabody College of Vanderbilt University, Department of Leadership, Policy, and Organizations, Peabody Box 514, 230 Appleton Place, Nashville, TN 37203–5721. E-mail: ken.wong@vanderbilt.edu

In the 1954 *Brown v. Board of Education* (1954) majority opinion, Chief Justice Warren found the claim that "segregation of white and colored children in public schools has a detrimental effect upon the colored children" (p. 494) was "amply supported by modern authority" (p. 494). Chief Justice Warren cited the research of several prominent social scientists, including Kenneth Clark and Gunnar Myrdal, in Footnote 11 to refute the *Plessy v. Ferguson* assertion of "separate but equal." The use of social science research was not a strategic innovation of the *Brown* opinion. In 1896, Justice Brown's majority opinion in *Plessy v. Ferguson* used quasi-psychological evidence to counter the plaintiff's argument that enforced segregation in the realm of transportation creates a badge of inferiority. Justice Brown claimed that feelings of inferiority were not linked to laws, but rather rest in the heads of Black people. Although Chief Justice Warren did not overrule the *Plessy* ruling in his *Brown* opinion, Warren declared that the findings of the *Plessy* ruling were inapplicable for public schools. Hence, Warren's *Brown* ruling set in motion the use of social science research to determine the effects of and solutions for educational inequity.

In light of the 50th anniversary of the *Brown* ruling, this article focuses on how the majority opinion in *Brown* set a precedent for the use of social science research in defining and examining inequity in education. This article argues that following *Brown*, social science research has gained prominence in its social function in shaping the debate in equal educational opportunity. Whereas *Brown* introduced racial desegregation in the governmental agenda, social science research since the 1960s has sustained the societal concerns on the challenge of inequality. In this article, we examine how the use of social science research in Equality of Educational Opportunity (Coleman et al., 1966), an extensive study of schools and schooling under the direction of James Coleman of Johns Hopkins and Ernest Campbell of Vanderbilt University during the mid-1960s, shaped the course of education research and policy toward the notion of equal educational opportunities. Further, this article discusses the more recent work of William Julius Wilson (1987) that shifts the equality of opportunity debate out of the courts and from individual and group opportunities to the equality of life chances.

This article shows that the contribution of social science research on educational equality goes beyond data analysis. Rather, the long-term impact of social science research lies in its ongoing efforts to reframe society's understanding of how the changing society reshapes schooling opportunities for all children.

Social Science Research and *Brown v. Board of Education*

Debate surrounds the inclusion of Footnote 11, the reference in Chief Justice Warren's majority opinion ruling in *Brown v. Board of Education* to social science data suggesting the detrimental effects of segregation on Black children. The debate centers on whether the sociological proof presented by Chief Justice Warren was essential to the *Brown* ruling, which has consequences for the legal interpretation of the opinion. If the social science research was critical to the ruling, then the *Brown* ruling would hinge on changes in social science evidence or methodology. However, if Chief Justice Warren used the social science research in *Brown* to merely support the legal basis of the argument that racial classifications violated the equal protection clause of the 14th Amendment, then the citation would be evidence of the use of social science research to mitigate social forces.

The use of social science research in legal opinions on racial issues arose before the *Brown* ruling. In the 1948 *Shelley v. Kraemer*, social science evidence was used by National Association for the Advancement of Colored People (NAACP) lawyers and cited in the ruling to strike down racially restrictive covenant rules (Kelly, 1987; Kluger, 1976; Levin & Moise, 1977). In the 1950 *Sweatt v. Painter*, the work of anthropologist Robert Redfield was used to refute the claim that Black people are innately inferior in a case involving enrollment of Black students in a Texas law school (as cited in Kelly, 1987; Kluger, 1976; Levin & Moise, 1977). As the NAACP worked to bring school desegregation cases to the U.S. Supreme Court, NAACP lawyers, such as Thurgood Marshall, used the technique of requesting testimony from academic experts in the social sciences. In fact, over 40 social scientists testified for the school desegregation cases leading up to *Brown* and filed the testimonies in an appendix to the plaintiffs' briefs in *Brown* (Kelly, 1987; Wisdom, 1977).

Writing about the role of social science research in litigation, Judge John Minor Wisdom of the Fifth Circuit Court of Appeals claimed that the importance of social science research was diminished in *Brown* because Chief Justice Warren did not make specific reference to the appendix of social scientists' testimonies. Wisdom (1977) stated

> The social science evidence was the kind of support a court likes to find in a record to lend factual and scientific aura to a result sustainable by other, perhaps purely abstract and sometimes formalistically legal, considerations, but dictated by the moral necessity of changing social attitudes. (p. 142)

If the opinion had extensively cited the research of social scientists, critics could claim that the decision was based on sociology rather than law. According to Wisdom, the limited citation of social science research in a footnote at the end of the *Brown* ruling shows that the evidence was not essential for the legal basis of the argument but rather was included to mediate social forces.

Chief Justice Warren's majority opinion in *Brown* did not overrule *Plessy v. Ferguson* across all social and economic arenas. However, the opinion did counter the separate but equal finding of *Plessy* by stating that *Plessy* had no place in schools where unequal facilities produced a sense of inferiority and violated the equal protection clause of the 14th Amendment. The use of social science research in footnote 11 supported this claim. In explaining the use of Footnote 11, Kluger (1976) quoted Chief Justice Warren's clerk, Earl Pollock:

> The only reason to have included footnote #11 was as a rebuttal to the cheap psychology of *Plessy* that said inferiority was only in the mind of the Negro. The Chief Justice was saying in effect that we know a lot more now about how human beings work than they did back then and can therefore cast doubt on that preposterous line of argument. (p. 706)

Again, the citation of social science research was merely a footnote and not an extensive review of the testimony of social scientists in the case. Kluger (p. 707) claimed that Chief Justice Warren used the footnote as a small, forceless token of dissent since the Court was unable to strike down *Plessy* outside of schools.

The reliability of social science evidence would be a critical issue if the data had been the basis of the *Brown* ruling. In fact, the research of Kenneth Clark that links children's ideas about self-esteem to race relations through the use of dolls has experienced significant criticism (Studies Challenge Belief That Black Students' Esteem Enhances Achievement, 2000). However, the legal basis of the *Brown* ruling is not dependent on the validity of the social science research cited in Footnote 11. The inclusion of social science research merely supports the legal basis of Chief Justice Warren's opinion and provides further information regarding the meaning of equal educational opportunities.

Although critics of the *Brown* ruling claimed that it was illegal due to its sociological rather than legal basis, it is clear from the interpretations of Wisdom and Kluger that the social science research was not imperative to the majority opinion in *Brown*. Chief Justice Warren's ruling in *Brown* was based on principles of law that found segregation in schools violated the equal protection clause of the 14th Amendment. The citation of social science evidence in the majority opinion supported the legal evidence but, more important, was necessary for allaying social forces toward the idea of equal educational opportunities. In the next section, this article examines the use of social science in the Coleman report to reconsider the meaning of equal educational opportunities.

Social Science Research and the Coleman Report

It would be an understatement to claim that the research design and findings of Coleman's 1966 report, Equality of Educational Opportunity (Coleman et al., 1966), have impacted social science research, the field of education, and the policy arena. The Coleman report not only reshaped the ways in which social scientists design and conduct research but it transformed how educators think about the purpose of education and significantly informed the policy arena. Coleman understood that his social science research had a significant impact on education policy and the public. In a 1983 interview, Coleman noted

> What has struck me is that there's media attention paid now to social research results, both by the media and apparently by the readers of the media. It seems to have been a long, slow process, a long slow buildup of public consciousness before there was a great deal of media attention to research results on equal educational opportunity. (Barber, 1987, p. 37)

This section examines one of Coleman's major research contributions to the social sciences, the Coleman report.

The purpose of this section is not to examine the validity of the Coleman report findings or research design, as considerable research, analysis, and critique exist. Rather, this section considers how the use of social science techniques in the Coleman report redefined equal educational opportunities. The historical context, the research design, and the findings of the Coleman report are each examined for their uniqueness in thinking about equal educational opportunities. In addition, this article assesses how the Coleman report has been used to impact educational policy in an attempt to fulfill the purpose of the ruling in *Brown v. Board of Education*.

Historical Context of the Coleman Report

The Coleman report originated 10 years after the *Brown* ruling in Section 402 of the Civil Rights Act of 1964:

> The Commissioner shall conduct a survey and make a report to the President and the Congress, within two years of the enactment of this title, concerning the lack of availability of equal educational opportunities for individuals by reason of race, color, religion, or national origin in public educational institutions at all levels in the United States, its territories and possessions, and the District of Columbia. (Coleman et al., 1966, p. iii)

Although Section 402 required the Commissioner of Education to conduct the survey of equal educational opportunities, the Civil Rights Act had been developed in the Justice Department without the input of the U.S. Office of Education (USOE). The requirement to conduct the survey was a Congressional mandate that the USOE had 2 years to complete.

In the 1960s, the USOE maintained a relatively weak role in American education (Murphy, 1971). Writing about the politics of the Coleman report, Grant (1973) commented as follows:

> The U.S. Office of Education had traditionally been an inventory taking agency. It seldom dared ask how well anyone was doing with what they had. ... The U.S.O.E. had a strong aversion to projecting an image that would smack of federal control or federal meddling in the schools. (p. 19)

Given the organizational restrictions of the USOE, the survey clearly could have been limited to taking inventory of educational resources without making connections between resources and various outcomes. However, when Chief Justice Warren ruled in *Brown* that the segregation inherent in separate but equal facilities created a sense of inferiority among Black students that violated the equal protection clause of the 14th Amendment, *Brown* made it clear that the notion of equal educational opportunities transcends a listing of school resources. In turn, the USOE had the chance to use the survey to probe deeper into the meaning of equal educational opportunities.

Commissioner Francis Keppel approached Coleman to conduct the elementary and secondary education components of the survey in 1965. Keppel decided to expand the functions of the USOE in order to conduct a thorough survey of equal educational opportunities. In turn, the USOE and Coleman would not perform a mere fact-finding study. Keppel intended for the project not only to include a national sample of student and teacher surveys and inventories of school resources but also to conduct student achievement tests. As the federal government had never facilitated national student achievement tests, the idea was initially received with intense resistance by local superintendents. In fact, 10% of the school districts asked to participate in the research project declined because of the student achievement tests, including Chicago, Los Angeles, and all of the school districts in Florida (Grant, 1973).

The research for the Coleman report coincided with the administration of Lyndon Johnson and the Great Society initiatives, which supported increased spending to remedy social problems. The federal compensatory program, Title I, was enacted through the Elementary and Secondary Education Act of 1965 in the same year Coleman began conducting research. The stated purpose of the Title I program was to allocate extra funds to schools with high concentrations of poverty in order to improve the educational opportunities of poor students (Murphy, 1971). The logic behind the Title I program was that increases in funds to high-poverty schools would enhance equal educational opportunities for poor students, though equal educational opportunity outputs had never been systematically measured.

As Coleman set out to study equal educational opportunities, the common belief was that his research would justify the reasoning behind the Great Society initiatives by finding large resource disparities between primarily White and Black schools that would explain the differences in academic achievement (Grant, 1973; Heckman & Neal, 1996; Kahlenberg, 2001). This input–output assumption guided Coleman's understanding of equal educational opportunities as he developed the research design. However, as an empirical researcher, Coleman remained willing to accept alternative findings about the relationships between inputs and outputs that ultimately altered the way in which equal educational opportunities are defined.

The Research Design of the Coleman Report

The Coleman report was monumental in terms of its research design. The sample included around 600,000 students, 60,000 teachers, and 3,100 schools across the nation, which was the second largest social science research project ever conducted in the United States (Coleman, 1990; Coleman et al., 1966). Because of the deadline set by the Civil Rights Act, all of the data collection and analysis had to be completed in less than a year, limiting the Coleman report to an observation of the education system at one point in time. In addition to the magnitude and the severe time constraints, the Coleman report was limited to a narrowly defined agenda set by Congress and the Civil Rights Act. Given the constraints, it is remarkable that Coleman and his research associates not only met the requirements of Section 402 but exceeded expectations in terms of producing findings that went beyond an inventory of school resources.

The analytical strategies used by Coleman were innovative for the social sciences at the time of the study. Coleman studied at Columbia University under Paul Lazersfeld, who established the logic of survey analysis versus purely descriptive analysis. High-speed computers that were able to analyze large data sets and conduct multivariate regression allowed Coleman to make use of the advantages of surveys with large sample sizes and multiple variables (Dreeben, 2000). In analyzing Coleman's contributions to the study of education, Heckman and Neal (1996) commented that the research of the Coleman report "demonstrated the value of large-scale data sets and empirical social science for evaluation social programs" (p. 84). Indeed, the accomplishments of the Coleman report set a precedent for the use of large-scale social science research projects.

The research design and analytical strategies of the Coleman report allowed Coleman to ask new research questions regarding the nature of equal educational opportunities. In a 1983 interview, Coleman stated

> Ordinarily, quality of schools had been defined in terms of inputs to the schools. We asked about outputs, using achievement outputs as criteria for judging the relative quality of schools. Even though that was not exactly a result, I think it had an important effect in reshaping the way in which educational research questions were asked after EEOC [Equality of Educational Opportunity]. (Barber, 1987, p. 34)

Although the validity of the methods used in the Coleman report have been critically analyzed by social scientists (Hanushek & Kain, 1972; Heckman & Neal, 1996), the research question posed by Coleman went nearer to replicating the intentions of *Brown* by going beyond assumptions that increases in school resources, such as separate but equal facilities, would improve educational opportunities. Rather, the Coleman report was designed to systematically measure the types of inputs that impact educational outputs. Designed in such a way, the findings of the Coleman report would influence the way the public understood education by redefining the nature of equal educational opportunities.

The Findings and Policy Implications of the Coleman Report

The Coleman report found two significant results that changed the notion of equal educational opportunities and consequently impacted the interpretation of the *Brown* ruling. The Coleman report exposed the underlying notions of equal educational opportunities by focusing on the notion that "the concept implied *effective* equality of opportunity, that is, equality in those elements that are effective for learning" (Coleman, 1990, pp. 26–27). First, the Coleman report found that school resources, including school facilities, curriculum, and teacher quality, do not show statistically significant effects on student achievement. Second, the most significant effect on student achievement was the background characteristics of other students, or peer effects (Coleman, 1990; Coleman et al., 1966).

The Coleman report findings regarding the influence of school resources, or school inputs, on student academic achievement surprised many education researchers. In terms of the effects of facilities and curriculum, the Coleman report stated

> Differences in school facilities and curriculum, which are the major variables by which attempts are made to improve schools, are so little related to differences in achievement levels of students that, with few exceptions, their effects fail to appear even in a survey of this magnitude. (Coleman et al., 1966, p. 316)

Though Coleman clearly establishes the general insignificance of school resources, the caveat to the research is that among the school resources that do show a slight relationship to student achievement, such as science laboratories, the variations in the facilities of Black students did create differences in student achievement. The Coleman report claimed, "Again, it is for majority whites that the variations make the least difference; for minorities, they make somewhat more difference" (Coleman et al., 1966, p. 22). The Coleman report may not have found statistically significant school effects on student achievement. Nevertheless, the findings suggest school resources have differential impacts on White and Black students.

In terms of the effects of teacher characteristics, including teacher quality, teachers' family education level, teachers' own education, and teachers' score on a vocabulary test show a weak impact on student academic achievement. Overall, the Coleman report found that differences in teacher quality have a cumulative effect on student achievement over the years and those differences influence the academic achievement of disadvantaged minority groups more than the achievement of White students. In addition, teachers' verbal scores and educational backgrounds show an impact on the academic achievement of minority students in the upper grades (Coleman et al., 1966, pp. 318–319).

Although the Coleman report found a relationship between the teacher quality school resource and student academic achievement, the second major finding of the report was that the background characteristics of students in the school have a larger statistically significant effect on student academic achievement. Coleman stated, "Attributes of other students account for far more variation in the achievement of minority group children than do any attributes of school facilities and slightly more than do attributes of staff" (Coleman et al., 1966, p. 302). This second finding indicates that the social composition of schools is critical to providing equal educational opportunities, which validates the *Brown* ruling for desegregation of public schools. Furthermore, the Coleman report makes clear that the social composition of a school impacts student achievement through the student body's educational background and aspirations rather than the racial composition:

> The higher achievement of all racial and ethnic groups in schools with greater proportions of white students is largely, perhaps wholly, related to effects associated with the student body's educational background and aspirations. This means that the apparent beneficial effect of a student body with a high proportion of white students comes not from racial composition per se, but from the better educational background and higher educational aspirations that are, on the average[,] found among white students. (Coleman et al., 1966, p. 307)

This second finding of the Coleman report had a significant bearing on the meaning of equal educational opportunities. However, as the courts and school district dealt with issues surrounding school desegregation, the results of the Coleman report were misinterpreted to equate racial integration with equal educational opportunities, ignoring the more significant influence of social class when understanding educational background and aspirations.

It should be noted that subsequent research has questioned the Coleman report findings that schools do not significantly impact student achievement (Alexander & Entwisle, 1996; Barr, Dreeben, & Wiratchai, 1983; Carver, 1975). Nonetheless, the critical issue for this article is how the social science research of the Coleman report reshaped the notion of equal educational opportunities and affected education policy. As the Supreme Court ruling in *Brown v. Board of Education* established that segregation created unequal educational opportunities by refuting the concept of separate but equal, the social science findings of the Coleman report have attained their largest impact in the courts. Coleman used the findings of the Coleman report to testify in the desegregation cases *Hobson v. Hansen* in Washington, DC, and *Keyes v. School District Number One* in Denver, Colorado. In addition, the findings of the Coleman report were used in *Beckett v. School Board of the City of Norfolk* and *Swann v. Charlotte-Mecklenburg* (Barber, 1987; Grant, 1973). In each case, the courts used the social science testimony of the Coleman report that an integrated school setting was critical to improving the equality of educational opportunities (Levin & Moise, 1977). As noted earlier, the courts focused on racial integration as opposed to social class integration. Even with the misinterpretation of the Coleman report findings, the social science research strengthened the legal basis for busing, which has impacted the public school system for the past 30 years with the intention of fulfilling the *Brown* ruling for equal educational opportunities.

Although the findings of the Coleman report were used to support the desegregation cases, the *Brown* ruling has experienced substantial legal setbacks over the years, which threaten the notion of equal educational opportunities. Kahlenberg (2002) documented the slow demise of *Brown* through three legal stages. The first phase occurred in the 1970s when the Supreme Court limited the reach of *Brown* to state-sponsored de jure segregation and eliminated the possibility of de facto segregation. In 1974, the Supreme Court ruled in *Milliken v. Bradley* that suburban districts were not to be held responsible for segregation in cities outside of their jurisdiction, which excluded the suburbs from desegregation orders. This ruling cemented the requirement of de jure segregation to trigger the equal protection clause under the 14th Amendment. The second phase took place in the 1980s and early 1990s due to the Supreme Court's 1968 ruling in *Green v. School Board of New Kent County*, which outlined the procedure for lifting desegregation orders once districts could prove that de jure segregation had been remedied. Across the country, desegregation orders have been lifted and districts declared "unitary." And most recently in the late 1990s, courts have been ruling against voluntary efforts to address de facto segregation based on racial classifications. In *Montgomery County Public Schools v. Eisenberg*, the Supreme Court let a Fourth Circuit decision stand, which struck down a voluntary transfer policy that used race as a classification.

It is important to note that the courts have only ruled on racial integration in school desegregation cases. The Coleman report findings indicate that the background factors that significantly affect student achievement are not limited to racial classifications but, rather, include social class. The 1996 Connecticut case *Sheff v. O'Neill* has come closest to addressing integration of social class by identifying poverty concentration as detrimental to the education experience. Nonetheless, the opinion in *Sheff v. O'Neill* failed to require integration based on classifications besides race.

If social science is to continue to set a precedent in influencing the concept of equal educational opportunity as it has in the *Brown* ruling and the Coleman report, social scientists may want to consider how to allay public concern about addressing the system of inequality. In the next section, this article examines Wilson's (1987) research that shifts the equality of opportunity debate out of the courts and from individual and group opportunities to the equality of life chances.

Equality of Life Chances

Wilson's research on the equality of opportunity has not been limited to the effects of schools. In his book, *The Truly Disadvantaged*, Wilson (1987) claimed that disadvantaged individuals endure concentration effects of poverty that can be characterized by the departure of middle- and working-class families from poor neighborhoods. The mass exodus of middle- and working-class families creates social isolation and cumulative discrimination in poor neighborhoods through diminished "social buffers" and "social networks" (Wilson, 1987, pp. 56–60). In turn, concentration effects of poverty amplify vicious cycles of unemployment, impede the potential benefits of schools, and create inequality of opportunities.

The social science research used by Wilson (1987) to formulate his theories on equality of opportunities is not as innovative as the methods used by Coleman at the time of the release of the Coleman report. As a matter of fact, Wilson merely used descriptive statistics from the U.S. Bureau of the Census and local community fact books to illustrate the changes in neighborhood demographics. Wilson did not attempt to find casual inferences between demographic information and equality of opportunity outcome variables. The work of Wilson has been included in this article to illustrate the areas that future social science research on the notion of equal educational opportunities may want to explore.

Wilson (1987) extended the understanding of equal education opportunity developed in *Brown* and the Coleman report to a broader notion of equality of opportunity. Similar to equal educational opportunities, for Wilson increases in resources are insufficient to remedy the inequalities of opportunity if individual background factors and social composition are ignored. Wilson's significant contribution to the debate on equality of opportunity rests in his use of the concept of equality of life chances to impact the cumulative effects of a system of inequality. Wilson found that the civil rights movement's focus on the equality of individual opportunity for individual minorities, and then the equality of condition for groups of minorities, led to concentration effects of poverty by assisting middle- and working-class minorities, but not the truly disadvantaged (Wilson, 1987, p. 112). In this line of argument, attempts to address inequality of opportunity have focused entirely on providing remedies for past discrimination rather than targeting truly disadvantaged individuals who suffer from the lack of competitive resources due to their economic-class background (Wilson, 1987, p. 117). In turn, defining equality of life chances addresses the system of inequality for the truly disadvantaged individuals.

Wilson (1987) drew his analysis from the work of James Fishkin regarding the principle of equality of life chances. In his book, *Justice, Equal Opportunity, and the Family,* Fishkin (1983) highlighted the inherent conflict between liberty and equality in the liberal assumptions of equality of opportunities. Specifically, equality of opportunity has been based on tensions between the principle of merit, which assumes procedural fairness in the evaluation of individual qualifications for positions, and equality of life chances, which states that background characteristics should not predict future positions. The critical issue for Fishkin is that the autonomy of the family creates a scenario in which it is incredibly difficult to maintain equal developmental conditions to ensure equality of opportunities (Fishkin, 1983). Hence, the notion of equality of opportunity must take account of the unfair advantages in the conditions by which individuals are able to develop talents and motivations based on their economic background.

Unlike the social science work used in the *Brown* ruling and the Coleman report to define equality of educational opportunity, the social science work of Wilson (1987) on equality of life chances has yet to significantly impact social policy. Wilson's work, however, has been included in this article in order to indicate where the future of social science research on equal opportunities may lie. Although the courts have been unwilling to remedy equal opportunities based on social or economic class characteristics, the work of Wilson suggests that inequality may not be resolved until class and social composition are considered.

Conclusion

As President Johnson stated in an address at Howard University on June 4, 1965

> We seek not just freedom but opportunity. We seek not just legal equity but human ability, not just equality as a right and a theory but equality as a fact and equality as a result ... To this end equal oportunity is essential, but not enough, not enough.

This seemingly ambitious conception of equality has been shaped and reshaped by social science research conducted by prominent scholars, including Coleman and Wilson, over the last 40 years. As we look forward to the next generation of social science research, we are cautiously optimistic that the broader societal role will be taken seriously by our colleagues. It is our hope that rigorous and innovative social science research methods will continue to be used to push the notion of equality to new levels.

References

Alexander, K. L., & Entwisle, D. R. (1996). Early schooling and educational inequality: Socioeconomic disparities in children's learning. In J. Clark (Ed.), *James S. Coleman* (pp. 63–80). Philadelphia: Falmer.

Barber, B. (1987). *Effective social science: Eight cases in economics, political science, and sociology.* New York: Russell Sage Foundation.

Barr, R., Dreeben, R., & Wiratchai, N. (1983). *How schools work.* Chicago: University of Chicago Press.

Beckett v. School Board of Norfolk, 308 F. Supp. 1274, U.S. Dist., 1969.
Brown v. Board of Educ., 347 U.S. 483 (1954).
Carver, R. P. (1975). The Coleman report: Using inappropriately designed achievement tests. *American Educational Research Journal,12*(1), 77–86.
Civil Rights Act of 1964, P.L. No. 88-352 (1964).
Coleman, J. S. (1990). *Equality and achievement in education.* Boulder, CO: Westview.
Coleman, J. S., Campbell, E. Q., Hobson, C. J., McPartland, J., Mood, A. M., Weinfeld, F. D., & York, R. L. (1966). *Equality of educational opportunity.* Washington, DC: U.S. Government Printing Office.
Dreeben, R. (2000). Structural effects in education. In M. T. Hallinan (Ed.), *Handbook of the sociology of education* (pp. 107–135). New York: Kluwer Academic/Plenum.
Elementary and Secondary Education Act of 1965, P.L. No. 89-10 (1965).
Fishkin, J. (1983). *Justice, equal opportunity and the family.* New Haven, CT: Yale University Press.
Grant, G. (1973). Shaping social policy: The politics of the Coleman report. *Teachers College Record, 75*(1), 17–54.
Green v. County School Board, 391 U.S. 430 (1968).
Hanushek, E. A., & Kain, J. F. (1972). On the value of Equality of Educational Opportunity as a guide to public policy. In F. Mosteller & D. P. Moynihan (Eds.), *On equality of educational opportunity* (pp. 116–145). New York: Random House.
Heckman, J., & Neal, D. (1996). Coleman's contribution to education: Theory and research styles and empirical research. In J. Clark (Ed.), *James S. Coleman* (pp. 81–102). Philadelphia: Falmer.
Hobson v. Hansen, 265 F. Supp. 902, DDC, 1967.
Johnson, L. (1965, June 4). *To fulfill these rights.* An address at Howard University.
Kahlenberg, R. D. (2001). Learning from James Coleman. *Public Interest, 144,* 54–72.
Kahlenberg, R. D. (2002). Socioeconomic school integration through public school choice: A progressive alternative to vouchers. *Howard Law Journal, 45,* 247–280.
Kelly, A. H. (1987). The school desegregation case. In J. A. Garraty (Ed.), *Quarrels that have shaped the Constitution* (pp. 243–268). New York: Harper & Row.
Keyes v. School District No. 1, 413 U.S. 189 (1973).
Kluger, R. (1976). *Simple justice.* New York: Knopf.
Levin, B., & Moise, P. (1977). School desegregation litigation in the seventies and the use of social science evidence: An annotated guide. In B. Levin & W. Hawley (Eds.), *The courts, social science, and school desegregation* (pp. 50–133). New Brunswick, NJ: Transaction.
Milliken v. Bradley, 418 U.S. 717 (1974).
Montgomery County Public Schools v. Eisenberg, 197 F.3d 123 (4th Cir. 1999).
Murphy, J. (1971). Title I of ESEA: The politics of implementing federal education reform. *Harvard Educational Review, 41*(1), 35–63.
Plessy v. Ferguson, 163 U.S. 537 (1896).
Shelley v. Kraemer, 334 U.S. 1 (1948).
Sheff v. O'Neill, 678 A.2d 1267 (Conn. 1996).
Studies Challenge Belief That Black Students' Esteem Enhances Achievement. (2000, March 26). *Washington Post,* p. A03.
Swann v. Charlotte-Mecklenburg Bd. of Ed., 402 U.S. 1 (1971).
Sweatt v. Painter, 339 U.S. 629 (1950).
Wilson, W. J. (1987). *The truly disadvantaged.* Chicago: University of Chicago Press.
Wisdom, J. M. (1977). Random remarks on the role of social science in the judicial decision-making in school desegregation cases. In B. Levin & W. Hawley (Eds.), *The courts, social science, and school desegregation* (pp. 134–149). New Brunswick, NJ: Transaction.

PEABODY JOURNAL OF EDUCATION, *79*(2), 136–140

Expert Report of Kent D. Syverud in *Grutter v. Bollinger*

Kent D. Syverud
Vanderbilt University Law School

Editor's Note: In *Grutter v. Bollinger*, __ U.S. ___; 123 S. Ct. 2325; 156 L. Ed. 2d 304 (2003), the Supreme Court rendered a landmark decision approving the use of race as one factor in admissions decisions at the University of Michigan Law School. The opinion of the Court discussed an expert opinion of Kent D. Syverud, Dean of the Vanderbilt Law School, concerning the educational benefits of diversity, noting that "when a critical mass of underrepresented minority students is present, racial stereotypes lose their force because non-minority students learn there is no 'minority viewpoint' but rather a variety of viewpoints among minority students." The expert report to which the Court referred was prepared at the Vanderbilt Law School in 1999 and attached as an Exhibit (in Volume 3 of the Appendix) to the Defendant University of Michigan Law School's Memorandum of Law in Support of Motion for Summary Judgment, May 3, 1999, Grutter v. Bollinger, C.A. No. 97–75928, in the United States District Court for the Eastern District of Michigan. The report was also referenced in the appendix to the Writ of Certiorari in the Supreme Court of the United States at 215a. What follows is the original expert report as submitted to the Court.

Reprinted with permission from *Michigan Journal of Race & Law*, *5*(1), 451–454, 2002.

Requests for reprints should be sent to Kent D. Syverud, Vanderbilt University Law School, 228 Law School Building, 131 21st Avenue, Nashville, TN 37203. E-mail: k.syverud@vanderbilt.edu

Expert Report of Kent D. Syverud
Grutter, et al. v. Bollinger, et al., No. 97–75928 (E.D. Mich.)

I am Kent D. Syverud. I have been Dean and Garner Anthony Professor of Law at the Vanderbilt University Law School since 1997. For 10 years, I was a professor at the University of Michigan Law School. For the last 2 years of my tenure there I also served as Associate Dean for Academic Affairs. In that role I worked with new and experienced teachers to improve the quality of teaching. I have also taught at the University of Pennsylvania Law School, the University of Tokyo Faculty of Law and Politics, and in Germany at programs sponsored by the Universities of Trier and Saarbrücken. I have taught and continue to teach courses in civil procedure, negotiation and drafting, and insurance law. I am the incoming editor of the *Journal of Legal Education*, which is the scholarly journal of the American Association of Law Schools. I frequently give addresses about law teaching, about the challenges of law teaching, to lawyers, law teachers, judges, and teachers at other universities. I have published an article on the challenges of teaching law students well. I have won teaching awards at the University of Michigan Law School, and, in my 1st year in my new position, at the Vanderbilt University Law School. Since 1991, I have regularly taught lawyers who are about to become law professors at the annual New Law Teachers Workshop of the Association of American Law Schools. Before becoming a law teacher I practiced law in Washington, DC.

I am not charging any fee for my expert services in this action. I am being compensated for my reasonable expenses. In the past 4 years, I have testified as an expert in three insurance matters: Dow Corning Corp. v. Hartford Accident & Indemnity Co. (Wayne County Circuit Court), Giant Eagle Inc. v. Federal Ins. Co. (W.D. Pa.), and Dow Chemical Co. v. Aetna (E.D. Mich.). I attach a copy of my current résumé, which includes publications, to this report as an exhibit.

At the beginning of my career as a law teacher, I was skeptical of efforts to consider race as a factor in law school admissions. I was also skeptical that considering race as a factor in admissions had a positive impact on the educational experience of law students. My views on whether law schools should consider race in admissions have changed. The change has been gradual, and the product of many experiences teaching many students in many settings. I have in particular had the experience of teaching the same subject matter to classes that are racially homogeneous and racially heterogeneous, and to classes where non-White students make up a tiny fraction of the enrolled students and where their numbers are more significant.

I have come to believe that all law students receive an immeasurably better legal education, and become immeasurably better lawyers, in law schools and law school classes where the student body is racially heterogeneous. It has been my experience from many conversations over the years that the vast majority of committed law teachers agree. When my students reflect on their law school experience, whether Black or White, Asian or Hispanic, conservative or liberal, they also often volunteer this conclusion. I now view this agreement as indicating that those people most directly involved in the law school classroom can see the difference that racial heterogeneity makes in legal education. I have many reasons for now believing that considerations of race in law school admissions are particularly vital to providing the best possible legal education and to training the best possible lawyers.

The first reason is the unique way learning happens in the best law school classrooms. Most 1st-year classes in law schools are conducted by the Socratic method, in which professors call upon individual students and engage in a dialogue of questions and answers in front of the entire class. There are many variants of this method, but most professors continue to single out individual students each day to answer a series of questions suggested by the assigned reading. In my own civil procedure class, I call upon each student several times a semester, usually questioning each student for 15 to 20 min. The purposes of this method are manifold; they include the desire to engage the student closely and carefully with a legal text and to make the classroom dynamic, lively, and interesting. At least as important, the method consciously seeks to make the students think, to learn from each other, and to learn to be able to see any set of facts from different points of view. Students are expected to draw upon their own backgrounds and experiences in answering questions and in making arguments. Rather than passively receiving the accumulated wisdom of the professor, students are required to grapple with their own viewpoints, and those of their colleagues, on an array of difficult situations posed by the professor and the text. The result is that, in the best classrooms, every voice is heard, and the quality of the education received is largely a function of the diversity of viewpoints and experiences among the students in the class.

It is my view, based on my experience, that racial heterogeneity dramatically enhances the ability of the best active, Socratic teaching to achieve its purposes. My best class sessions, by far, have been characterized by direct and often painful dialogue between students who are forced by the method to confront and make explicit their deepest unexamined convictions about legal issues, and also to engage in discussion with those who, because of different experiences and often because of different race, do not share those convictions. Those class sessions produce the most careful thinking and, when handled with care, are the most challenging and appropriate education I can offer. It has been my experience that racial diversity in the Socratic classroom strongly fosters the kind of thinking that the best lawyers need to be able to do.

For a related reason, racial heterogeneity in a Socratic classroom produces better lawyers. As a law teacher, I am constantly struggling with the need to teach new students the obligations of a lawyer to become a zealous advocate for a client and a skilled negotiator with adversaries and others. A basic component of excelling in these roles is the ability to understand the views, goals, and tactics of a client or adversary. Good advocacy first requires understanding both the client and the adversary. Yet most of my students come to law school with strong advocacy skills and poor listening skills; they assume they already know what the viewpoint of a client or adversary must be in every situation. In particular, they often assign to people of different races and ethnic backgrounds viewpoints that are uninformed by experience or by direct dialogue with a client or adversary. They are often very wrong. They don't know what they don't know, and it is my job to show them what they have to learn, every time, from every individual client or adversary.

Nothing teaches this lesson better than a classroom where, because of abundant racial heterogeneity, common assumptions about viewpoints of different races are constantly confronted by frank discussion that at times confirms and at times profoundly confounds those assumptions. I have seen this demonstrated repeatedly, both in my civil procedure classes taught via the Socratic method and in the upper level skills class I teach on negotiation.

There is abundant criticism of legal education for failing to teach students the skills they will need to succeed as lawyers. It is an important responsibility of law schools to teach students to become able negotiators, problem solvers, managers, counselors, investigators, and mediators. It also is vital that the lawyers we train be able to participate to the fullest in a democratic society in which they will have a vital role, as officers of the court, in preserving justice. It has been my experience that skills instruction is enhanced dramatically for all students by the interaction in class of future lawyers of all races and by the different and at times unpredicted viewpoints different people bring to the discussion. It is also my experience that civil democratic discourse among lawyers of all races, in public and in court, is something that, once experienced in the law school classroom, is valued outside it and across my students' careers.

Racial heterogeneity thus helps make better lawyers at the same time it assures that classroom discussion will not become so theoretical as to be divorced from the real differences in viewpoints that characterize many of the clients my students will need to serve.

Some examples from my teaching experience may better explain why I have come to hold these views. In my civil procedure course each year, I teach students how the finder of fact, whether judge or jury, is selected in the American federal and state systems, as well as under systems in other countries. I teach jury selection by having 6 to 12 students in the class assume the role of potential jurors, who are questioned by classmates serving in the role as defense and plaintiff's counsel. Male student jurors pretend to be their own fathers; female student jurors pretend to be their own mothers. The students answer the searching voir dire questions accordingly, often revealing unexpected differences in backgrounds and viewpoints that are shocking and enlightening to the class. When challenges are exercised by the plaintiff and defense counsel, it is often the case that both Black and White students strike both Black and White jurors. The reasons they give, and the analysis that ensues, is remarkable to all students. The ensuing discussion of the peremptory challenge is incomparably richer than would be possible without racial heterogeneity, and the students, I believe, are incomparably better trained to understand the roles they will serve in American civil trials.

I have found that racial heterogeneity improves the quality of my classes even and especially when the subject seems far removed from issues traditionally associated with race in American law. In insurance law, I have found that my teaching of the regulation of insurance products aimed at consumers changes dramatically when the makeup of the class is racially diverse. In civil procedure, my teaching of remedies (including the remedy of garnishment) and of attorneys' fees and costs has been significantly improved, for all students, by having a diversity of views expressed among my Black students as well as among my White students.

For all these reasons, I now believe racial heterogeneity is a very important contributor to a quality legal education for all students, and to the training of the best lawyers. I think a law school without significant representation of Black, White, Asian, and Hispanic students in the student body will provide a significantly poorer education than a law school blessed by such a representation. And I think a lawyer trained in a law school that is racially homogeneous, will be, in the coming decades, ill equipped to serve the functions the best lawyers will need to serve in our democracy.

PEABODY JOURNAL OF EDUCATION, *79*(2), 141–156

Educating Culturally Diverse Learners with Exceptionalities: A Critical Analysis of the *Brown* Case

Festus E. Obiakor
Department of Exceptional Education
University of Wisconsin–Milwaukee

Cheryl A. Utley
Juniper Gardens Children's Project
University of Kansas

The *Brown v. Board of Education* case of 1954 set the stage for addressing problems of educational and social inequities. It challenged prejudicial exclusion and supported nondiscriminatory exclusionary policies in general and special education programs. However, about 50 years later, culturally diverse learners are still excluded in educational programs through misidentification, misassessment, miscategorization, misplacement, and misinstruction–misintervention. It appears that 1 step forward and 2 steps backward have been taken. In this article, the authors examine the *Brown* case and its impact on the historical contexts of special education as they affect culturally diverse learners with exceptionalities.

Requests for reprints should be sent to Festus E. Obiakor, Department of Exceptional Education, University of Wisconsin–Milwaukee, Milwaukee, WI 53201. E-mail: fobiakor@uwm.edu

The educational rights and opportunities for culturally diverse learners with exceptionalities have been of grave concern to educators, policymakers, and society (National Research Council, 2002). For more than 50 years, the judicial system has been involved in the arena of special education because of disproportionate representations of culturally diverse learners in special and gifted education programs. The 1954 landmark case of *Brown v. Board of Education* (1954) in Topeka, Kansas, was the most significant school inclusion case requiring that schools make a "good faith" effort to desegregate schools "with all deliberate speed" (Dooley & Voltz, 1999, p. 19). The intent of the *Brown* case was to uphold the 14th Amendment and redefine issues related to equal access of educational programming. This case recognized that separate educational facilities were inherently unequal and unconstitutional. To a large measure, it failed to favor discrimination in school admissions on grounds of race or color. Of interest, although this case was supposed to extinguish practices that are discriminatory and protect the educational rights of children and youth, there continues to be the issue of how to effectively educate culturally diverse learners with exceptionalities (Dooley & Dooley, 2002).

After 3 decades of the *Brown* case, Staples (1984) discovered some apparent inequities at all educational levels. He noted that "the ideology of equal opportunity masks the reality of a country stratified along racial, gender, and class lines" (p. 12). He was also saddened by what he called the *new racism*, which (a)Êtends to deny the existence of racism or the responsibility for it, (b) defends phony meritocracy, and (c) relies on standardized tests that are not valid predictors of quality performance. Staples's frustrations reflected outcries of people regarding problems associated with misidentification, misassessment, mislabeling, misplacement, and misinstruction–misintervention (MacMillan & Reschly, 1998; Obiakor, 1994, 1999). As MacMillan and Reschly acknowledged, the outcry of the people was not merely because culturally diverse learners were disproportionately represented in special education classes but because they were also put in classes that were stigmatizing, degrading, and less effective than their previous general education classes.

For culturally diverse learners with exceptionalities, the question has been simple and consistent, that is, how can we provide equitable educational programs that help them to maximize their fullest potential? However, the responses have been inconsistent, disingenuous, and sometimes racist (Jackson, 1988). Today, although the reform rhetoric continues, many culturally diverse learners with exceptionalities continue to be disproportionately represented in special and gifted programs (Obiakor, 2001). One is left to wonder if researchers, educators, and policymakers are really interested in solving these problems or if they are interested in the politics of the problems. In this article, we examine the impact of the landmark *Brown* case on the historical contexts of special education as they affect culturally diverse learners with exceptionalities.

The *Brown* Case: Impact on General and Special Education

The landmark *Brown* case sets the stage for recognizing inherent inequities in traditional general and special education programming and policies. Historically, this case was significant in education and disability policy. Turnbull and Turnbull (2000) confirmed that

1. *Brown* is an example of how the educational rights of students with disabilities are social and policy issues cast in the guise of constitutional litigation to be resolved by the courts.
2. *Brown* demonstrates that difficult educational issues can be fought on civil rights battlefields. Just as *Brown* was the first successful case on the battlefield of racial desegregation of schools, it was the seed that gave birth to other civil rights battles and set the tone for challenging governmental discrimination against certain persons because of their unalterable personal characteristics such as race, sex, and disability. In reality, *Brown* gave rise to the right to education for children and persons with disabilities.
3. *Brown* demonstrates that the principles of equal protection and due process under the 5th and 14th Amendments have significant effects on public education.

Apparently, *Brown* initiated the legal foundation for federal education and civil rights legislation, especially for culturally and linguistically diverse persons with disabilities. The *Brown* case has far-reaching effects on general and special education. According to Turnbull and Turnbull (2000), the *Brown* case dealt with the following critical issues confronting general and special education today:

1. Denial of equal educational opportunities is wrong and cannot be condoned.
2. Separateness in education is unconstitutional and can be challenged.
3. Right-to-education cases can be upheld in courts.
4. Stigmatization and its detrimental educational consequences can be challenged.

5. The function of schools to meaningfully educate all students can be upheld in courts.
6. Public policy against invidious state action can be advanced and instituted.
7. Obtaining a quality education can be advanced through legal avenues.

Historically, the struggle for equality has been at the forefront for most culturally diverse persons in the United States. Though there are pockets of restructuring and reform programs that have buttressed academic success of culturally diverse learners, the undergirding principle of equitable educational programming for these learners remains a problem. Consider the endemic predicaments confronting them in school programs. First, standardized instruments are consistently used to misjudge their intelligence or place them in restrictive special education programs (Hilliard, 1992, 1995; Obiakor, Algozzine, & Ford, 1994; Obiakor & Ford, 2002). Second, teacher expectations of them are frequently inaccurate, unrealistic, and negative (Obiakor, 1999, 2000, 2001). Third, they are consistently perceived to have "low" or "negative" self-concept or self-worth (Obiakor, 1992, 1999). Fourth, they continue to lack realistic role models who understand their history, symbols, cultural values, and learning styles in school programs (Harvey & Scott-Jones, 1985; Ogbu, 1990). And fifth, schools in their neighborhoods are still viewed as "bad" or "poor" schools (Obiakor, 2001).

Directly or indirectly, added pressures have been put on school reform programs for culturally diverse learners with exceptionalities. It is imperative that reformers understand traditional general and special education problems before initiating change policies. Issues related to equal education for all cannot be discussed without acknowledging that traditional educational programs foster historical inequities. It is important to ask, What reform and restructuring lessons have been learned from history? What efforts must be made to design programs that foster quality and equity? How can general educators understand the relationship between what they do and what happens to students in special education? For culturally diverse learners, these questions must be answered to initiate and design equitable and quality programs at all educational levels.

In its truest fashion, special education was intended to be individualized and tailor-made for each child with a special need. In 1975, the Education of All Handicapped Children's Act was instituted to ensure that all children, despite their exceptionality, would have the right to enter into the public education system and receive a free and appropriate education. For the past 26 years, only the letter, not the spirit, of this legislation has been carried out by many general and special educators. As a result, many scholars (e.g., Daniels, 1998; Russo & Talbert-Johnson, 1997) have questioned whether or not this was a form of resegregation under the guise of educational reform. Of interest, special education was intended to buttress regular education (Shapiro et al., 1993), and on the surface, it seemed to have great face value. For example, consider the fact that special education laws (e.g., the 1990 Individuals With Disabilities Education Act and its 1997 reauthorization) required (a) special education classrooms to maintain a lower teacher-to-pupil ratio than regular education classrooms, (b) special expenditures that are 2 to 4 times higher than those of general education, (c) specially tailored programs designed specifically for the child, and (d)Êspecial services to be delivered by well-prepared teachers (MacMillan & Reschly, 1998). With these excellent intentions, one would not expect inclusion, exclusion, and disproportionate placements to be critical issues today. In reality, school districts are now challenged with regard to teacher–pupil ratio, inadequate expenditures, inappropriately designed programs, and poorly prepared teachers (Obiakor, 2001; Obiakor & Ford, 2002). A logical conclusion is that pertinent court cases (e.g., the *Brown* case) and subsequent legislative efforts have not yielded the desired outcomes for culturally diverse learners.

Analyzing the Special Education Process in the Context of the *Brown* Case

As indicated, the *Brown* case opened doors for nondiscriminatory exclusion or inclusion of students. It is in this spirit that special education was instituted to leave no child behind. A critical analysis of the special education process reveals a process that is inadequate, misleading, unethical, and dangerous (Obiakor & Johnson, 1997). The use of controversial methods (e.g., intelligence tests) has been debated in courts over the past 4 decades. As indicated, these inadequate assessments and discriminatory tests are still used with great regularity (Obiakor, Harris-Obiakor, Obi, & Eskay, 2000; Ysseldyke & Marston, 1999). It is no wonder that the disproportionate representation of culturally diverse learners in special education programs has attracted national attention (Artiles & Trent, 2000; Obiakor & Utley, 2001; Patton, 1998; Utley & Obiakor, 2001). To effectively analyze how "special" special education has responded to the *Brown* case, the intricate steps of special education (i.e., identification, assessment, categorization, placement, and instruction) must be briefly examined.

Identification

As early as the 1960s and 1970s, many concerned scholars and educators warned that special education would be a disservice to certain students; the manifestation of this prophecy still holds true in this new millennium for many students from diverse ethnic, socioeconomic, and linguistic backgrounds (Obiakor, 2001). The identification of a student sets the stage for further legally mandated activities not routinely addressed in regular education classrooms. Once a child has been identified as having an educational disability, the law mandates that general and special education teachers use several referral and assessment strategies before interventions are set in motion. Interestingly, students with different behavioral and learning styles are misidentified as having problems. Based on multiple sources of information (e.g., classroom observations and records), decisions should be made as to what form of intervention is needed (i.e., temporary placements in a resource room and/or teacher-based classroom interventions). Unfortunately, the overall effectiveness of examining multiple sources of information during the identification process has been overlooked (National Research Council, 2002). Logically, overlooking multiple sources of information leads to misidentification, which invariably leads to exclusion in the educational process, a phenomenon that the *Brown* case attempted to deal with.

Grossman (1998) acknowledged that most general and special educators do not believe they are biased against those outside the mainstream society. These educators tend to forget that schools are a microcosm of the larger society. He further noted that people see what they expect to see and that the propaganda of the media has vilified those outside the mainstream culture. As a consequence, teachers judge ethnic minority and "poor students'" behaviors as more deviant than those of European American children, even when they are exactly the same. In a recent study, Sbarra and Pianta (2001) reported that kindergarten and first-grade teachers differ in their perceptions of appropriate behaviors between culturally diverse and Caucasian students. Furthermore, they observed that the differences expressed were based on the cultural biases of teachers. Many culturally diverse parents trust and rely on certified educators to detect various exceptionalities; however, some teachers play on the subjective nature of the current system and abuse this initial referral protocol as a means of getting rid of selective students they deem as incorrigible (Obiakor, 1999, 2001; Obiakor, Algozzine, et al., 2002). Ironically, these teachers are more likely to bequeath praise and congratulatory remarks and attentiveness to European American students in comparison to culturally diverse students (see Grossman, 1998; New, 1996; Sbarra & Pianta, 2001). Frequently, inappropriate identification is followed by inappropriate assessment, another gross injustice that is in antithetical to what the *Brown* case attempted to combat.

Assessment

General and special educators have continued to use outdated materials and assessment instruments despite court decisions, outcries of parents, and school failures. The current assessment procedure is based on a myopic strategy (Boykin, 2000) and a "one-size-fits-all" paradigm (Obiakor et al., 2000) despite the great heterogeneity inside and outside schools. An assessment measure is frequently designed to present valuable information to the specialist to determine the needs of the child; however, assessment tools used in special education cases are designed to produce scores used to determine eligibility (Obiakor, Algozzine, et al., 2002; Utley, 2002). The irony of the process is that many creators of these same instruments (e.g., Alfred Binet) warned that a single number could not describe an individual's intelligence and could produce a brutal pessimism (Kwate, 2001; Onwuegbuzie & Daley, 2001). For instance, Kwate stated that IQ scores are inherently meaningless and misleading and have outlived the usefulness they once had. Moreover, most of these assessment tools have been unable to assess culturally diverse children's giftedness, and thus, they do serious harm to them by preventing them from maximizing their fullest potential. Clearly, the misassessment of culturally diverse learners using instruments that are not discriminatory goes contrary to what the *Brown* case dealt with.

Scholars (e.g., Allen & Graden, 1995; Obiakor, Algozzine, et al., 2002; Ysseldyke & Marston, 1999) have suggested that schools approach assessment from a developmental perspective and not from a deficit perspective. In a search for pathology, educators and psychologists have spent more time assessing culturally diverse children to declare them eligible for categorical labels and special education placements (Gardner, 1993; Gould, 1981). Misassessment destroys the self-confidence of students and fails to identify their specific strengths and weaknesses. More than 2 decades ago, Heller, Holtzman, and Messick (1982) confirmed that a valid assessment is marked by its relevance to and usefulness for instruction. If the quality of educational programming becomes the conceptual basis for testing, then traditional methods of assessment conflict with the practical issues of testing. Studies of the effectiveness of specific instructional strategies derived from diagnostic and placement decisions are virtually nonexistent (Kavale, 1981; Newcomer & Hammill, 1976). As a result, two critical questions continue to be, Why then are assessment tools advocated and used even when they are culturally and linguistically biased? and Who benefits from the use of these biased tools? Sadly, rather than minimize the use of biased tools, the aggressive push for testing has been magnified by the promulgation of the 2001 No Child Left Behind Act. Obiakor (2003) concluded that

> The *No Child Left Behind Act* will leave many children behind. Its embodiments are complex and its wisdom is weak. To leave no child behind, there must be a comprehensive support model that taps on the energies of students, families, schools, communities, and governments in the educational process. Clearly, many children will not benefit from the *No Child Left Behind Act*. The beneficiaries will be (a) educational bureaucrats, (b) test manufacturers and producers, (c) testing professionals and bureaucrats, (d) politicians, and (e) those who perpetuate phony meritocracy and fraudulent multiculturalism. (p. 3)

Categorization

There is a great deal of ambiguity regarding the criteria for categorical labeling in special education. Very often, biased general and special education teachers predict an ominous cloud of doom for culturally diverse learners who fail to conform to their individual standards. For instance, the etiology of learning disabilities (LD) is a psychological enigma. Many schools use an arbitrary IQ–achievement discrepancy, which is not empirically supported, to determine eligibility. Therefore, criteria for the same diagnosis can vary within the same city and state. Not long ago, Ysseldyke and Marston (1999) stated that psychometric measures could not reliably differentiate between students with LD and those who are low in achievement (LA); furthermore, the LD criteria are inadequate in discriminating between LD and LA students (Graden, Casey, & Christenson, 1985). Ysseldyke and Marston's findings confirmed previous findings by Gresham, MacMillan, and Bocian (1996). Apparently, the ambiguity found in the lack of empirical evidence to differentiate between children with mild cognitive disability and those with academic difficulties has been substantiated by several empirical investigations (see Gresham et al., 1996; Ysseldyke & Marston, 1999).

It appears that the benefits of the *Brown* case have been silenced and even lost, especially when one looks at many of the urban schools today. Culturally and linguistically diverse learners are still excluded and miscategorized. In his classical book, *The Futures of Children: Categories, Labels, and Their Consequences*, Nicholas Hobbs (1975) acknowledged that words and labels are needed to classify students but that they make victims out of students. In other words, words and labels exclude students who look, act, and learn differently. As he pointed out

> Categories and labels are powerful instruments for social regulation and control, and they are often employed for obscure, covert, or hurtful purposes: to degrade people, to deny their access to opportunity, to exclude "undesirables" whose presence in some way offends, disturbs familiar custom, or demands extraordinary effort. (p. 11)

Hobbs's views were later reiterated by Ysseldyke, Algozzine, and Thurlow (2000) when they wrote

> Labeling students is not a benign activity nor is it a necessary evil, as school officers and others sometimes claim. Despite a presumed need for them, labels are an unfortunate by-product of a system that attaches money to acts, thus resulting in classifications and categories. Labels are often irrelevant to the instructional needs of students. Furthermore, labels become real attributes that prevent meaningful understanding of actual individual learning needs. By causing some to believe that students labeled as having mental retardation cannot perform certain tasks, the act of classifying condemns these students to a life of lesser expectations and performance. Labels require official sanction. Resources diverted to the process of identifying and classifying students are extensive. Time and money spent on labeling are time and money not spent on teaching. Time spent being labeled is time not spent being taught or learning. (p. 110)

Placement

As indicated, the *Brown* case was against exclusion from educational programs. The worst kind of exclusion for many culturally and linguistically diverse learners today is the misplacement that results from misidentification, misassessment, and miscategorization. It has been proven that special education has a disproportionate number of culturally diverse learners diagnosed with various disabilities (Reschly & Ysseldyke, 1995; Sparks, 1999; Strickland & Ascher, 1992). Some scholars (e.g., Patton, 1998) have acknowledged that special education is structurally flawed and does not have the best interest of culturally diverse learners at heart. Between 1980 and 1990, special education as a whole increased among all racial groups: European Americans increased 6%, African Americans increased 13%, Hispanic Americans increased 53%, and Asian Americans/Pacific Islanders increased 107.8% (U.S. Department of Education, 2000). Earlier, in her investigation, Harry (1992) discovered that the national data can be a little misleading. For instance, it was reported that African Americans make up 16% of the general enrollment and 21% of special education enrollment. Yet, when probed deeper, the African American population, which composed 16% of the general school population, made up 35% of the Educable Mentally Retarded category, 27% of the Trainable Mentally Retarded category, and 27% of the Seriously Emotionally Disturbed classification (see Harry, 1992). In addition, although some special education categories appear objective (e.g., vision, hearing, and traumatic brain injury), some are not objective (e.g., learning disabilities and mental retardation), and some even seem desirable (e.g., gifted and talented programs where culturally diverse learners are unfortunately underrepresented).

It is sad to note that mandated laws in special education are seldom treated as law (Utley & Simon, 2003). Frequently, they are treated as suggestions or proposals! It is no surprise that low-achieving culturally diverse learners are placed in special education classes before academic interventions are attempted. The paradox is that the intervention for these learners has been the actual placement into retrogressive special education settings. Obiakor (1999), Patton (1998), and Russo and Talbert-Johnson (1997) agreed that these learners are placed in educational structures that are not conducive to their academic success. In other words, culturally diverse learners are more likely to be pathologically labeled, administered punitive disciplinary procedures, placed in alternative educational facilities, and subsequently placed in special education (National Research Council, 2002). Unfortunately, in these placement settings, they receive stigmatizing labels, isolation from peers, and patronizing teachers. In fact, for many culturally diverse learners with exceptionalities, misidentification leads to misassessment, misassessment leads to miscategorization, miscategorization leads to misplacement, and misplacement leads to misinstruction– misintervention (Obiakor, 1994, 1999, 2001; Obiakor & Johnson, 1997). One is left to wonder if the *Brown* case had any useful far-reaching impact on today's general and special education.

Classroom Instruction and Interventions

The question is, How can a student who is unfairly excluded in educational programs or inappropriately placed in stigmatized environments receive appropriate instruction–intervention? When a teacher provides a systematic instruction, students have opportunities to attain new skills and activities. If general and special educators are to meet challenges posed by demographic changes, they will need help in creating effective instructional environments that promote academic productivity and appropriate social behavior for an increasingly diverse student population (Obiakor & Ford, 2002). In particular, they will need information about the process of designing, implementing, and evaluating interventions and a broad range of strategies useful for classroom applications. Obiakor (2001) and Orlich, Harder, Callahan, and Gibson (2001) have argued that "good" teaching must incorporate

1. The school milieu.
2. A holistic view of instruction.
3. Equity as the big picture.
4. Sequencing and organizing of instruction.
5. Goals, standards, and outcomes for instruction.
6. Management of the classroom environment.
7. The process of questioning.
8. Inquiry, teaching, and higher level thinking.
9. Small-group discussions and cooperative learning.
10. Monitoring of student success.

Undoubtedly, the phony definition of "good" teaching–intervention has been very harmful to many culturally diverse learners. The school sometimes is not viewed as a learning community where individuals from different cultural, racial, and socioeconomic backgrounds come together (Ford, Obiakor, & Patton, 1995). "Goodness" is rarely used to define schools in culturally diverse neighborhoods, even though the majority of the general and special education teachers who teach culturally diverse learners are Anglo Americans (Obiakor, 2001). Apparently, these teachers are culturally disconnected from these children whom they teach. Earlier Diaz (1992) explained that cultural experiences can have an effect on a student's learning style and should be considered within a teacher's curriculum. However, Diaz noted that, although certain characteristics can be attributed to culture, the educator must be careful not to stereotype all persons within a culture simply because they belong to that particular cultural group. By focusing on the specific ethnic groups with which one works, one can develop a culturally tailored curriculum and intervention strategy. If a general and special education teacher is aware that a particular child from a specific culture learns more by a verbal strategy than a visual method, then he or she can make modifications to meet this need and, thus, maximize the learning potential. The variation of learning style is only one culturally related difference within a variety of cultural groups (Gilliland & Reyhner, 1988; Obiakor, 2001; Sparks, 1998). Though the

Brown case set the stage for incorporating individual differences through its anti-exclusionary message, today's school programs continue to devalue behavioral, learning, cultural, and linguistic styles different from mainstream styles.

Conclusion

In this article, we have examined the *Brown* case and its impact on the historical contexts of special education as they affect culturally diverse learners with exceptionalities. It appears that we have consistently talked about responding to individual differences and effective educational solutions for culturally diverse learners with exceptionalities, but, very often, these differences are viewed as deficits. Our experiences tell us that educational programs for culturally diverse learners have failed to yield measurable dividends that are supposed to be derived from the *Brown* case. Consequently, we believe it is the responsibility of general and special educators to implement effective identifications, assessments, categorizations, placements, and interventions with culturally diverse learners.

In this new millennium, as educators, we must reengage ourselves toward the historical lessons of the *Brown* case. We must make everyone accountable to educating culturally diverse learners with exceptionalities. As it appears, the more things change, the more they remain the same—and we wonder why we continue to take one step forward and two steps backward! This dangerous phenomenon leads us to ask this critical question, How can we avoid the mistakes of the past in school programs for culturally diverse learners with and without exceptionalities? We believe realistic special education programs are necessary for culturally diverse learners; however, we also believe many of these learners do not deserve to be in such segregated and stigmatizing programs. To avoid past mistakes that resulted in the *Brown* case, we must begin to understand that traditional educational programs are loaded with discriminatory practices, unrealistic expectations, disproportionate representations, and illusory conclusions. In addition, we believe our paradigms must be shifted and our resolve must be stronger if we are to create effective interventions and learning environments for culturally diverse learners with and without exceptionalities (Obiakor, Grant, & Dooley, 2002; Obiakor, & Utley, 1997; Slavin, Madden, Dolan, & Wasik, 1996).

Because race has continued to matter in the United States (see West, 1993), court cases such as the *Brown* case must be followed by federal government initiatives to maximize the fullest potential of culturally diverse learners with and without exceptionalities. From our perspective, we reaffirm the following:

1. There must be a national commitment to improving the education of poor and minority families and children in low-performing schools to reiterate the historical significance of the *Brown* case.
2. Several policies must meet the needs of children, families, and communities to foster empowerment in order to maintain the legacy of the *Brown* case.
3. Innovative problem-solving strategies are needed to engage schools, families, and communities in comprehensive interagency planning to foster school, community, and family partnerships. These partnerships will increase multiple voices that the *Brown* case was bent on highlighting in school programs.
4. There must be an emphasis on maintaining a knowledge base that is grounded in research and evaluation. Without such a knowledge base, the *Brown* case would not have been successful. As researchers, we must learn the facts when we are in doubt, and we must move beyond emotions as we learn the facts.

References

Allen, S. J., & Graden, J. L. (1995). Best practices in collaborative problem solving for intervention design. In A. Thomas & J. Grimes (Eds.), *Best practices in school psychology* (Vol. 3, pp. 667–678). Washington, DC: National Association of School Psychology.

Artiles, A. A., & Trent, S. C. (2000). Culturally/linguistically diverse students, representation of. In C. R. Reynolds & E. Fletcher-Janzen (Eds.), *Encyclopedia of special education* (2nd ed., pp. 513–517). New York: Wiley.

Boykin, A. W. (2000). Talent development, cultural deep structure, and school reform: Implications for African immersion initiatives. In D. S. Pollard & C. S. Ajirotutu (Eds.), *African-centered schooling in theory and practice* (pp. 143–161). Westport, CT: Bergin & Garvey

Brown v. Board of Educ., 347 U.S. 483 (1954).

Daniels, V. I. (1998). Minority students in gifted and special education programs: The case for educational equity. *The Journal of Special Education, 32*, 41–43.

Diaz, C. (1992). *Multicultural education for the 21st century*. Washington, DC: National Education Association.

Dooley, E. A., & Dooley, K. L. (2002). Legal foundations of special education for African American learners. In F. E. Obiakor & B. A. Ford (Eds.), *Creating successful learning environments for African American learners with exceptionalities* (pp. 17–26). Thousand Oaks, CA: Corwin.

Dooley E. A., & Voltz, D. L. (1999). Educating the African American exceptional learner. In F. E. Obiakor, J. O. Schwenn, & A. F. Rotatori (Eds.), *Multicultural education for learners with exceptionalities* (pp. 15–32). Stamford, CT: JAI.

Education of All Handicapped Children's Act of 1975, Pub. L. No. 94-142.

Ford, B. A., Obiakor, F. E., & Patton, J. M. (1995). *Effective education of African American exceptional learners: New perspectives*. Austin, TX: Pro-Ed.

Gardner, H. (1993). *Multiple intelligences: The theory of practice*. New York: Basic Books.

Gilliland, H., & Reyhner, J. (1988). *Teaching the Native American*. Dubuque, IA: Kendall/Hunt.

Gould, S. J. (1981). *The mismeasure of man*. New York: Norton.

Graden, J. L., Casey, A., & Christenson, S. L. (1985). Implementing a prereferral intervention system: II. The data. *Exceptional Children, 51*, 467–496.

Gresham, F. M., MacMillan, D. L., & Bocian, K. M. (1996). Learning disabilities, low achievement, and mild mental retardation: More alike than different. *Journal of Learning Disabilities, 29*, 570–581.

Grossman, H. (1998). *Ending discrimination in special education*. Springfield, IL: Thomas.

Harry, B. (1992). *Cultural diversity, families, and the special education system*. New York: Teachers College Press.

Harvey, W. B., & Scott-Jones, D. (1985). We can't find any: The elusiveness of Black faculty members in American higher education. *Issues in Education, 3*, 68–76.

Heller, K. A., Holtzman, W. H., & Messick, S. (1982). *Placing children in special education: A strategy for equity*. Washington, DC: National Research Council.

Hilliard, A. G. (1992). The pitfalls and promises of special education practice. *Exceptional Children, 59*, 168–172.

Hilliard, A. G. (1995). Culture, assessment, and valid teaching for the African American student. In B. A. Ford, F. E. Obiakor, & J. M. Patton (Eds.), *Effective education of African American exceptional learners: New perspectives* (pp. ix–xvi). Austin, TX: ProEd.

Individuals with Disabilities Education Act of 1990, Pub. L. No. 101-476 and 1997 reauthorization, Pub. L. No. 105-17.

Hobbs, N. (1975). *The futures of children: Categories, labels, and their consequences*. San Francisco: Jossey-Bass.

Jackson, J. L. (1988). In pursuit of equity, ethics, and excellence: The challenge to close the gap. In K. Ryan & J. M. Cooper (Eds.), *Kaleidoscope: Readings in education* (5th ed., pp. 444–448). Boston: Houghton-Mifflin.

Kavale, K. (1981). Functions of the Illinois Test of Psycholinguistic Abilities (ITPA): Are they trainable? *Exceptional Children, 47*, 496–510.

Kwate, N. A. O. (2001). Intelligence or misorientation? Eurocentrism in the WISC–III. *Journal of Black Psychology, 27*, 221–238.

MacMillan, D. L., & Reschly, D. J. (1998). Overrepresentation of minority students: The case for greater specificity or reconsideration of the variables examined. *The Journal of Special Education, 32*, 15–24.

National Research Council. (2002). *Minority students in special and gifted education*. Washington, DC: National Academy Press.

New, C. A. (1996). Teacher thinking and perceptions of African-American male achievement in the classroom. In F. A. Rios (Ed.), *Teacher thinking in cultural contexts* (pp. 85–103). Albany: State University of New York Press.

Newcomer, P. L., & Hammill, D. D. (1976). *Psycholinguistics in the schools*. Columbus, OH: Merrill.

No Child Left Behind Act of 2001, Pub. L. No. 107-110.

Obiakor, F. E. (1992). Self-concept of African American students: An operational model for special education. *Exceptional Children, 59*, 160–167.

Obiakor, F. E. (1994). *The eight-step multicultural approach: Learning and teaching with a smile*. Dubuque, IA: Kendall/Hunt.

Obiakor, F. E. (1999). Teacher expectations of minority exceptional learners: Impact on "accuracy" of self-concepts. *Exceptional Children, 66,* 39–53.

Obiakor, F. E. (2000, October). *Transforming teaching–learning to improve student achievement.* Position paper presented at the Best Practice conference, Institute for the Transformation of Learning, Marquette University, Milwaukee, WI.

Obiakor, F. E. (2001). *It even happens in "good" schools: Responding to cultural diversity in today's classroom.* Thousand Oaks, CA: Corwin.

Obiakor, F. E. (2003, May). *To assess or not, is that the question? Who benefits from the No Child Left Behind Act? Personal perspectives.* Paper presented to the Institute on Multicultural Relations, University of Wisconsin–Milwaukee, Milwaukee, WI.

Obiakor, F. E., Algozzine, B., & Ford, B. (1994). Education reform and service delivery to African American students. In S. G. Garcia (Ed.), *Addressing cultural and linguistic diversity in special education: Issues and trends* (pp. 1–9). Reston, VA: Council for Exceptional Children.

Obiakor, F. E., Algozzine, B., Thurlow, M., Gwalla-Ogisi, N., Enwefa, S., Enwefa, R., & McIntosh, A. (2002). *Addressing the issue of disproportionate representation: Identification and assessment of culturally diverse students with emotional or behavioral disorders.* Arlington, VA: Council for Exceptional Children, Council for Children With Behavioral Disorders Division.

Obiakor, F. E., & Ford, B. A. (2002). *Creating successful learning environments for African American learners with exceptionalities.* Thousand Oaks, CA: Corwin.

Obiakor, F. E., Grant, P. A., & Dooley, E. A. (2002). *Educating all learners: Refocusing the comprehensive support model.* Springfield, IL: Thomas.

Obiakor, F. E., Harris-Obiakor, P., Obi, S. O., & Eskay, M. (2000). Urban learners in general and special education programs: Revisiting assessment and intervention issues. In F. E. Obiakor, S. A. Burkhardt, A. F. Rotatori, & T. Wahlberg (Eds.), *Advances in special education: Intervention techniques for individuals with exceptionalities in inclusive settings* (pp. 115–131). Stamford, CT: JAI.

Obiakor, F. E., & Johnson, M. J. (1997). Children and youth at risk: From understanding to intervention. *Emporia State Research, 40,* 1–15.

Obiakor, F. E., & Utley, C. A. (1997). Rethinking preservice preparation for teachers in the learning disabilities field: Workable multicultural strategies. *Learning Disabilities Research and Practice, 12,* 100–106.

Obiakor, F. E., & Utley, C. A. (2001). Culturally responsive teacher preparation for programming for the twenty-first century. In C. A. Utley & F. E. Obiakor (Eds.), *Special education, multicultural education, and school reform: Components of quality education for learners with mild disabilities* (pp. 188–207). Springfield, IL: Thomas.

Ogbu, J. U. (1990). Understanding diversity: Summary statements. *Education and Urban Society, 22,* 425–429.

Onwuegbuzie, A. J., & Daley, C. E. (2001). Racial differences in IQ revisited: A synthesis of nearly a century of research. *Journal of Black Psychology, 27,* 209–220.

Orlich, D. C., Harder, R. J., Callahan, R. C., & Gibson, H. W. (2001). *Teaching strategies: A guide to better instruction* (6th ed.). Boston: Houghton Mifflin.

Patton, J. (1998). The disproportionate representation of African-Americans in special education: Looking behind the curtain for understanding and solutions. *The Journal of Special Education, 32,* 25–31.

Reschly, D. J., & Ysseldyke, J. E. (1995). School psychology paradigm shift. In A. Thomas & J. Grimes (Eds.), *Best practices in school psychology* (Vol. 3, pp. 17–31). Washington, DC: National Association of School Psychology.

Russo, C. J., & Talbert-Johnson, C. (1997). The overrepresentation of African-American children in special education: The resegregation of educational programming? *Education and Urban Society, 29,* 136–148.

Sbarra, D. A., & Pianta, R. C. (2001). Teacher ratings of behavior among African American and Caucasian children during the first two years of school. *Psychology in the Schools, 38,* 229–238.

Shapiro, J. P., Loeb, P., Bowermaster, D., Wright, A., Headden, S., & Toch, T. (1993, December 13). Separate and unequal. *U.S. News,* pp. 1–8.

Slavin, R. E., Madden, N. A., Dolan, L. J., & Wasik, B. A. (1996). *Every child, every school: Success for all.* Thousand Oaks, CA: Corwin.

Sparks, S. (1998). Multicultural practice in mental retardation and developmental disabilities. In A. Hilton & R. Ringlaben (Eds.), *Best and promising practices in developmental disabilities* (pp. 171–184). Austin, TX: Pro-Ed.

Sparks, S. (1999). Educating the Native American learner. In F. E. Obiakor, J. O. Schwenn, & A. F. Rotatori (Eds.), *Advances in special education: Multicultural education for learners with exceptionalities* (pp. 73–90). Stamford, CT: JAI.

Staples, R. (1984, March/April). Racial ideology and intellectual racism: Blacks in academia. *The Black Scholar,* 2–17.

Strickland, D. S., & Ascher, C. (1992). Low-income African American children and public schooling. In P. W. Jackson (Ed.), *Handbook of research on curriculum: A project of the American Educational Research Association* (pp. 609–625). New York: Macmillan.

Turnbull, H. R., & Turnbull, A. P. (2000). *Free appropriate public education: The law and children with disabilities* (6th ed.). Denver, CO: Love.

U.S. Department of Education. (2000). *Twenty-second annual report to Congress on the implementation of the Individuals with Disabilities Act.* Washington, DC: U.S. Government Printing Office.

Utley, C. A. (2002). Functionalizing assessment for African American learners in general and special education programs. In F. E. Obiakor & B. A. Ford (Eds.), *Creating successful learning environments for African American learners with exceptionalities* (pp. 27–40). Thousand Oaks, CA: Corwin.

Utley, C. A., & Obiakor, F. E. (2001). *Special education, multicultural education, and school reform: Components of quality education for learners with mild disabilities.* Springfield, IL: Thomas.

Utley, C. A., & Simon, M. (2003). The federal role in transforming general and special education. In F. E. Obiakor, C. A. Utley, & A. F. Rotatori (Eds.), *Advances in Special Education: Vol. 15. Effective education for learners with exceptionalities* (pp. 17–42). New York: JAI.

West, C. (1993). *Race matters.* New York: Vintage.

Ysseldyke, J. E., Algozzine, B., & Thurlow, M. L. (2000). *Critical issues in special education* (3rd ed.). Boston: Houghton Mifflin.

Ysseldyke, J., & Marston, D. (1999). Origins of categorical special education services in schools and a rationale for changing them. In D. J. Reschly, W. D. Tilly, & J. P. Grimes (Eds.), *Special education in transition: Functional assessment and noncategorical programming* (pp. 1–18). Longmont, CO: Sopris West.

PEABODY JOURNAL OF EDUCATION, *79*(2), 157–179

Immigrants and Education in the U.S. Interior: Integrating and Segmenting Tendencies in Nashville, Tennessee

Daniel B. Cornfield
Department of Sociology
Vanderbilt Institute for Public Policy Studies
Vanderbilt University

Angela Arzubiaga
College of Education
Arizona State University

On the occasion of the 50th anniversary of *Brown v. Board of Education* (1954), recent global immigration to the U.S. interior compels local education systems that are relatively inexperienced with immigration to address new integrating and segmenting tendencies expressed by the growing and diversifying number of immigrants from Africa, Asia, and Latin America. The authors

The research for this study was conducted under contract No. 14830 for the Immigrant Community Assessment (ICA) with Metropolitan Government of Nashville and Davidson County, Tennessee, to whom we are grateful for their support. We are also grateful to our ICA coprincipal investigators, research assistants, community advisory board, and community collaborators for producing the research.

Requests for reprints should be sent to Daniel B. Cornfield, Vanderbilt University, Department of Sociology, UN Station B, 351811, Nashville, TN 37325–1811. E-mail: daniel.b.cornfield@vanderbilt.edu

discern 4 patterns of integrating and segmenting tendencies from self-proclaimed education needs expressed in focus groups by African, Asian, and Latin American immigrant residents of Nashville, Tennessee. Integrating tendencies were expressed more frequently than segmenting tendencies by group participants. Results suggest further integration of immigrants into the Nashville education system can be achieved with policies that overcome economic, linguistic, child care, scheduling, and discriminatory barriers to adult and children's education.

The 50th anniversary of the U.S. Supreme Court decision *Brown v. Board of Education* (1954) is an apt occasion for assessing sociologically the status of "integration" as a principle and objective for organizing education in local settings. Nationally, *integrating* and *segmenting* tendencies simultaneously challenge local school systems to develop optimal models of group relations in student bodies and with respect to teacher staffing. *Integrating tendencies* are community pressures for policies and practices that encourage the mixing of students and teachers of multiple social backgrounds (e.g. social class, ethnicity, race, nativity, gender, religion) in concrete teaching and learning settings. Integrating policies and practices include public education, busing, and affirmative action. *Segmenting tendencies*, in contrast, are community pressures for policies and practices that separate students and teachers of particular social backgrounds from their counterparts of other social backgrounds in concrete teaching and learning settings. Segmenting policies and practices include private schools; home schooling; single-sex and single-race schools; neighborhood-based schools; and suburbanization of the middle-class, school-age population in a metropolitan area.

Increasing global immigration to the U.S. interior challenges many local communities and school systems to address contradictory integrating and segmenting tendencies. With little or no immigration history and experience in incorporating recent African, Asian, and Latin American political refugees and economic migrants, local communities of the U.S. interior must accommodate to the needs of immigrants by strengthening and adjusting social services and educational institutions accordingly.

In this article, we examine the expression and patterning of integrating and segmenting tendencies in a local community of the U.S. interior. Specifically, we examine variations across immigrant ethnic groups in their self-proclaimed educational needs in Nashville, Tennessee. After presenting our theoretical framework, we describe immigration trends in Nashville and present our recently collected focus group data on immigrant educational needs. The focus group data consist of immigrant responses to our questions about their educational needs for adults and children. Distinguishing ethnic groups by their reasons for immigrating and their reception by the local community suggests how the increasing mix of integrating and segmenting tendencies challenges educational institutions in Nashville and, more generally, other local communities of the U.S. interior.

Theoretical Framework

The formation of immigrant interests and life chances may follow a set of variable nonlinear paths constituting "segmented assimilation" (Bean & Stevens, 2003, p. 100). Following Portes and Rumbaut (1996), immigrant interests and life chances are shaped by the interaction between their *mode of incorporation* and *context of reception*. As applied to an immigrant ethnic group, *mode of incorporation* refers to a "series of common characteristics of socioeconomic origin and reasons for departure that tend to be associated with different courses of adaptation once in the United States" (Portes & Rumbaut, 1996, pp. 14, 82–84). Portes and Rumbaut presented four modes of incorporation that may vary within and between immigrant ethnic groups: (a) labor migrants, (b) professional migrants, (c) entrepreneurial immigrants, and (d) refugees and asylees (Portes & Rumbaut, 1996, pp. 14–25). *Context of reception* consists of the opportunity structure for immigrants. According to Portes and Rumbaut, "the most relevant contexts of reception are defined by the policies of the receiving government, the conditions of the host labor market, and the characteristics of [immigrants'] own ethnic communities" (p. 84).

We argue in this article that the patterning of integrating and segmenting tendencies with respect to self-proclaimed, immigrant educational needs reflects the mode of immigrant incorporation into Nashville society and the local context of reception. Self-proclaimed educational needs, we argue, are expressions made by an economically and politically disadvantaged minority group of immigrants and refugees who are attempting to gain access to educational opportunities that are asymmetrically distributed in the local community.

Furthermore, immigrants, refugees, and host communities engage in *cultural practices* and constitute *cultural communities*. Cultural communities are characterized by their inheritance of beliefs and behavioral practices (Shweder et al., 1998). Communities' beliefs and behavioral practices are enacted within cultural practices. However, beliefs and behavioral practices are not static or fixed in time but rather undergo changes. Individuals participate in cultural practices in varying ways that change over time and over historical change in a community's organization and relationships with other communities (Cole, 1998; Gutiérrez & Rogoff, 2003). In the case of immigration, both the host communities' and the immigrant communities' participation in daily face-to-face cultural practices shape the beliefs and the behavioral practices of communities. Behavioral practices are locally instantiated and constrained by people's varied participation in the practices of dynamic cultural communities.

C. Suárez-Orozco and Suárez-Orozco's (2001) conception of two spheres of culture is helpful for analyzing immigrant beliefs about their self-proclaimed educational needs. M. Suárez-Orozco (2000) differentiated between *instrumental culture* and *expressive culture*. He explained

> by instrumental culture, I mean the skills, competencies, and social behaviors required to earn a living and contribute to society. By expressive culture, I mean, the realm of values, worldviews, and the patterning of interpersonal relations that give meaning and sustain the sense of self. (Suárez-Orozco, 2000, p. 20)

Identification of immigrant self-proclaimed education needs within these two broad constructs can indicate the integrating or segmenting tendencies of immigrants' self-proclaimed educational needs. We discuss, later in this article, how our findings indicate that the immigrant communities, overall, expressed interest in acquiring skills related to instrumental culture or the skills and competencies to earn a living and contribute to the host society. Our findings support the notion in education research that immigrants value education as a means toward success within the host society (see Delgado-Gaitán, 1993; Gándara, 1995; Goldenberg, Gallimore, Reese, & Garnier, 2001; López, Scribner, & Mahitivanichcha, 2001). In this sense, immigrants' values of education are integrating tendencies. In contrast, though, the context of reception of the host communities might include educational options within cultural practices that segregate cultural communities from each other, creating in this manner segmentation of educational opportunities.

We maintain that some beliefs of immigrant and refugee communities' self-proclaimed needs related to expressive culture or that which sustains the sense of self may propitiate segmenting tendencies within particular communities. However, these segmenting tendencies and the context of reception are mutually constituted. The psyche—sense of self—which is sustained by expressive culture and the context—of reception—are mutually constituted. Within Nashville, for example, the recentness of immigration, the existence of few enclave economies, and the numerical disadvantage of the immigrant communities indicate that certain elements of the expressive culture of immigrants might not find resonance within the cultural practices of the host communities and the educational system.

Integrating and Segmenting Tendencies in Nashville

Nashville is a useful case in point for discerning the patterning of integrating and segmenting tendencies that arises with global immigration in the U.S. interior. Global immigration to Nashville is historically recent and the infrastructure of private and public social services and education is evolving to accommodate the growing and diversifying number of noncitizen immigrants and refugees. After discussing the modes by which immigrants have been incorporated in Nashville and characterizing Nashville as a context of reception, we present our focus group data on the self-proclaimed educational needs of Nashville immigrants. We conclude this section by discerning four patterns of integrating and segmenting tendencies from the self-proclaimed education needs of Nashville immigrants that are linked to their modes of incorporation in Nashville and the local context of reception.

Modes of Incorporation in Nashville

Immigration is relatively new in Nashville, and the foreign-born are a relatively small group lacking in economic and political resources. The Nashville immigrant community consists of an unknown mix of refugees and immigrants, and an unknown number of undocumented workers, especially from Mexico and Central America. Many others are refugees from Africa, Asia, and the Middle East. Recently, the *New York Times* reported that refugees have been resettling in Nashville and other cities "where the cost of living is relatively low and entry-level jobs are available" (Swarns, 2003, p. 23). Statistical data on patterns of employment by occupation, industry, and ethnicity are unavailable for Nashville's foreign-born population.

According to the 2000 U.S. Census,[1] the number of Nashville–Davidson County residents who were born outside of the United States tripled between 1990 and 2000, having grown to roughly 40,000, or 7% of the county

[1]The U.S. Census Bureau's online American FactFinder program is the source of all Census data reported in this article. See especially the on-line Summary File 3 data sets of the 2000 U.S. Census for Nashville–Davidson County, Tennessee, at http://factfinder.census.gov/servlet/DTSubjectShowTablesServlet?_ts=92679127275

population, by 2000, which was slightly below the U.S. average. In contrast, the percentage who were born outside of the United States was 60% in Miami, 40% in Los Angeles, and 35% in New York City. Many foreign-born residents of Nashville originated in Africa, Asia, and Latin America. Sixty-one percent were born in Mexico or Central America. Some 5% of Nashville residents—native and foreign-born—identified themselves to the Census as "Hispanic." Of all foreign-born Nashville residents in 2000, two thirds had arrived in the United States during the 1990s, whereas 58% of all foreign-born residents in the United States arrived in the United States before 1990. Three fourths of Nashville's foreign-born residents were not citizens, compared to 60% of all foreign-born residents in the United States. Twenty percent of the foreign-born in Nashville were officially poor, almost twice the 13% poverty rate of Nashville's native-born population.

Among Nashville's foreign-born population, English-language speaking ability is variable. In 2000, roughly one third of Nashville's foreign-born residents, especially those who are ages 18 to 64, were what the U.S. Census termed "linguistically isolated"—they lived in households where no member over the age of 14 spoke English "very well." At the same time, over 70% of Nashville residents whose native language was not English spoke English "well" or "very well."

Nashville as a Context of Reception

As a context of reception, Nashville is a state capitol with a full-employment service economy. According to the U.S. Bureau of Labor Statistics (2003), Nashville's annual unemployment rate has not exceeded 4% over the last decade. Ninety percent of the Nashville labor force are wage and salary workers (i.e., not self-employed) who are mainly employed in service occupations of all skill levels—professional and nonskilled—in such industries as health, entertainment and tourism, education, social services, finance, and government. Federal government resettlement assistance is available for political refugees (but not for immigrants). Although mutual aid is not uncommon within Nashville's foreign-born communities, private ethnic enclave economies are not prevalent. Monolingualism predominates among natives and local institutions. We infer from some of the adverse interpersonal experiences reported in this article by the focus group participants that an unknown amount of prejudice against cultural practices that differ from the dominant North American cultural practices exists in Nashville.

The foreign-born population in Nashville is more residentially integrated than Nashville's Black population. Measuring residential segregation in Nashville with 2000 Census data, the index of dissimilarity for foreign-born residents was 37%, indicating that 37% of foreign-born residents or natives would have to move to another Nashville neighborhood in order to become residentially integrated with respect to the other group. In contrast, the 2000 Black–White index of dissimilarity for Nashville was 55%. According to the 2000 U.S. Census, almost 60% of Nashville's foreign-born residents live within the southeast quadrant of the city in the emerging international corridor along Nolensville and Murfreesboro Roads. The U.S. Census also shows that Nashville's foreign-born ethnic groups tend to reside in different census tracts within the southeast quadrant and that each foreign-born group constitutes no more than a minority of residents within any one census tract.

Data

The data from which we infer expressions of integrating and segmenting tendencies by Nashville's foreign-born community are from the 2002–03 Immigrant Community Assessment (ICA) that we conducted under contract with Metropolitan Government of Nashville and Davidson County, Tennessee (hereinafter referred to as *Metro*). The ICA is a social service needs assessment of immigrant and refugee residents of Nashville. The ICA included focus group discussions with adult immigrants and refugees about the availability, accessibility, and adequacy of a wide range of social services in Nashville. Metro stipulated that the focal ethnic groups of the ICA were to be Arabs, Kurds, Laotians, Latinos, Somalis, and Vietnamese. Local ethnic community organizations helped the researchers to recruit individual focus group participants. All in all, 16 linguistically homogeneous focus groups were conducted with the aid of professional interpreters in seven languages among 137 individual participants, mainly on the premises of local ethnic community organizations.

In this article, we report the results of the focus group discussions about "adult education" and "children's education." Focus groups were asked to respond to the following questions about the two education policy domains:

> Let me pursue this a little further with you by asking you about several daily life topics. For each topic, please tell me how [ethnicity] like or don't like any social services they may have used in Nashville. I would

like to know how easy to get to, expensive, and helpful the services are, or if the service is not important to [ethnicity].

What about schools? How does [ethnicity] like or not like schools in Nashville?

Prompt: How about for you? What has been your experience with schools in Nashville?

Results

Overall, the focus group participants' self-proclaimed needs with respect to adult education and children's education suggest that Nashville immigrants treat educational attainment as a vehicle for becoming integrated and upwardly mobile in the general local community. Most of the expressed educational needs reflect integrating tendencies, whereas a minority of these needs reflect segmenting tendencies.

In order to analyze the patterning of these self-proclaimed educational needs, we present them separately by educational policy domain, that is, adult education and children's education. Within each policy domain, we classify the educational needs in terms of M. Suárez-Orozco's (2000) spheres of culture, that is, instrumental and expressive culture, and by type of tendency, whether an integrating or segmenting tendency.

Adult Education

All of the adult education needs were instrumental–cultural needs for gaining access to existing educational opportunities. These opportunities include English-language instruction, higher education, and technical and vocational training classes. The needs pertained to overcoming economic, legal, and scheduling barriers to, as well as the constraints of child care responsibilities on, gaining access to these opportunities.

Integrating tendencies. Integrating tendencies are reflected in the need to overcome economic, legal, and scheduling barriers to obtaining higher education and technical and vocational training. Immigrants and refugees were interested in opportunities for higher education and technical–vocational training classes. For example, a woman in a Spanish-speaking group commented that "I've been trying to get computer classes but I haven't found any." A man in an Arabic-speaking group commented on how refugees' "ambition" to continue their education is not addressed by refugee programs:

> In refugee programs in their internal program those who come here and they have ambition to continue their education, they will not give any advice to that person. They will take you to a factory to work you out, they will call for you to find a job, and they will not lead you to continue your study.

A man in a concurring Spanish-speaking focus group made the case for government-supported training that would ultimately benefit both "parties":

> I think, just like the lady mentioned, just as they have the disposition, right? And resources to give us an education, English in this case ... I think if the government can support us in some areas, like a technical degree, like he was saying plumber, electrical, I feel we could be better prepared, and this would be a benefit for the state, because we could perform in a more qualified job; then the companies, could have a better, I don't know ... we could do a better job. We could be more capable to perform in any field that we're trained for; then it is beneficial for both parties, right? We ... because we have the education, and the companies because they have qualified people.

A man in a Somali focus group stated

> There are classes here going on at the [X]. It was a new program not a one that existed before. We need more classes and increased time. The availability of classes is only two days. We need help on that and we need more hours. We also need to learn vocational skills.

Immigrants and refugees noted the barriers to obtaining higher education posed by their legal status and their unrecognized prior training or certifications when enrolling in schools. For example, a man in an Arabic-speaking group noted

> To apply for any university they will ask you for your certificates, you cannot get anything back from Iraq, for example we have a friend he has a Master's degree, he escaped from Iraq and cannot go back home of course and they will not give him his certificates, this is first point he could not get his certificates to continue his education. The other point, some other universities will accept him as a student but it is so expensive

he cannot go and study there, to get a loan we got a loan in [education services provider] it was $500 a month, to work full time and pay for your study is difficult.

Another Arabic-speaking man added,

They deal with all students the same as far as the documents concerns because if somebody comes from other countries as a political asylee, he left everything and it is difficult for him to get his documents.

A Laotian woman noted the implications of her legal status for studying at a university:

English?! I mean, I basically I, I can understand read and I have something to say. Umm, I go to [education services provider] and when I first applied to [education services provider] umm, I did not know that I being considered an international student. I've been here ... when I applied I was umm ... I guess, living in the United States for nineteen years and umm ... of course, I mean I did not know ... [Inaudible] you're an international student; you're not accepted yet because you're an international student and I had to go take like an English proficiency test to prove you can speak ... I mean in a way I kind of think was very, I don't know, absurd because I've been here for nineteen years, went to school for thirteen years, I mean, why can I not speak write umm ... but then they; they were like, OK no. We still have to have proof that you can read and write and understand English very well, so I had to go take this test and pay money, which I did not want to spend because I can speak, read and you know ... Yeah! And you know, fluently! And I had to do that. And then the international students at [education services provider] which, I ... I don't know why, I think in a way it's kind of umm ... discriminating that they make international students pay more than, umm ... I guess, citizens at [education services provider]. And I'm still considered an international student because I am not a citizen. And so, I am like, well ... you know, well I can understand but ... that is, that is very ... and that kind of delayed the process, that delayed me getting the classes that I needed ... [Inaudible] ... and so I was very ... [Inaudible].

In another group, a Sorani-speaking (Kurdish) woman also noted financial barriers to educational opportunities:

Some of us we don't have a kid problem, but the problem is you have to pay to go to school which we can't afford. I work part time and I probably

> have to pay three quarters at least to go [to] school, I would like to go because I was a teacher back [in country of origin school] and you can't get a job that you want.

Segmenting tendencies. In light of the monolingual character of instruction in Nashville and the separation of English-language instruction from other types of instruction, the need to overcome economic, scheduling, and child care barriers to obtaining English-language instruction reflects segmenting tendencies. Immigrants and refugees emphasized the importance of speaking English and shared the view that learning English is a primary concern. The words of a Spanish-speaking woman exemplify the sentiment shared by the majority: "In Nashville, the most important thing is speaking English." An Arabic-speaking woman also commented

> If you can develop some schools that can teach us English that will help and employment especially for our husbands is very [difficult] now employment is not that much especially for our husbands who does not speak that good English and a lot of employers they now require English.

Another Arabic-speaking woman commented in response to the group moderator's[2] question as follows:

> GM: Can you suggest to us what would be the best thing to help when you first come to America? What's the best thing for you?
> AV: The best thing at first would be free schools and they have to teach us the language and I think that's more important thing in the United States. If a person can't speak the language he can ... [Inaudible] ... himself in the U.S. because he doesn't know anything. There's freedom here in the U.S. and they can help us with driving and teaching everything like open up schools for Arabic people. They need to learn because language is more important than everything.
> GM: Does everybody agree with that?
> AT: Yes.

Laotians stated that if English classes were available they would attend:

[2]GM refers to the focus group moderator, CM refers to the comoderator, and all other initials are substitutes for actual names. The pseudonym letters have no relationship to the person's name or role in the group.

GM: Are ... are there English classes available to you?
LD: Uh. ... We don't know if there are any, any available.
LE: OK, if the government provided English classes somewhere and provide transportation there would people going to those places.

The constraints of child care responsibilities on gaining access to English-language instruction were especially salient for Kurdish and Arab women refugees. This need emerged in focus group conversations with Sorani-speaking (Kurdish) women. A Sorani-speaking woman commented as follows:

> When we were in Arizona we had a lot of helps, and a lot of helps was offered in Arizona. First, that was really important back in Arizona was education, then they were providing day care for of our kids. I think this is not only my problem but all of our problem. All the people that are here in this group meeting have a language barrier. We don't have the same opportunity to learn English all at the same time. I think that's my problem and everybody else's. Thank you.

In another conversation with Sorani-speaking women, the following discussion occurred:

KL: I have another question, too. There was a teacher coming to my house and she was helping me with the language ... to teach me the language, but now she doesn't come any more. If there is a way that you can help to provide a teacher to come home and teach me English, it will be very good because I have kids and I can't go to school.
GM: So in terms of learning English for some of you, you are homebound and want to have that option at least ... that is important?
KK: Yes, very, very important.

Arabic-speaking women stressed that they would prefer access to women-only workplaces that would also provide day care and language classes for them. The isolation women experienced was a constant theme in their discussions:

AK: Can I speak? As far as we [are] concerned those of us we don't speak English and who take [children crying; inaudible] care of our children with the day care situation we don't know and who will take us to our job places, because we don't know how to drive.

Later, another woman added

AH: We wish, although, we don't think this will happen, but we wish if there is a place that can employ us, all the women, and they can provide like a day care center or anything to keep our children. At the same time they could just teach us some English that would be helpful.

The discussion continued:

GM: You have mentioned that maybe um ... there would be place that would offer day care and it would be like work for ... for women ... did you ... did I understand correctly you said for women only working?

AG: Yes, like a place we can benefit from and can serve and just for women and day care center at work and we will see each other. This may reduce the stress.

Another Arabic-speaking woman commented on the need for day care:

AS: I want to study here and learn English. We speak Arabic and we need some classes to teach us English language.

CM: Are there any classes available and do they have people who speak Arabic teaching the classes?

AS: Until now we haven't seen anything like but what about our kids? Where do we have to leave them if we go to those classes?

Children's Education

Focus group participants' needs in the domain of children's education were presented as both instrumental and expressive–cultural needs. Most of the needs were presented as instrumental–cultural needs, and all of these reflected integrating tendencies. The needs that were presented as expressive–cultural needs reflected segmenting tendencies. Integrating tendencies were more frequently expressed than segmenting tendencies by the focus group participants.

Integrating tendencies. The three chief needs in the domain of children's education that were associated with integrating tendencies were the need to (a) facilitate transfer credits and grade level placements for foreign-born students, (b) strengthen communications between parents and schools, and (c) protect foreign-born students from harassment by native students at school. These needs were expressed by all ethnic groups, and especially by African, Middle Eastern, and East Asian refugee groups. They are integrating tendencies insofar as they seek to better incorporate foreign-born students and their families into the Nashville public schools.

Regarding grade-level placements, an Arabic-speaking woman reported the following:

> AQ: I went to Jordan when I was in ninth grade. I took English class there and I got 50 percent passed the class, but when I came back to Florida they told me that you have failed the class 60 percent is the passing grading here. Now I'm not getting any credit for that and I've failed the class.
>
> GM: Is this because you transferred class from …?
>
> AQ: Yeah, they told me it has not been translated to pass the class it only says 50 percent grade … [Inaudible].

A Somali man also noted

> For example when a boy go to school and they are told how the system works. … The way we are used to in Somalia was when a teacher is like here in the U.S. the teacher has different teaching ways. They have a lot of materials to teach with … for example, a learning center. The kids need lot of help to go to and we are not used to this American teaching. Sometimes they come 16 of age and placed into class, depending on age, and forced to go to higher grade, while his knowledge is not there. When a student stops here, learns here, they may not get anything and are out of hope. They might not benefit from the U.S. and then go into being Americanized in bad way or go choosing different ways and choosing to destroy themselves. We were expecting to get help after schooling that is what we are interested in. After schooling helps like other states with many other communities, like Ohio. We have the space from our own expenses and we need help.

Several focus group participants expressed a need to improve communications between home and school. In the following excerpts drawn from a focus group conducted in Vietnamese, parents' lack of information about school activities and home–school connections is evident:

VD: My children go to school, every time there is a meeting, I was asked to attend, and I don't know what to say. I don't understand what they are talking about.

GM: Are your children in ... in public schools?

VD: Yes, my children are in second grade and the school keep asking me to attend the meeting, and I don't know anything, when they come home at night I don't know how to help them with their homework. For instance, I go to the doctor with my children, they give me an application. So, I don't know English. Some nurses are very good. I say, I don't understand, they help me. But some are not; they won't help me ... and told me to change my appointment, make another appointment and find an interpreter.

In a Laotian focus group, participants discussed similar matters related to home–school connections:

> Wait. I, I think that, you know, like when we ask them socially, I don't think they [other Laotian parents] really would know how things were socially because you know how they have stuff at school where you can go talk to the teacher or, you know, PTA, whatever all that stuff. They're not involved with that kind of stuff because ... [Simultaneous talking; inaudible] they, if they went, they wouldn't understand and I think that, you know, that's a disadvantage for them because they won't know exactly what's going on in their child's school. Like for us, now that I have a daughter, I know, like I would probably know more than what they taught their kid's ... [Simultaneous talking; inaudible] ... understand more, so ...

Several refugee groups especially sought protection for their children from harassment by other students at schools. An Arabic-speaking man commented as follows in regard to 9/11:

> Before 9/11 we thought the school system, the programs for the immigrant students especially Muslims, after 9/11 we discovered that some of our kids we thought that they have certain programs for Muslim kids who have certain needs and wear certain clothes they have certain programs for them, but after 9/11 we discovered that it was not that good and they were not protective more or they were not protective from school for the kids who have certain needs, most of the problems happened after 9/11 were in schools not in factories or companies or in the streets.

In a Vietnamese focus group, a woman shared the following:

I have an issue. My children ... my friend's children ride the bus. The American children, black and white the same, threw things and spit on our children and so they fought back after being hit three or four times. The bus driver did not know who was at fault. She took the children to the office to see about who was to be expelled. The children got expelled, as well as my friend's children. When I arrived at school, they would not meet me so I had to go to a court. Really, my children and my friend's children only hit three or four times by the boys and they were so angry, they fought back. We end up having to go to court. Due to the fact that my children do not speak English, while the other kids do ... we were to blame. He was not allowed to attend the school.

In a Somali group, participants also discussed harassment on the buses:

GM: Do any of you have children that have problems with the buses? [Simultaneous talking] That you want to tell us about? [Simultaneous talking] Do you want to tell me about that?
SY: We have had a problem in the past when our children are riding the bus. There was a misunderstanding between the Somali and American children. They always are arguing.
GM: What kind of misunderstandings? [Simultaneous talking]
SY: The clothing that we Muslims wear. They ask many questions why they are wearing the clothing while it's cold or hot. Making fun of the different culture.
GM: Is that usual or is it a matter of the clothing or are there other things also?
Participants: Cultural. Misunderstandings.
SY: I have two children that are in high school and they have a similar problem with children asking if they are related to Osama Bin Laden and my children don't even know who he is. One of my girls always tells me that she is afraid that one of the boys is going to kill her because they think I'm related to him when she doesn't even know whom he is. If the girls finally want to tell the teacher they don't because they are afraid because if they do they might get beaten after school so they feel helpless and they can't speak out. [Simultaneous talking]
CM: Have you talked to the teachers ... did you talk to the teachers at the school about these problems ...? [Simultaneous talking]
GM: Did you talk to the teachers? [Simultaneous talking]

SCC: Nothing can help them because the teachers will tell you that ... [Simultaneous talking] it was outside of the school.

Harassment was also a theme brought up in a Laotian focus group:

LF: And my children have been kind of provoked by their, not friends, but the children about the same age. And they do not want you to have arguments, but they have to. Sometimes they fight. I wonder why the school does not really take care of these problems. The school let the children do things like that, like fight each other. They should not do that. And when they fight together the school blames the parent.
GM: And have you had interactions with school officials?
LF: Many times.
GM: And are you able to communicate well with school officials ... or how does that normally go?
LF: Yes, I talk to the teachers and the director. I am not sure whose fault it is it might be, the school's or my children's.

Segmenting tendencies. Segmenting tendencies were associated with expressive–cultural needs for preserving refugees' ethnic and religious cultural practices. These needs include establishing separate ethnic and religious educational institutions and having public schools accommodate to cultural practices. For example, a Somali man stated

> We are...trying to save the education of our kids maybe to have uh ... a charter school or similar to a charter school. We are not getting to do that because of lack of space here. There is a culture clash and we need room to handle all of it.

The following comments by a Somali parent suggest that the desire for private school education is linked to the harassment experienced by Somali schoolchildren at school:

SGG: I had two children that I took from that school and put them in a private school because they always are having trouble on the bus. The kids are always asking question like are they related to Osama Bin Laden because you look like him and then the children come home and ask me who is that man that these kids are calling me? They cry and say that's not my dad or uncle. My response to them is that I don't know who this man is so I don't

> know why they say those things. The main thing is that I moved my children to a private school.

Similarly, another Somali parent commented

> Two years ago my children had a problem. Before this, I told the principal I had a problem. But one day I was called to come to the school and saw my child with his teeth ... [Inaudible]. When I asked what happened and whose fault it was the teacher told me she did not see whose fault it was, however, all the children said it was his fault. I said that because he cannot speak the language, everything would be his fault because he can't defend himself. I spoke to the principal on several occasions and she said that if I sent my child to private schools, they would understand the culture better.

In a Sorani-speaking (Kurdish) group, participants commented on the importance of religious education:

> GM: What ... what in schools um ... right now, do you like and what do you not like? [Simultaneous talking]
> KN: I want my kid to ... whatever she learns ... to learn the religion with it too.
> GM: Is that ... for all?
> KP: Yes.
> GM: So then ... what you see is uh ... is the problem is that there is no teaching of Islamic faith within the school?
> KN: Yes.

In a Behdini-speaking (Kurdish) group, a participant discussed several differences between the ideal education for the children and incidents in school:

> We are very concerned with the schools because we don't want our kids just to go there. There are very good things in the schools here because they teach our kids like computers and more. At elementary school they don't have any problem but when they get to middle school or high school level, we have a problem with engaging girls with boys and that is against our religion and our culture. One day I went to school to pick up my son for early dismissal, they were watching a movie and boys and girls were close to each other and sitting close together we don't like that as Muslims. In our culture and religion it is not allowed to have boys and girls sitting close to each other. Always when there is a class activity in-

side or outside they are always engage a boy with a girl. In our schools back home up until college we have boys separate from girls but here indirectly they are teaching our kids to have boyfriends and girlfriends. That's what our understanding is. What we need is a school with separate classes for boys and girls and there are places in the United States that have such a school.

A woman added

> One example is that they enforce the holidays. In our culture we don't have Valentine and Halloween but they make the kids to exchange cards. I told my brother and he said everybody does that why shouldn't I? So they enforce those holidays indirectly. One other thing that I saw in my little brother's book said something about Islam that it wasn't true. I tried to contact the author but I didn't get anybody. The stuff was written about Islam was not correct.

An Arabic-speaking focus group identified practices in physical education classes that were inconsistent with their cultural and religious practices:

AQ: At school when we have PE [physical education] or tennis class, we have to wear shorts.
AP: Yeah, that's a problem.
AQ: Yeah, for both of us my sister and me. We can't wear shorts and if we don't wear it, we'll fail the class.
GM: So they said if you don't wear shorts you're going to fail the class?
AQ: Yeah, in the summer but I had my class in winter so I didn't have to wear shorts.
AP: They [school officials] said if you don't wear shorts you have to go to the office and sign out.
AQ: Like you'll get suspended or you've done something against the school if you aren't wearing it. We are going to [education services provider] and you have to wear school shorts and shirts.
AP: You have to buy them from the school.
AQ: We keep telling them that we can't wear shorts and she said "well you aren't wearing scarf so why don't wear shorts?" I said " No we can't wear shorts."
CM: So have they actually failed you in these classes or do they understand if you are... [Inaudible]

> AQ: They don't understand... [Inaudible] until my dad wants to go and explain it to them.

A Behdini-speaking (Kurdish) woman stated a need for public support of a private school that would preserve traditional cultural practices:

> The important thing is if we could get a private school for our kids. We want to keep our religion for our kids. We wish to get some support or help from the government because our community is getting bigger in Nashville. There are almost seven thousand Kurdish people here. All the people from Pakistan or anywhere else wants that school also. If we could get that private school for our kids [it] would be better. We can't provide a private school for our kids because it's very expensive. Every child needs at least eight to nine thousand dollars to continue school.

Patterns of Integrating and Segmenting Tendencies

In sum, four patterns of integrating and segmenting tendencies can be discerned in the self-proclaimed educational needs of the focus group participants. The patterning of integrating and segmenting tendencies, in turn, is linked to the structure of opportunities and obstacles afforded immigrants and refugees by local Nashville society, and to the modes by which foreign-born residents are incorporated into Nashville.

The first pattern is that integrating tendencies associated with instrumental–cultural needs accounted for the majority of the educational needs expressed by most of the ethnic groups who participated in the focus groups. These needs consist mainly of overcoming barriers—economic, scheduling, child care, linguistic, legal, and discriminatory barriers—to becoming students integrated into mainstream, educational institutions.

The second pattern is that some of the segmenting tendencies expressed by the focus group participants were associated with instrumental–cultural needs and shaped by the segmental organization of education in Nashville. These needs mainly pertained to overcoming the range of barriers to obtaining English-language instruction, which is offered apart from other educational services in local mainstream educational institutions. In this case, the tendency is effectively defined as "segmenting" by the segmental organization of English-language instruction in the local educational system. Focus group participants, however, viewed English-language instruction as a prerequisite for navigating, becoming integrated into, and succeeding in the general society of Nashville.

The third pattern is that some of the segmenting tendencies were associated with expressive culture and defensive reactions to harassment of foreign-born residents by natives. For example, some of the focus group participants sought the establishment of private schools for their ethnic groups in order to protect their school-age children who were being harassed by native students in public schools.

The fourth pattern is that some of the segmenting tendencies were associated with expressive culture and preferences for preserving and immersing school-age children in their ethnic and religious cultural practices. Several of the Muslim refugee groups, for example, advocated the establishment of private schools for Muslim students in order to preserve Islamic religious practices and customs that local public schools were unable or unwilling to accommodate.

The expressions of educational need by the focus groups suggest that the patterning of integrating and segmenting tendencies arises from the cultural practices, the structure of opportunities, and the obstacles to educational attainment afforded Nashville residents, and the needs and interests of a growing and diversifying number of immigrants and refugees. Integrating tendencies are linked to a local opportunity structure of educational, social welfare, and economic institutions that distribute educational opportunities unevenly among socioeconomically and culturally diverse groups, generating a demand for greater incorporation into the educational system by an economically and politically disadvantaged minority of immigrants and refugees. Segmenting tendencies are linked to a segmentally organized delivery of English-language instruction for immigrants and refugees who desire greater access to such instruction; to culturally discriminatory harassment and rejection of foreign-born students in public school settings; and to the cultural preferences of refugee families for educational institutions whose objectives are to preserve traditional culture and religion and that public schools are unable or unwilling to accommodate.

Conclusion

On the occasion of the 50th anniversary of *Brown v. Board of Education*, the case of Nashville suggests that global immigration to the U.S. interior is yielding a new mix of integrating and segmenting tendencies in local communities and education systems. As pressures for more integrated and segmented incorporation of immigrant families into a local public and private education system, these tendencies emerge from an uneven structure of educational and economic opportunities afforded local residents, and the needs and interests of an economically and politically disadvantaged minority of immigrants and refugees.

Our Nashville focus groups indicate that integrating tendencies are more prevalent than segmenting tendencies among immigrants and refugees and that integrating tendencies are linked to the desire of immigrants and refugees to overcome economic, child care, legal, linguistic, and discriminatory barriers to obtaining educational opportunities. Segmenting tendencies are associated most with refugees who have been culturally harassed by natives and whose deep identification with their religious and cultural practices leads them to develop their own private, culturally distinct educational institutions.

From the perspective of the Nashville focus group participants, integrating tendencies in local communities of the U.S. interior like Nashville pose several policy challenges for realizing the integration of immigrant and refugee families into local education systems. These policy challenges pertain to overcoming the barriers to gaining access to educational opportunities. These economic, scheduling, child care, legal, linguistic, and discriminatory barriers call for an increase in social support resources for:

1. Making education more affordable to immigrants and refugees.
2. Facilitating communication between families and schools with bilingual advocates.
3. Reducing the constraints of child care responsibilities on adults who interact with schools as parents and as adult students in higher education, technical, vocational, and English-language programs.
4. Promoting tolerance and preventing harassment of immigrants and refugees in schools.
5. Rationalizing the process by which students who lack transcripts of education attained in other countries are placed in the local educational system.

The case of Nashville has several implications for future research on the integration of immigrants and refugees into local education systems of the U.S. interior. First, research is needed to measure the prevalence of integrating and segmenting tendencies among the foreign-born, as well as natives' attitudes about these tendencies, in local communities. Second, in order to estimate the magnitude of policy responses to integrating tendencies, indicators of immigrant integration in local school systems should be developed and inventories taken of the extent and ethnic patterning of immigrant integration in educational systems and of the supply of existing social support resources for integrating immigrants in local educational systems. Third, more research is needed on the causes and mechanisms by which the local community opportunity structure, cultural norms and prejudice, and the cultural preferences of immigrants and refugees shape the mix of integrating and segmenting tendencies in local education systems. Pursuing this research agenda can help develop the policies for increasing the requisite social support for making educational opportunities more accessible to immigrants and refugees in the U.S. interior.

References

Bean, F., & Stevens, G. (2003). *America's newcomers and the dynamics of diversity.* New York: Russell Sage Foundation.

Brown v. Board of Educ., 347 U.S. 483 (1954).

Cole, M. (1998). Can cultural psychology help us think about diversity? *Mind, Culture, and Activity, 5,* 291–304.

Delgado-Gaitán, C. (1993). Parenting in two generations of Mexican–American families. *International Journal of Behavioral Development, 16,* 409–427.

Gándara, P. C. (1995). *Over the ivy walls: The educational mobility of low-income Chicanos.* Albany: State University of New York Press.

Goldenberg, C., Gallimore, R., Reese, L., & Garnier, H. (2001). Cause or effect? A longitudinal study of immigrant Latino parents' aspirations and expectations, and their children's school performance. *American Educational Research Journal, 38,* 547–582.

Gutiérrez, K., & Rogoff, B. (2003). Cultural ways of learning: Individual traits or repertoires of practice. *Educational Researcher, 32,* 19–25.

López, G., Scribner, J., & Mahitivanichcha, K. (2001). Redefining parental involvement: Lessons from high-performing migrant-impacted schools. *American Educational Research Journal, 38,* 253–288.

Portes, A., & Rumbaut, R. (1996). *Immigrant America: A portrait* (2nd ed.). Berkeley: University of California Press.

Shweder, R., Goodnow, J., Hatano, G., LeVine, R., Markus, H., & Miller, P. (1998). The cultural psychology of development: One mind, many mentalities. In W. Damon (Series Ed.) & R. M. Lerner (Vol. Ed.), *Handbook of child psychology: Vol. 1. Theoretical models of human development* (5th ed., pp. 865–937). New York: Wiley.

Suárez-Orozco, C., & Suárez-Orozco, M. (2001). *Children of immigration.* Cambridge, MA: Harvard University Press.

Suárez-Orozco, M. (2000). Everything you ever wanted to know about assimilation but were afraid to ask. *Daedalus, 129,* 1–30.

Swarns, R. (2003, July 20). U.S. a place of miracles for Somali refugees. *New York Times,* pp. 1, 23.

U.S. Bureau of Labor Statistics. (2003). *Local area unemployment statistics, Davidson County, Tennessee.* Retrieved October 1, 2003, from http://www.bls.gov/lau/home.htm

For Product Safety Concerns and Information please contact our EU representative GPSR@taylorandfrancis.com
Taylor & Francis Verlag GmbH, Kaufingerstraße 24, 80331 München, Germany

www.ingramcontent.com/pod-product-compliance
Ingram Content Group UK Ltd.
Pitfield, Milton Keynes, MK11 3LW, UK
UKHW021300190926
475701UK00009B/91
9780805895506